The Art of Memory

REMEMBERING
WHAT NOT TO FORGET

Bill E. Beckwith, Ph.D.

To my wife
Pamela,
For transforming my life
Into a world of
Color, beauty, art,
And love

Acknowledgments

I gratefully acknowledge my mentor and friend, Dr. Curt Sandman, who took a chance on me by becoming my thesis advisor at Ohio State. I approached other faculty who probably were put off by my ponytail (an attempt to save money while in school) and Fu Manchu ("freak" in the terminology of the time). Curt provided an excellent role model for my professional growth as well as support and guidance. Importantly, he taught me how to write, as I am sure he got writer's cramps from editing my early writings. He provided the intellectual freedom from which I have grown more than he can know.

I also wish to thank Dr. Tom Petros. Tom was instrumental in my intellectual, spiritual, and personal growth. We spent time designing research, going to movies, attending scientific meetings, and running in the dead of winter in North Dakota. We ran through snowdrifts, frigid temperatures, and on the frozen Red River. He is one of the most authentic persons I have ever met.

I wish to acknowledge Dianne Nelson. Dianne spent endless hours editing, clarifying, and improving this manuscript. In addition, she provided invaluable support and encouragement that allowed me to feel that this work will be helpful to all who choose to read it. She was so much more than just an editor but also a friend I have never met in person.

Finally, I express my appreciation to Mary Anne Maier, who edited my earlier book in 2004, *Managing Your Memory*, and referred me to Dianne. I also am deeply appreciative for the support and guidance given by Cass Leoncini. She read through the very rough first manuscript and guided me through the publication process for *Managing Your Memory* and *The Art of Memory*.

CONTENTS

INTRODUCTION

"…memory provides our life with continuity. It gives us a coherent picture of the past that puts current experience in perspective. The picture may not be rational or accurate, but it persists. Without the binding force of memory, experience would be splintered into as many fragments as there are moments in life…. We are who we are because of what we learn and remember."
(Eric R. Kandel, 2006)

I am seventy-eight (where did the time go?) and am revisiting my views and reminiscences on life and memory. It's been more than ten years since I last read my book, *Managing Your Memory* (second edition). It gave me an eerie feeling. There they were — my thoughts and misunderstandings concretely staring me in the face.

First, I noticed "dissociation" (which often happens when I review my previous publications). It didn't feel like my work but rather the work of someone else. Next, I was shocked by weaknesses in the narrative. Despite positive feedback from many who read the book, some of the text lacked clarity. However, the *essence* of the work held up well. I originally planned to write a book that was approachable and readable and that stated general principles rather than to create a text that would soon be out of date. I feel that I mostly achieved that goal with the earlier book. And then, I was in lock-down due to the coronavirus (COVID-19) pandemic of 2020 – 2021. That allowed me to contemplate, rethink, and reprocess my understanding of memory, assessment, teaching, neurological disease, aging, and life. This was my chance to rewrite and revise the text to increase clarity as well as to update and to expand discussions.

My interest in memory and emotion originated from the aftermath of the drowning death of my brother, Dick, when I was nearly four years old. I had nightmares most nights throughout my childhood. These dreams often had images of the funeral that I couldn't recall in normal consciousness. I was also puzzled about my parents' reactions and idealization of

Dick. Added to this, I was dyslexic and was slow in learning to read (I scored at the twelfth percentile on a national reading test administered as part of admission to Ashland College). Nor could I spell well, despite hours of detention to write out words (spell checkers became a blessing). Indeed, much of my understanding of learning and memory stem from my efforts to master university-level courses and overcome my limitations.

The final event that caught my attention was an exercise required in my senior English class. I had to memorize a passage from *Macbeth* and recite it in front of the class. I still can feel the terror, as I was very shy and avoided speaking up or asking questions in classes. I successfully memorized the passage — in fact, I overlearned it. However, fear prevailed when I stood in front of the class, and I did poorly, only to be able to recall it perfectly thirty minutes later.

From these beginnings, I decided to major in psychology and earn a Ph.D. from The Ohio State University (my master's degree was in experimental psychology; I specialized in learning and memory with an emphasis on psychoneuroendocrinology — how's that for a mouthful?). I was a university professor in my early career, during which I published many research papers and contributed several book chapters on learning and memory. As an educator (teaching students from preschool age to junior high, college, and graduate education), I had the privilege of mentoring hundreds of undergraduate and graduate students (mainly at the University of North Dakota). I briefly returned to teaching at the University of North Georgia during 2017 and 2018.

During the last twenty-five years of my career before retirement, I helped found and develop a memory clinic, a behavioral health department at a retirement community, and, later, a private practice specializing in memory in southern Florida. I was able to apply my academic skills to real-life problems as well as broaden my knowledge of memory and emotions. I developed a comprehensive memory evaluation and treatment center where I consulted with thousands of older people who had both excellent memory (sometimes referred to as the "worried well," but I prefer the "proactive well") and declining memory (from various etiologies such as head injury, stroke, Alzheimer's disease, and Parkinson's disease).

At the same time, I contended with changes in the efficiency of my own memory as I aged and with the onset of Parkinson's disease in my sixties.

My conclusion from decades of experience with memory is that *trying to remember doesn't work*. You must plan on *how* you will remember. You must develop your plan before you need it. Better memory takes effort and evaluation.

Writing this book helped me to translate this experience and knowledge into a practical guide, not only for you but also for myself. Despite the changes brought by aging, most of us will not become demented. *We do have a say in how we age*. We can make self-enhancing lifestyle choices that move ourselves toward self-actualization.

***

An array of aids and techniques underlie good memory, allowing you to learn, retain, and execute new information and skills. As will be elaborated later, some memory systems benefit from practice/repetition, or "mental aerobics," while others do not. Even though I've learned many skills and gained much information during my life, I have always had to put time and effort into this process. You will come to know this as **The One-Minute Rule** — anything given less than one minute of thought will fade from your memory.

As I grow older, I use more notes, rely on a more detailed calendar, and keep myself better organized. I also have to increase my efforts with each passing year. Despite the changes from aging, I've developed an evolving plan in which I can successfully engage, enjoy my life, and recall my experiences. If I practice what I preach (and I do not develop a memory disorder), I will learn and grow as long as I live, despite having Parkinson's disease.

This book is not a textbook. Rather, it distills information that has helped me to develop my personal and professional appreciation of normal and abnormal memory as well as to understand how to better manage my own memory. This book is practical rather than academic. Therefore, I am not using a scholarly format for referencing ideas. You will find many helpful sources in the Annotated Bibliography at the end of the book.

Individuals who have experienced memory loss resulting from neurological disorders (head injury, Alzheimer's disease, Parkinson's disease, Lewy body disease, stroke) as well as medical disorders (kidney disease, heart disease, diabetes, cancer) will benefit from the information in this book. Even young persons who don't experience memory loss will find valuable ideas here, as will individuals who, like me, are trying to handle the normal changes in memory efficiency as we age. With all of these challenges, there are no easy ways to a better memory. Although some exercises and experiences can strengthen or reinforce long-term memory and habits, unfortunately, no exercises will strengthen short-term memory.

The strategies in this book that reinforce and strengthen memory will help support memory whether you are ten or ninety years of age. You will find help, whether you apply the principles in this book for home, school, or work. You will feel strengthened in facing the changes of aging as well as the challenges of illnesses that interfere with memory. The practical techniques you will learn involve spending more time and effort in *deciding* what is important to learn and track. You will gain confidence in your ability to cope with information and to compensate for changes as you mature.

This book has three major sections. The first consists of nine chapters that will help you (1) to better understand how memory works; and (2) to develop and use specific techniques that will propel you to more effectively learn and remember new information, remember what needs to be done and when, and remember where to go and how to get there. These chapters describe what memory is as well as the factors that influence forgetting. They also discuss the changes that can be expected during aging and the practices that have been proven to support learning and memory regardless of age.

The second section (Chapters 10 and 11) describes disorders of memory and the concepts of Mild Cognitive Impairment, dementia, and Alzheimer's disease. They are the most technical and clinical chapters in the book. The third section (Chapters 12 through 15) discusses managing controllable factors (such as diet and exercise) that may improve mental operations as we age and may slow down memory decline. In these chapters, you will also learn how to plan ahead, whether or not you have risk factors associated with memory disorder or have mild changes in memory beyond those of normal aging. The main message of this last section is to *be proactive about your memory. Stop trying to remember. It does not work. Rather, plan how you will remember and how you and significant others can live a more engaged life.*

We insure ourselves against financial contingencies as best we can. We create a financial road map for retirement. We also must get organized to protect ourselves against the inconveniences of aging and possible fading memory skills. If you have vulnerabilities for developing conditions such as Alzheimer's disease or stroke, planning ahead becomes critical for successful management of your future. Unfortunately, if you wait until you need the skills described in the first part of this book, you may no longer be able to learn them. That's why it's important to develop good memory "hygiene" so that *you will have the skills before they are needed.*

According to a *New York Times* article, many elders (a description I am increasingly finding distasteful but accurate for myself) fear developing Alzheimer's disease more than they fear their own death. This need not be the case, as Alzheimer's disease progresses over the course of decades. The early phases of the disease create annoyances and inconveniences that can be well managed by careful, advanced planning, ideally beginning in at least middle age. *It is never too early to plan ahead.* Your memory is the best it will ever be. Now is the time to learn memory management skills *before* you need them. If you don't experience a decline in memory, you have lost nothing. Instead, you have developed habits that will give you a well-remembered life. Design a plan to preserve your past for active conservation of your future. That is what this book is all about.

* * *

The past is consumed in the present
and the present is living
only because it brings forth the future.
— James Joyce, A Portrait of the Artist as a Young Man

A Methodological Note
For Evaluating Research

A caveat to keep in mind: Few definitive answers are found in science. Random assignment, the gold standard for inferring causal connections, does not really address many of the issues discussed in this book. We have to accept correlational data as a guide that has no definitive proof. Who wants to be in the placebo group from birth? In addition, some data sets are enormous, thereby generating trivial findings. Does a statistically significant treatment that improves recall by 1.5 words really change your life? This is true of many of the studies that guide our healthcare decisions. This is not a criticism of many excellent studies but reflects the complexity of the issues and multifactorial nature of causation in biological systems.

We live in a world overrun with data — it is the age of computers and information. Hence, we are endlessly confronted by statistics. I wrote this book during a presidential election, a time when we are barraged by polls. What percentage of women, men, blacks, Hispanics, etc. is likely to vote for which candidate? How do news agencies project winners? What is the error of a poll? How good is the poll?

Maybe you follow trends in the stock market. How is the Dow Jones doing? How is the S&P 500 doing? How is the NASDAQ doing? What are index funds, and how are they constructed? How do you best choose mutual funds or individual stocks? What are the trends over ten years, and why would you need to know?

If you follow baseball, you want to know the batting average and earned run average of your favorite players or teams on base percentage. If basketball is your sport, you may follow field goal percentages, rebounds per game, or percentages of shots made at different parts of the court. What is your metric for ranking a quarterback's performance in American football, and how good is that metric? Fantasy fans, too, are constantly seeking data and statistics.

How do you know if a social program is working? Do tax cuts hurt or help? Which people do they hurt or help? How are our schools doing? How useful are IQ tests? Achievement tests? How do you know if a medical treatment works? How can you determine the relative efficacy of drugs? How do you decide the tradeoff between benefits and costs?

These are just some examples, but the point is, data run the world. Statistics are everywhere. And statistics are tools for describing the world (descriptive statistics) and generating probabilities to help you make rational decisions (inferential statistics).

You could take a statistics course to get a better understanding and working knowledge of this subject to make yourself a more rational decision-maker/consumer. But, as I can attest, formal courses and textbooks are mostly dry and mathematical rather than intuitive. Furthermore, the technical and computational aspects of statistics can be completed faster and more accurately by modern computers than by humans.

Instead of taking a statistics course, I recommend reading *Naked Statistics: Stripping the Dread from the Data* by Charles Wheelan (2013, New York: W.W. Norton). You may also want to read *How to Lie With Statistics* by Darrell Huff (1954, New York: W.W. Norton), the model for Wheelan's book. Both of these are intuitive and humorous rather than mathematically driven. They are easier to read and more understandable than other books on statistics.

The real function of the theoretical and applied sciences is to answer meaningful and well-asked questions. As Wheelan points out for data collection, "garbage in, garbage out," no matter how well the statistics are done. There are no "nearly significant findings." Statistics provide estimates of probability of being wrong; hence, they are tools for making better decisions.

What is the point of statistics? According to Wheelan, and I quote:

- To summarize large quantities of data.
- To make better decisions.
- To answer important social questions.
- To recognize patterns.
- To catch cheaters and to prosecute criminals.
- To evaluate the effectiveness of policies, programs, drugs, medical procedures, and other innovations.
- To spot the scoundrels who use these very same powerful tools for nefarious ends."

PART I

WHAT IS MEMORY AND HOW DO YOU MANAGE IT?

CHAPTER ONE

Plan How You Will Remember

*"Anything given less than one minute of thought
will fade from your memory."
(Douglas Herrmann, 1990)*

*"Every indication is that, rather than a neatly separable hierarchy
like a computer, the mind is a tangled hierarchy
of organization and causation.
Changes in the mind cause changes in the brain, and vice versa."
(Ari Schulman, 2009)*

I'm often asked, "How can I improve my memory?" or "Can I do exercises to improve my memory?" Whether you are simply looking to do better in school or work, or you are anticipating or already experiencing the inefficiencies of memory that result from aging (or are beginning to develop clinically significant memory loss), these are the wrong questions to ask. That's because memory is not a single skill. "Memory" is a general term that covers a multitude of abilities ranging from remembering your name, knowing how to swim, and recognizing pathogens via your immune system.

Most of us have a "good" or a "bad" memory. Some of us master new information quickly, while others need to spend more time and effort to learn and remember new information. We all have strengths and weaknesses for remembering different kinds of information or skills. For example, you may have a good memory for dates but a poor memory for when to take medications. You may have a good memory for driving a car with an automatic transmission but a poor memory for driving a car

16

with a manual transmission. In other words, what is generally referred to as "memory" is actually a complex set of capabilities with an array of personal strengths and weaknesses. I remember my name, the date of my birth, and my siblings' names. I remember many facts and concepts that I learned during my education. I remember vacations that I have taken but often do not recall specific details, such as what I did on which day. I remember odors (my wife's perfume), tastes (strawberry shortcake), and feelings (sadness from deaths of persons or pets for whom I have cared). There are many avenues to remembering. As you can see, not all memories are in the form of words or concepts. They may be in the form of images, tastes, odors, feelings, abilities, spatial patterns, sense of familiarity, immune responses, allergies, and genetic codes. I know and can recall much more than I can say, which is to say that not all memories are based on language (e.g., I don't tell myself how to drive a car or how to swim).

Memories have different ways of being organized and stored in the brain and body (e.g., information, knowledge, skills, reflexes, immune responses, DNA). Memories are structured and recalled in accordance with your personal experiences, your biases, and your likes and dislikes. Furthermore, different kinds of memories operate through different rules depending on their function. On the one hand, short-term memory skills cannot be strengthened like a muscle. On the other hand, repetition increases the strength of long-term memory and therefore may be viewed through the metaphor of training a muscle. This book will help you to better manage your short-term memory as well as your long-term and working memory.

Consider the following questions about your own memory. The more often you answer "yes," the better your memory "hygiene," or memory management skills. If you answer "no" to several of the questions, you may have some work to do.

1. Do you use a timer or alarm to remind you to do something?

2. Do you ask someone else to remind you to do something or to help you remember?

3. Do you write things on a calendar? Do you include pleasurable activities? Do you include appointments? Do you include routines that you wish to build?

4. Do you have a "to do" list? Do you update it each day? Do you have more items on the "to do" list than you can possibly manage in a day?

5. When you are stumped about a word or a name, do you go through the alphabet one letter at a time to see if it brings to mind the word or name?

6. Do you repeat something out loud in order to remember it?

7. Do you write it down to help you remember it?

8. Do you use routines to help you remember important things?

9. Does everything have a place, and is everything in its place?

10. Do you make lists to recall what to buy at the grocery store? Do you remember to take the list with you?

11. Do you mentally elaborate on something that you want to remember? Do you try to form associations? Do you try to conjure up an image, a story, or a rhyme?

12. Do you put things that are important to remember in a prominent place to remind you to do something or to take something with you?

13. Do you repeat information to yourself at increasingly longer and longer intervals so that you will remember it? Do you plan practice opportunities to help keep important skills sharp or to develop new skills that you wish to acquire?

14. Do you take notes to help you remember? Do you organize your notes and keep them in a convenient (and routine) place for easy use? Do you update and review them often?

15. Do you use your smartphone to help you remember?

CHAPTER TWO

Frequently Asked Questions About Memory

"No one has ever seen a memory and no one is ever likely to see one.
In our everyday conversation, we use that word to talk about things we do.
We remember our first day in class or forget where we parked the car.
We recognize an old friend or recall a pleasant day at the beach.
All these things have to do with memory."
(Wingfield and Byrnes, 1981)

The key to improving memory is to spend time attending to, contemplating, and rehearsing/practicing information/skills. Most learning does not occur in one pass unless it is emotionally charged. It takes time to master the organizing and practicing of what you want to learn. It takes effort and intention. Experiences and skills that you ponder and practice are much less prone to being forgotten. Lebron James and Tom Brady did not develop their skills overnight or by osmosis. Albert Einstein did not formulate the theory of relativity in a single flash. If you are unfortunate enough to develop a memory disorder (reviewed in Chapters 10 and 11), *you need to learn, integrate, and practice habits before you need them.*

Everyone will experience decreased memory efficiency as they age. The best way to deal with these changes is to actively develop memory strategies (such as having a takeaway spot or reminder system like a smartphone application [app]) to improve your quality of life. It is important to understand that if you wait until you *need* to master the techniques described below, it may be too late to learn how to use them. You will best remember information when you take the time to develop a strategy for learning and remembering. For example, my wife Pamela and I recently took a trip to Paris. I had studied French in college for a year, so I decided to "try" to relearn enough French by using an app on my iPhone. However, I violated my own rule. I didn't spend the time or make the effort to plan for how I was going to *remember* vocabulary and dialogue. The trip was wonderful; my mastery of French was not.

You can start building better memory habits by addressing the following questions. At the same time, you will be introduced to the basics of memory aids and memory enhancement.

ARE THERE DIFFERENT KINDS OF MEMORY?

I remember things that I want and need to do; for example, if I need to pick up some things at the supermarket on the way home from work, hopefully I've made a plan on how to remember the list. I remember skills (how to ski, how to ride a bicycle). I remember routes (how to get home from work), names (my wife's name is Pamela, my cats' names are Vanna and Gracie), and facts (the capital of North Dakota is Bismarck, the capital of South Dakota is pronounced "pier"). I remember movements (swimming, walking).

Therefore, yes, there are many different kinds of memory systems — short-term, long-term, procedural, explicit, and implicit — and different networks and codes to organize each one. I'll discuss these types of memory in Chapter 3.

WHAT CHANGES CAN YOU EXPECT
IN MEMORY AS YOU AGE?

Senility is not an unavoidable consequence of aging. However, your memory will become *less efficient* as you grow older. I already see changes in the reliability and efficiency of my memory as I approach eighty compared to when I was in my forties, fifties, and sixties. I am much more vulnerable to distraction (absentmindedness, blocking, and sluggish word finding) than I used to be. I need a much more detailed calendar. I am not doomed to dementia (although as I age, the risk becomes greater because I have Parkinson's disease), but I will need to incorporate better plans on how to remember as the years pass. I'll talk about these changes in Chapter 4.

IS FORGETTING NORMAL?

The answer is simple: Yes. We all forget, no matter how young or old we are. Memories generally fade with the passage of time. We mainly recall the gist, the essence, but not the details. Very few of us have a photographic memory (eidetic imagery), and those who do are usually quite young. In fact, individuals who retain this skill may not find such detailed memories a blessing. Those with a photographic memory are often frustrated by the details they cannot help but recall. They may have difficulty seeing the forest for the trees.

Forgetting is a normal part of memory and must be acknowledged and planned for. If you know the factors that increase the likelihood of forgetting, you can compensate for or work around them. Many of us (although some of us are night owls) will do better in challenging mental tasks that require memory and dependable attention in the mornings rather than in the evenings. This may reflect, in part, the effects of fatigue as the day wears on. Also, we are more likely to recall information that is well organized. We better remember to pay the bills if they are organized into folders and if paying bills is marked on the calendar or set as a smartphone reminder each month. We are more likely to recall a phone message if we write it down and then repeat the message back to be sure we got it right. This, too, adds repetition to help better reinforce the memory. I'll cover the factors that increase forgetting in Chapter 5.

WHO AM I?

This is a basic philosophical question that we need to address and read-dress throughout life. We all have skills, knowledge, and routines. What we pay attention to and remember depends upon who we are, our past experiences, our knowledge, and our needs. Our plans and routines are the skeletons upon which we can structure memory skills.

For example, I shave first thing in the morning. Therefore, I put a note on the mirror where I shave to help me remember something that is important to do that day. Similarly, I place a new medication that I need to take in the mornings next to my razor. This increases the likelihood that I will take it routinely. Here's another example: I have already developed adequate computer skills. This means that I can use computers to help me recall what I need to do or to know. When I give talks and seminars, I use a well-honed PowerPoint from my computer to provide the blueprint for what I want to discuss. The slides also help my audience to recall the major ideas that I make, because they see as well as hear the information I'm presenting. Long-term memory is discussed in Chapter 7.

WHAT IS ABNORMAL FORGETTING?

Abnormal forgetting is being more forgetful than your peers. As an example, I am seventy-eight years old. I would be abnormally forgetful if, on a difficult memory test, I recalled much less information than other seventy-eight-year-olds who have taken the same memory test. As an extreme example of abnormal forgetting, consider that it is okay to occasionally forget where you parked your car. However, it is not okay to forget that you have a car.

Abnormal forgetting is not the same thing as having "no" memory. People with abnormal forgetting may recall many things very well, but they have certain memory skills that are poor (e.g., they can remember their social security number and date of birth but forget the names of their grandchildren or the way to the supermarket). Usually, abnormal forgetting is manifested by failure to adequately learn new things or adjust to change. Abnormal forgetting also refers to forgetting what you have to do (forgetting to take a new medication, forgetting appointments). In clinical cases, it is someone who forgets that they forget. Abnormal forgetting is discussed in Chapters 10 and 11.

What Kinds of Skills Should Be Assessed During Memory Evaluation?

During a formal memory evaluation, information needs to be obtained not only from the person who has memory concerns but also from a knowledgeable family member or friend, if possible. This is because your confidence in your ability to remember may not reflect reality.

A challenging memory test is the best way to determine your ability to learn new information. This memory test must examine your ability to recall newly learned information immediately as well as after a delay. You should also have your ability to recognize newly learned information tested, because even if you have difficulty recalling information, you may still do well in recognizing it (you will benefit from using structured external memory aids).

A careful history of who you are (e.g., education, work skills, leisure skills) is another important part of a memory evaluation. Also, this history should uncover information on the unfolding of your concerns. This part of the evaluation helps to assess your long-term memory skills, and your companion can verify your answers. Other mental skills that the evaluation should test are language, construction (e.g., draw a clock, copy overlapping pentagons, arrange blocks into patterns), problem solving, and executive skills (e.g., planning, judgment, intelligence). A clear understanding of the current state of your skills in these areas allows a management plan to be developed that uses your strengths to shore up any of your weaknesses (for example, if my writing is unintelligible, I should not write notes for myself, but I can use my smartphone to dictate notes).

Memory evaluations are complex and take time. If the memory test is too easy, it is a waste of time, because it may not catch any problems when they are quite mild (like many memory screenings such as the Mini-Mental State Exam in current use). The most important aspects of an evaluation are to review and explain the findings with you, your family, and/or your companion. Ideally, these individuals will *observe all components* of the evaluation to gain a better understanding of what you are dealing with. The goal of these assessments is to help you and your family and friends understand the nature and parameters of any problems.

These evaluations aren't done so that someone might "look bad," such as when another person wants to get an edge in a court appearance or seeks benefits in legal proceedings. Instead, the results of memory evaluation serve as a teaching aid so that a logical and effective treatment plan can be developed that meets the needs of you and your family. Your family needs to review and understand the test scores so that they can help you with your everyday skills and with any anticipated future changes. I discuss evaluations in more detail in Chapters 10 and 11.

WHAT ARE THE GOALS OF MEMORY MANAGEMENT?

First, you must ask yourself, "Which kind of memory do I want to improve?" The answer then becomes simpler, because the techniques that improve one kind of memory (how to ski) differ from those used to improve another kind of memory (tracking when to take the cake out of the oven). Memory can be improved by better use of existing memory strengths (such as using a calendar or a scheduling program on a smartphone) and development of new memory strategies. I've said this more than once, but it's important, so allow me to repeat it: *Plan ahead. Learn skills before you need them.*

The major rules of memory enhancement are simple:

1. Dedicating more time to learning and rehearsing/practicing.

2. Organizing, reviewing, and associating items to be remembered.
3. Developing routines.
4. Liberally employing external memory aids.
5. Minimizing and planning for factors that contribute to forgetting.

General rules for memory enhancement will be discussed in Chapter 8.

WHAT SPECIFIC TECHNIQUES CAN BE SUCCESSFUL FOR IMPROVING MEMORY?

Specific techniques will allow you to become more efficient at learning and recalling new as well as old information. These techniques use assistive strategies. They include using external aids such as timers, calendars, computers, smartphones, and other people. I'll discuss these techniques in Chapter 9.

CHAPTER THREE

What Is Memory?

"For those with a [normally] functioning memory, amnesia is a condition that is almost impossible to conceptualize. Try to envisage the erasure of all past autobiographical memory. Remembering reactivates the pattern of neuroactivity originally generated and replays the memory with an awareness of the present. Remembering is therefore an act of creative re-imagination, and if this fact is denied, the future is also unimaginable. Without the ability to remember, how can we place ourselves in the world around us, hold on to an understanding of self, recognize the ones we love (benefit from experience), own any part of what is experienced, and know who we have become? Memory is intrinsically connected to identity, and to a large extent, is what makes us truly human."
(Jules Morgan, 2017)

"There is a common language to be found between artist and scientist, because in a sense, both search for interpretations, mechanisms, patterns, and experiences."
(Jules Morgan, 2017)

Many clients have sought my council stating, "There is something wrong with my memory" (or they are concerned about their partner's or parents' memory). However, as I ask them questions about their date of birth, name of the high school from which they graduated, or their address and phone number, they provide the correct information. Furthermore, they are well groomed and dressed, suggesting that they recall how to care for themselves. They look well fed and fit, which implies that they remember to eat and exercise. They are on time for their appointments, indicating that they have recalled (or wisely used a manual or electronic calendar) when they were to meet with me. They find their way to my office, which presumes that they have adequate route-finding memory. They probably recall social conventions, because they interact with me in socially appropriate ways. They can still swim if they ever learned in the first place. They recognize familiar persons, suggesting that they have memory for faces. They have good language skills. Still, they report that they are concerned about how their "memory" is working and fear that their memory is failing. Without proper evaluation, I can't adequately address their concerns (more on that later).

Many of us have a sense that memory is an overall capacity or ability and that our "memory" is good or bad. Hence, we speak of fear of "losing our memory." However, as we saw in the last paragraph, *the brain has a multitude of memory systems/skills, and each system/skill has unique properties of operation.* Most of us have good memory in some areas (e.g., spelling, recalling words to music) and poor in others (e.g., spelling, route finding, recalling words to music). We have memory systems for language, movement, and music. We remember the multiplication tables, our family history, and the locations of many familiar places. We recall our personal history and have memory of self. We have skills such as touch typing or riding a bicycle, and we recollect sounds, sights, tastes, and odors. We have memories of emotions. We know when to take medications and when the trash will be collected. *Memory is clearly not a general skill — it is a concept that subsumes many skills or types.*

Anterograde Amnesia: The Case of HM

When we complain of "losing" our memory, we usually mean our "short-term memory." This is the memory system that allows us to learn new information. Aging, as well as disorders of memory, often produce malfunctions of short-term and working memory (discussed later). The most well-known and thoroughly studied clinical case of short-term memory failure is that of HM (Henry Gustoff Molaison). HM was born on February 26,

1926, in Manchester, Connecticut. He was hit by a bicycle while stepping off a curb to cross a street on July 3, 1933 or 1934 (he was seven or eight years old). He landed on the left side of his head and ended up with a gash just above his left eyebrow as well as a concussion. He lost consciousness for about five minutes.

Soon after the injury, HM started to have mild seizures; his first grand mal seizure occurred on his fifteenth birthday. These seizures became increasingly more frequent. He was able to complete high school but was unable to hold a sustained job. Medications did not stop the seizures. In 1953, at the age of twenty-seven, in an attempt to control his seizures, HM became the first and only human known to have his hippocampi (brain structures that rest beneath the temporal lobes of the cerebral cortex) removed by a neurosurgeon named William Scoville.

The surgery did reduce the severity of HM's seizures, but it created a new and unexpected problem: Time simply stopped for him. Post-surgery, HM was unable to learn new facts (e.g., he could not learn the names of new presidents after 1951). Many researchers and clinicians spent considerable time with HM over the last fifty-five years of his life, but he still could never learn the names of staff, caregivers, and researchers, even those who worked with him over long periods of time. He recalled people from before the surgery but not new people. Nor could he learn new routes, such as how to get to and from his room. After the surgery, he lost about two years of his past memories. As far as he was concerned, he remained subjectively a twenty-five-year-old man. He reported the constant feeling as if he was "awakening from a dream." Although he was able to learn some procedures after the surgery (such as how to trace figures while looking at them in a mirror), he was not aware that he knew how to do this task or how he had ever done it. HM had lost a critical skill of memory: storing new information.

On a general level, we could say that HM "lost his memory." However, he did not have a *total* loss of memory. He still knew who he was and how to care for himself until much later in his life. He still knew the past facts of his life, could learn new skills (although, as mentioned, he did not know that he knew them), and had the stores of knowledge that he had possessed before the surgery. HM, wheelchair bound, demented, and mute, died December 2, 2008 at the age of eighty-two.

This type of memory disorder, surgically produced in HM's case, is known as *anterograde amnesia*. It is the type of memory loss that most of us refer to when we say that someone has lost his or her memory, though HM's case was much more severe. Most clients with memory loss whom I have seen and assessed have a milder form of anterograde amnesia. In Alzheimer's disease, and in what we will later discuss as Mild Cognitive Impairment, we are dealing with short-term memory loss, or anterograde amnesia. In this most common type of memory disorder (Alzheimer's disease), a person's ability to learn new information is impaired. Imaging (MRI) usually shows atrophy of the hippocampus, but damage to other brain structures in the thalamus and limbic system may also be found.

WHAT IS MEMORY?

According to *Merriam-Webster's Collegiate Dictionary* (10th edition, 1998), memory is "the power or process of reproducing or recalling what has been learned and retained." Alternatively, memory is "the store of things learned and retained from an organism's activity or experience as evidenced by modification of structure or behavior or by recall and recognition." Note that *memory is a persistent transformation in the "structure of the brain" and the "behavior" that results from "experience" or "learning,"* In other words, memory is the capacity to learn and to retain new information (requires short-term memory), to recall the information or skills when needed (long-term memory), and to recognize instances of familiarity when we are exposed to parts of information or experiences in the future.

Humans evolved about 2.5 million years ago. They developed a proportionately large brain that permitted them to move up the food chain. This was accompanied by the first cognitive revolution (as is beautifully described by Harari, 2015) that began 30,000 to 70,000 years ago and was marked by inventions such as boats, oil lamps, needles, banks, credit, and art. The big brain of humans also formulated legends, myths, politics, and religion. These creations, in turn, laid the foundations for modern institutions. What's important to understand is that the brain's memory systems evolved tens of thousand of years ago. "Ever since the cognitive revolution, there hasn't been a single natural way of life for *Homo sapiens*. There are only cultural choices, from a bewildering palate of possibilities" (Harari, 2015, p. 41). In the words of Stephen J. Gould, "Biological (Darwinian) evolution continues in our species, but its rate, compared with cultural evolution, is so incomparably slow that its impact upon the history of *Homo sapiens* has been small" (Gould, 1981, p. 324).

The memory systems we have today are the ones that evolved for survival in prehistoric times. These systems are static. Our memory abilities in the past several hundred years have arisen from our *cultural creativity*, which, in turn, has relied on the growth of external memory strategies (associations) and tools (smartphones) over time. Think of how ancient art, language development, growth of the printed word, and the rise of computers have expanded our memory capacity. Human memory did not evolve to handle the massive amounts of data and information that we cope with every day in the modern world. Indeed, memory sets limits on the speed and breadth of our ability to learn and remember. It leads us to become overwhelmed and stressed when we're confronted with the massive amount of information available in today's information-rich world.

Learning how to cope with the limits of this ancient biological hardware involves understanding the structure of human memory. Grasping these concepts will help you later to disentangle changes in memory that result from normal aging as well as those that occur as a result of memory disorders. This is the first step toward developing strategies that will improve your memory operations.

In your daily life, you depend primarily on the following kinds of memory:

- Sensory
- Primary

- Working
- Prospective
- Short-Term
- Long-Term
- Procedural
- Emotional

Learning about these types of memory can show you how you can retain some memory skills even if you have a memory disorder.

SENSORY MEMORY

Sensory memory is a temporary impression left on our sense organs after we perceive it. It is sort of like an after-image. Sensory memory is very transient and is quickly lost. It is a momentary total representation of a stimulus, such as a word or image heard or seen, that is rich in details: a face observed, a sound heard, a touch felt. It endures for less than a second and is passive. Sensory memory works in all of us unless we lose one of our senses (e.g., hearing) or suffer brain damage such as a stroke or head injury.

Managing sensory memory requires that we do what we can to keep our senses as sharp as possible; this will assist our memory processes later in the chain. The most obvious way to manage sensory memory is to wear hearing aids and/or eye corrections. While our sensory memory can become less efficient (e.g., cataracts, hearing loss), this is not the type of memory that leads us to say we have problems with our memory.

PRIMARY MEMORY

Primary memory is a second kind of temporary memory. This is the memory system that allows us to look up and dial a phone number that we will no longer need. It holds about seven (plus or minus two) pieces of information that will remain available as long as we rehearse (repeat the information in our mind).

We lose information in primary memory through interference as new information displaces the old. Hence, we forget the phone number we just called as we begin our conversation. Distraction also interferes with primary memory. If we go into another room for something and get distracted (a common occurrence), we may forget why we went into the room in the first place. Primary memory lasts for only seconds (up to about a minute) because, unless we actively rehearse the information without distraction, it can hold only a limited amount of information. While our primary memory can become less efficient, this is not the kind of memory that commonly leads us to say we have memory problems.

WORKING MEMORY

Working memory is a third type of temporary memory system. Working memory and primary memory are not distinct systems, but they do somewhat different tasks. One way to understand these functions of memory is to think of primary memory as a passive system that holds information (like a buffer) and working memory as an active system that manipulates the information, such as decoding speech sounds into language and multitasking. If primary memory allows us to hold seven items, working memory helps us to manipulate them in the context of past learning and our present situation. One way to test our working memory is to try repeating a phone number we know backwards.

Working memory allows us to decipher information and to track multiple things at the same time. For example, working memory helps us to listen to a lecture while taking notes. We can interpret the meaning of the words and concepts the speaker is using. We also are able to track what we have to do and when we have to do it. In fact, we need working memory for understanding language and keeping to our plans. With working memory, we can drive a car to wherever we wish to travel. (Remember that we are always driving for five cars — the one we are in as well as the ones in front, in back, to the left, and to the right of us.)

Working memory is highly influenced by attention and interference. Decline in working memory rather than primary memory is something for which we must all compensate as we age. Our working memory is related to yet another temporary memory function that is named prospective memory.

PROSPECTIVE MEMORY

All of us must be able to track events (plans with visitors, appointments and engagements, the need to return someone's call) and time (how long the cake needs to bake, when we need to go to an appointment or engagement, when we need to take medications). This is the function of prospective memory, which is another temporary memory system. It, too, is connected to working memory because it requires sharing attention over time. We are all subject to growing less efficient in prospective memory as we age. Prospective memory allows us to monitor and interact with our future, whereas other memory functions/systems that we have discussed so far connect us to the present and past.

SHORT-TERM MEMORY

Short-term memory is another relatively temporary memory system. Short-term memory holds information that endures for minutes to hours to days. Short-term memory constantly interacts with sensory, primary, working, and prospective memory. It is the *harmony* of these systems that allows us to function smoothly most of the time in our everyday life.

With short-term memory, we can store new knowledge and procedures. It helps us to learn new names, facts, and skills. We are also able to link the past, present, and future. HM's surgery produced severe deficits in his short-term memory (i.e., anterograde amnesia). Short-term memory becomes less proficient with aging and is susceptible to many kinds of injuries and illnesses (such as Alzheimer's disease, head injury, or hypoxia). Short-term memory allows the accumulation of information and skills that builds long-term memory. Short-term memory does not improve with practice. It is not like a muscle.

LONG-TERM MEMORY

Long-term memory is a more or less *permanent* memory and/or habit. It is based on information, procedures, and skills already stored by the brain that is available for use at later times. It is our personal history, our store of knowledge, our enduring self, and our persisting skills.

Long-term memory changes as a result of experience. It is like a muscle in the sense that the more we exercise it, the stronger it becomes. Mental exercises and stimulation are sometimes referred to as "memory aerobics" and are believed by some to protect memory and to ward off Alzheimer's disease. However, mental exercises have been shown to strengthen long-term memory, not short-term, working, primary, sensory, or prospective memory. Doing crossword puzzles builds skills of long-term memory but does not strengthen or improve short-term memory ability or efficiency. Long-term memory (despite its many foibles) works quite well even in many who have early-stage memory disorders. Thus, long-term memory is the strength that we can build on to compensate for change during aging or if we detect or anticipate memory disorders in their very early stages.

PROCEDURAL MEMORY

Procedural memory is the memory of skills and procedures. We recall how to walk, dress, chew, and swallow. We remember how to ride bicycles, how to swim, or how to touch-type. These are not activities that we have to think about doing. Procedural memories unfold without thought. Once learned, they are automatic. Indeed, if we try to think about the elements involved in a skill such as walking, we interfere with the process and may stumble or get our legs crossed up (remember the first time you drove a stick-shift car if you learned on an automatic transmission?). We are not used to thinking in order to walk, drive, or dress; we just do it.

Procedural memories are developed and strengthened by repetition and practice. As we age, it takes us more time to build procedural memories. For example, those who learn to ski when they are young are generally much better skiers than those who learn when they are adults. It is much easier to learn languages when we are young than when we are adults. This is because the process of learning languages seems to be different and more automatic for children, whereas adults learn a language more through rote memory. I have often marveled at the computer skills of those growing up with computers compared to me learning to use a computer as an adult.

Procedural memory is another strength, along with long-term memory, upon which we can build compensatory strategies even if we develop memory loss.

DECLARATIVE VERSUS PROCEDURAL MEMORIES

The memory systems described so far make our life smooth and allow us to learn and to interact with our world. These systems allow information and skills to enter into our repertoire of knowledge, behaviors, and sense of self. Another important distinction that is helpful in understanding how memory works is that between declarative and procedural memory.

Declarative memory is based on language use and imagery. It is episodic (recalling the date or events) or semantic (recalling a fact or piece of personal information from our knowledge system). Declarative memory allows us to *know that we know.* For example, HM didn't know he had learned to trace a star in its mirror image.

Procedural memory represents memory that *allows us to do*; it permits us to "know how." HM improved his skill at mirror drawing with practice but claimed that he had never done this before. Another example is a survivor of a near drowning who was left with severe anterograde memory loss. Prior to the drowning, she did not know how to sew. Part of her rehabilitation was to learn to sew. She became skilled at making dresses. However, if she made a dress today, she would deny making it or even being able to sew by the next day.

EMOTIONAL MEMORY

Emotional memory is the array of feelings and reactions that we have to situations and people. Emotional memory may be positive (feelings of love toward our spouse, joy of accomplishment) or may be negative (waves of sorrow during grieving, being fearful, and feeling apprehension when the plane in which we are flying encounters turbulence). Emotional memory can be triggered by cues, incidents, or thoughts. For example, if we have speech anxiety, standing (or merely thinking about standing) in front of an audience may make us very anxious and elicit the desire to run away or to avoid giving speeches. Indeed, public speaking ranks very high on the list of fears for most of us, despite the fact that there is no objective harm in public speaking.

Emotional memories continue to function in many people who live with progressive dementia disorders. For example, seeing a sad movie may set an emotionally sad tone for the day in nursing home residents who have Alzheimer's disease, whereas viewing an uplifting movie may set a positive tone. However, in both cases, the residents have no recollection of having even seen a film and cannot tell you why they are having their feelings.

Emotional memory is processed quite differently from factual memory and keeps working well into progressive dementias.

FLASHBULB MEMORIES

I vividly recall where I was when I heard about the attacks of 9/11. Indeed, I can "see" the interaction as well as "hear" my wife's voice when she called. I was with a client who told me of the events, and I recall my disbelief and confusion. I can still see the look on her face. I remember how it seemed like forever before the reality began to set in. Finally, I recall my wife's call and insistence that I cancel my talk that was scheduled in the afternoon.

The destruction of the twin towers and other powerful events bring to mind vivid memories that feel as if they are formed instantly and in great detail. The explosion of the *Challenger* shuttle, the OJ Simpson trial, and the assassination of President Kennedy are other examples of events that generate these intensely felt memories.

Roger Brown and James Kulik first labeled this type of memory in 1977 as "flashbulb" memory. These memories are stored instantly and feel as if they are photographs. They feel more vivid, complete, and accurate than do everyday memories.

But ten years after 9/11, research clearly indicated that flashbulb memories are not as accurate as they feel unless a person was actually present at the event. Those in Manhattan at the time of the attacks can recount every sight, sound, and smell. The rest of us are more likely to forget or misremember facts we had at the time. For example, my wife and I were recently discussing the attack, and I had forgotten there were four planes rather than two.

As with most long-term memories, flashbulb memories erode over time. They are subject to factual distortion about how we first learned of the events and the actual details of the events. For example, Duke University researchers assessed students' recall both of 9/11 and of everyday events immediately after the attack. A third of the students were asked to recall these events again a week later, another third after six weeks, and the final third after thirty-two weeks. Both flashbulb and everyday memories changed in consistency and accuracy over this period of time. Despite the objective degradation after as small an interval as weeks, flashbulb memories *feel* as if they are more accurate and consistent than regular memories.

In short, flashbulb memories are not necessarily more accurate, but we perceive them to be. *Everyday memories are processed through the hippocampus* (circuit of short-term memory), which allows us to learn new things like names, what we have to do at 3:00 today, or what we did last night.

Emotionally laden memories sidestep this circuit. Strongly emotional events activate the amygdala, which labels an event as emotionally important. The experiences that trigger the amygdala are related to survival (either real or perceived threats) or strong negative feelings (e.g., personal attack or loss) or positive emotions (e.g., falling in love or seeing the Grand Canyon for the first time).

"SM," ANOTHER CASE STUDY; A DIFFERENT MEMORY SYSTEM

Another example of the effect of brain systems on memory (in 1994) comes from a woman known by the initials "SM." SM suffered complete bilateral destruction of the amygdala resulting from Urbach-Wiethe disease in late childhood. She was married and had three children. As a result of the illness, and notwithstanding being able to experience emotions like happiness and sadness, SM was unable to feel fear in situations that elicit fear in most of us. Experimenters exposed her to snakes, spiders, the world's scariest houses, and a series of horror films. She also completed questionnaires regarding death and public speaking, which trigger fear in most of us. When presented with these provocations, despite saying she hated snakes and spiders, she did not experience fear or show avoidance. Instead, she touched them despite being mystified by her own behavior. She was "overcome by curiosity."

The point here is that *memory does not operate in a sterile context.* We learned from HM that *the hippocampus mediates short-term memory.* SM's behaviors indicate that *the amygdala mediates fear learning and gives emotional tone to our memories.* Memory can be powerfully driven by emotions (consider posttraumatic stress disorders). Managing memory includes managing emotions. We shall discuss this topic further in Chapter 14.

***

Although other important complications and nuances of memory have not been addressed here, I hope this discussion has helped to clarify some important distinctions and functions of memory. As we age, our memory systems change. These changes do not necessarily reduce our ability to enjoy life, to learn new information, or to monitor what we have to do. However, the growing inefficiency of short-term and working memory as we age provides us with some amusement (we develop "old-timer's" disease, we suffer from "CRS" — can't remember s----) and some annoyances. The next step in appreciating the complexity of memory is to learn how the efficiency of our mental operations changes as we age.

CHAPTER FOUR

Normal Changes in Memory As We Age

*"Isn't it so astonishing, the number of things I can remember,
as the number of things I can remember that aren't so?"*
(Mark Twain)

*"Interventions focused on promoting physical activity in midlife promise to
help people reach old age healthier, reduce the trends of chronic illness and
poor health behavior prevalence, reduce societal costs, and increase individual
quality of life." (Infurna, Gerstof, and Lachman, 2020)*

As I look into the mirror each morning, I am aware that I have changed. I don't look like I did when I was thirty, forty, fifty, sixty, or seventy. The changes are obvious. My hair is white, no longer salt and pepper or gray; my hairline is receding. I have more wrinkles. My skin has markings and blemishes that I did not have when I was younger. I don't always like these changes, but there they are anyway. Consider how HM must have felt when he looked into a mirror with the memory of a twenty-five-year-old man and saw the reflection of a seventy-seven-year-old man.

What are not so obvious are the changes that have occurred in my internal organs. My bones have become less dense. My muscle strength and endurance have declined. My liver, kidneys, and heart have declined. All of these bodily organs will continue to become less efficient as I continue to age.

My brain will also change as I age. It will shrink. In fact, human beings have the largest number of cells that we will ever have in our brain by age two. The normal brain at age twenty weighs about 1,400 grams (three pounds). By the ninth decade of life, the normal brain will shrink to about

900-1,000 grams. It will have some very tiny strokes and "blemishes." Indeed, it is very common to see reports from brain-imaging (e.g., MRI) studies with descriptors such as "age-associated" or "age-consistent" atrophy and small-vessel disease. I have already most likely developed some plaques and tangles in my brain (the pathology currently associated with Alzheimer's disease). These changes will cause my cognitive skills (learning, perceiving, attending, problem solving) to become less efficient but will not necessarily lead me to develop dementia or senility as I age, even if I live into my 100s. My wife's great aunt is 102 (her sister died at 103) and still lives alone, cares for her apartment, and drove to church until her 102nd birthday.

THE FORGOTTEN CHILD — MEMORY LOSS OCCURS IN THE VERY YOUNG AS WELL AS IN THE OLD: INFANTILE AMNESIA

"My four-year-old grandson has near-photographic memory for outings from a year ago.... Soon that will disappear. By the time he is eight, he will remember almost nothing from his first four years."
(Thomas Insel, "NIH Director's Blog," August 19, 2013)

Think back. What is your earliest memory? Most of us have no memories from the first three to four years of life and recall little from before ages seven to eight. There are exceptions. For instance, author Ray Bradbury claimed that he recalled details from his birth. Children and teens retain earlier memories than adults; therefore, the loss of these memories — or at least the ability to verbalize them — is "progressive." Furthermore, the memories we have from these early times are often recollections from photos or stories told to us by others rather than by our own exact recall. The phenomenon is called *infantile amnesia.*

Infantile amnesia is poorly understood. On the one hand, it presents a paradox: We cannot recall early experiences, yet they exert a powerful influence on the person we become (a major contribution by Freud). Early experiences set the tone for the development of our intellectual, social, and physical skills. On the other hand, *there is a distinction between availability versus accessibility of memory*. Just because early experiences cannot be put into words does not mean they are forgotten.

Much of our understanding of infantile amnesia comes from asking teens or adults to retrospectively recall childhood experiences. Accurate recall of past memories is often very poor when compared to the facts (ever compare stories of growing up with your siblings?). Verifying the accuracy of early memories is difficult. Only longitudinal studies that follow children from childhood can better clarify these early processes of memory.

Babies as young as six months of age can recall experiences for anywhere from six minutes to several months. Preschool-age children typically recall events from several years back. So how does infantile amnesia happen? One contributory factor is that the memory systems of the brain have not yet fully matured. The brain is growing rapidly early in life and is in the process of constantly rewiring itself, which may write over early memories. Also, our language and conceptual skills of the brain are developing at least until early adulthood, which changes the way we express memories, as we always know more than we can say.

Despite recall of language and habits, children under the age of three rapidly forget episodes — that is, who, what, and when. This is called *episodic memory* and is the foundation of much of our autobiographical memory. Episodic memory requires the hippocampus and related circuits to reach a certain level of maturity that does not happen before at least age seven. Episodic memory may also need the nurturing of experiences that occur between the ages of two to four to fully foster the development of the hippocampus.

The other critical factor in episodic memory appears to be language development. Narrative and reminiscence underlying autobiographical memory requires the complex use of language. During the ages of one through six, children progress from one-word sentences to fluency. Interestingly, this is also the span of infantile amnesia. Children's ability to verbalize events predicts how well they recall experiences years later.

It seems clear that infantile amnesia arises from the complex maturation of the brain. It does not appear to be a true forgetting, as these early experiences do impact what we become, as suggested by Freudian theories. As the brain wires its language and memory systems, a paradoxical loss of the ability to recall early experiences occurs.

A Rock Star's Memory Lapse: More Common Than You Think

Dr. Gary Small, a UCLA memory expert, wrote an article entitled "Paul McCartney's Memory Lapses." Apparently, Paul McCartney (who is too old to be a baby boomer) admitted that he has times when he cannot recall the lyrics to his old songs — the ones he has been performing for years. Dr. Small used the article to discuss "normal memory loss associated with aging." The article intrigued me, so I pursued other examples of singers experiencing memory lapses for lyrics. It is not only the aged rockers who forget lyrics.

The examples are legion. I will present only a few. Mick Jagger, age sixty-five at the time, repeated a verse from "Ruby Tuesday" in a 2006 concert in Glasgow. A nearly three-minute YouTube video of Elvis (who was forty-two when he died) shows him unable to recall the lyrics for a song he was performing. Finally, Jenny McCarthy, age thirty-seven at the time, forgot the lyrics of the national anthem she was performing for a NASCAR race. Apparently, you don't have to be "old" to forget well-rehearsed lyrics. It is clear that age is not the common thread for this type of forgetting. So don't feel so badly if you temporarily forget your phone number or social security number — it happens to all of us. These lapses are not "age-associated memory loss" or "impending mental decline." Indeed, there is no such thing as "normal memory loss." Like with all things, aging reduces our effiiency, not our competency.

As I pursued this further, I was pleased that most performers solve this problem by liberally using *external memory supports*. One good way to reduce forgetting is to *make a plan for remembering* (e.g., a notation in a calendar or a post-it note). Performers have clear and specific plans to help them remember during concerts. Paul McCartney compensates by using a teleprompter. Mick Jagger, if he needs it, uses an onstage monitor to help him remember his lyrics. He also wisely adds the name of the city where he is performing and cues for his ad-libs between songs. Actually, this method was pioneered by Frank Sinatra. He used an onstage teleprompter while he was performing until the age of eighty.

These lapses are not necessarily the beginnings of Alzheimer's disease. Alzheimer's disease starts with failure to learn new things and is not the same as temporary memory lapses. A good memory evaluation can tell the difference. I don't have to feel guilt any longer for using PowerPoint slides to pace and manage my talks. I am in good company.

MEMORY LOSS AND MENTAL DISABILITY ARE NOT A NECESSARY OUTCOME OF AGING

Many of us will retain good memory and mental skills throughout our life. Indeed, aging is not the antithesis of personal growth and creativity, as some suggest. Our knowledge and vocabulary will increase as we age. And our fixed skills (crystallized intelligence) will remain intact.

Rather, as we age, we experience a decline in *working memory* (can't multitask as well as in the past) that will make us process information, solve problems, and think more slowly. This, in turn, will slow the speed at which we can acquire new information as well as reduce the amount of information that we can manage at any one time. We will also have more trouble directing our attention away from irrelevant information. For example, we may no longer be able to read while the radio is playing in the background.

These are the general inefficiencies that accompany aging. Knowing and planning in advance for these changes allows you to manage your memory better no matter how old you are. Often these changes are subtle. The talents of a twenty- or thirty-year-old in the workplace are different from those of a sixty- or seventy-year-old in the same workplace. Given normal aging, the former will excel in tasks that require speed, short-term memory, and working memory, while the latter will excel in tasks that require synthesis and experience.

It is important to plan for the changes that will occur as you age and put in place methods to compensate well *before* you need them.

AGING PRODUCES GREATER DIFFICULTY IN DIVIDING ATTENTION

I have already noticed this in myself. I can no longer read in a noisy environment. I must have a quiet place to absorb what I am reading. If I have background music while I work or read, the music must not contain words, and I need to play it at the "right" volume. I can no longer have the television on while I read anything that requires concentration. I have difficulty following a conversation if a second conversation is going on in the background. I lose my place in a conversation more often now than I used to. I need a more detailed calendar to track what I must do. It's a mistake for me to read my e-mail while I am on the phone. If I am asked to take a new or an additional medication, I have trouble consistently recalling that I need to do so if I don't use a pillbox.

AGING REQUIRES YOU TO SPEND MORE TIME AND EFFORT IN LEARNING SOMETHING NEW

I find this especially annoying when I am trying to learn a new name. I have always had a poor memory for names, but now I realize that I have to see a new acquaintance multiple times before I can recall his or her name. Fortunately, I do much better with faces, and people are forgiving about my repeatedly having to ask for their name. If I am learning new information, taking notes and reviewing them helps even more than it did in the past. I need to travel new routes a few times to get them down well, especially when I travel to new places. The changes are quite subtle, but clearly I spend more time learning new things than I did in the past.

AGING LENGTHENS THE TIME REQUIRED TO BRING A PIECE OF INFORMATION OR A WORD TO MIND

I think more slowly as I age. My wife and I are movie buffs. We often discuss movies that we've seen. I now take longer to recall the names of movies or the names of actors. Sometimes I remember the name of the movie a day or so after I originally tried to recall it (at least my brain keeps searching despite my unawareness).

This also occurs in conversations when I must choose an alternate word for the one I really want to use but can't bring to mind at the moment. The words or concepts I want often come to me after the conversation has turned elsewhere. I am especially likely to block with proper names and nouns. Despite the fact that my vocabulary will continue to grow at least into my seventies (I should be at about my upper limit), my speed of finding words will decline for each decade I continue to live. Many confuse the slowness of word finding with loss of memory. People I know who are older than seventy are often aware of these changes and find them very frustrating. These changes can be one of the signs of a condition called primary expressive aphasia (or may sometimes accompany the onset of Alzheimer's disease), but often they are not necessarily a result of memory loss. Freud referred to these incidents as "tip of the tongue" phenomena.

AGING PRODUCES MORE UNINTENDED WORDS

Sometimes I use substitute words or wrong words, especially nouns, for the concepts that I want to express. I recently was listening to a news broadcast in which a well-known and experienced anchor used the wrong word in a story and was apparently unaware he had even made this substitution. Seeing him made me feel a whole lot better when I recently was making a point about memory in a lecture and said "spring" when I meant to say "fall" as the current season. I am sure that I have used wrong words that neither my audience nor I even noticed.

Aging Is Not All Loss and Decline

There is a strong bias against aging and the aged. Consider the following **MYTHS**:

- **Aging is mostly accompanied by loss and decline.** This attitude leads to a bias in the practices of hiring and terminating older workers. In fact, most mental decline occurs after age eighty with great variability. Many older adults are frequent caregivers of grandchildren or adult children with disabilities. Others are productive workers or active volunteers.

- **The way we grow older is genetically determined.** Actually, as much as 70 percent of the variance in changes in memory associated with aging and cognition is determined by the use of alcohol and tobacco, physical activity, and cognitive engagement earlier in life. (See the comment below about a study of identical twins.)

- **It's all downhill after age sixty-five.** It's true that adults aged sixty-five to seventy-four, seventy-five to eighty-four, and eighty-five or older face numerous risks (e.g., strokes, heart disease, diabetes) as they age. *However, aging is a much more elastic process than previously thought.* Those of us who are middle-aged and older have more control over the *way* we grow older than we believe. We need to realign our personal and community efforts by ramping up the focus on prevention (e.g., not smoking, wearing helmets when cycling, and controlling blood pressure) and on engagement in healthy behaviors (e.g., exercising, mostly eating a Mediterranean diet, and staying socially and intellectually engaged), starting at least in middle age.

If we can avoid severe physical and cognitive disability, we can take actions to better control our destiny. We may even delay the clinical onset of such ailments as Alzheimer's disease, osteoporosis (loss of bone mineral density), diabetes, and sarcopenia (decrease in muscle mass, function, and strength). Extensive longitudinal research on memory has produced a number of findings that give us a more accurate and hopeful outlook of becoming old(er):

- The most robust finding in aging research is the dramatic variability between individuals. Many of us do quite well as we age.

- The biggest hit from aging is a decline in speed (mental and physical) associated with aging. This decline compromises tasks that measure *fluid intelligence.* (The tests that measure this decline all have a time requirement, whereas tests that measure vocabulary, information, or similarities reflect *crystalized intelligence*).

- Primary mental abilities remain intact until we reach our sixties. Marked decline does not start for most of us until we reach our eighties. (But keep in mind that many of us in our eighties and beyond do quite well until our death.)

- We experience improvements in the "Big Five" personality traits of agreeableness, conscientiousness, and mental stability.

- Average seniors maintain a positive sense of emotional well-being, emotional stability, and emotional complexity.

- Genetics accounted for only 30 percent of the variance in identical twins. That leaves 70 percent to nongenetic influences such lifestyle and environment. Genetics are not destiny.

- Our behavior and neuroplasticity are what really make the difference. For example, half of the risk for developing Alzheimer's disease is explained by seven risk factors that are subject to lifestyle interventions:

    - Hypertension
    - Diabetes
    - Obesity
    - Smoking
    - Depression
    - Cognitive inactivity or low educational achievement
    - Physical inactivity

- Regular physical activity, defined as at least thirty minutes of moderate physical activity five days a week, produces meaningful health benefits:

    - Better cardiovascular, respiratory, and musculoskeletal health
    - Improved resistance to type 2 diabetes and cancers
    - Improved cognitive and emotional function
    - Lower risk for depression

- Cognitive training in speed of processing, inductive reasoning (e.g., scientific reasoning), and episodic memory improved cognitive functioning in seniors (although the benefits did not generalize beyond the tasks trained).

- Regular aerobic activity over a twelve-month period was associated with increased levels of brain-derived neurotropic factor, hippocampal volume, neurogenesis, and neuroplasticity in previously sedentary adults, and improvement on memory test scores. No benefits occurred from toning or stretching exercises.

HOW OLD IS TOO OLD TO WORK?

This question used to be easier to answer. Prior to 1900, people worked until they could no longer work. The Social Security Act changed that. After 1935, older workers could draw benefits and retire at age sixty-five. When I reached the age of sixty-five, and much to my surprise, I was often asked when I was going to retire. I had no plan to retire at an arbitrary age. For me, retirement is a decision that *unfolds*, contingent upon circumstances (e.g., size of desired nest egg, health, cognitive abilities, family desires) over many years.

The question of being too old to work cannot be answered based on chronological age. Rather, it is based on financial resources, desired lifestyle, need for engagement and challenges, and functional (physical and mental) abilities. I had several clients doing well into their eighties and beyond. One was still CEO of his company at the age of ninety. Another an accountant was still successfully working full time at the age of eighty-two. And there was a bowler older than 100.

Work enhances economic security and well-being. Some argue that work improves brain health, but the issue is complicated in that those who have better brain health may be able to work successfully for a longer period of time. Work satisfies the need for engaging intellectual and social needs. Work adds a sense of accomplishment and achievement. Older workers do a good job of adapting to the normal physical and mental changes of aging. Many older workers have greater institutional knowledge and problem-solving experience than younger workers.

Rather than assume that older workers should retire when they reach a certain age, we should be helping those who are able and desire to continue to work. Chronological age matters little. What matters is the functional capacity to do the job and enjoy it.

The eighty-two-year-old accountant I mentioned above, along with his wife, noted "minor" changes in memory. He was also taking inordinately long to do the books — but he was still very competent. We completed a memory evaluation, and he was diagnosed with Mild Cognitive Impairment. We put together a plan that allowed him to retire from work on his own terms before he began making mistakes and was forced to retire. We also worked on a plan for adding activities that filled the hole left by retirement.

As we age on the job, we need to attend to our physical health. Most workers have annual physicals, and many workplaces have wellness programs that may be particularly helpful to older workers. We also need to routinely have our memory and cognitive skills (as part of corporate wellness programs) evaluated as we continue in the workforce. This may be especially important for professionals who serve others. We cannot take our mental skills for granted. We need to be sure our memory is still serving ourselves and/or our clients well. We can work into our seventies, eighties, and beyond as long as we want and are able to do so.

How Long Will You Live?

Aging is not a disease. Aging is a process that unfolds over time. One way to help manage the changes of aging is to have some idea of the possible length of time for which you are planning. No matter what you eat, how much you exercise, or tend to your overall wellness, you are unlikely to change your life expectancy by more than a few months on average. You will not live forever. However, the intent of this book is to *help you make changes in the quality of the life you have in front of you.*

A multitude of life-expectancy calculators are available online. The social security website (ssa.gov) has a life-expectancy calculator, while the Livingto100 website (developed from the New England Centenarian Study) is more elaborate. The number can be used to calculate ballpark figures (the omnipresent average) for life planningss (finances, tending to your bucket list).

Unavoidable Changes From Aging

1. Functional loss (muscle strength, aerobic capacity, cardiac function, senses)
2. More affected by heat and cold
3. Recover more slowly from altered sleep and meal patterns
4. Longer time to recover from injury
5. Less able to ward off illness
6. Slowing of reaction time/reflexes
7. Speed of thinking and moving slows down
8. Vision declines (need more light, accommodation declines)
9. Hearing declines (high pitch first, then low pitch)
10. Difficulty locating the source of a sound
11. Difficulty understanding a conversation
12. More interference from background noise
13. Changes in the efficiency of cognitive skills

Modifiable Factors That Influence Aging and the Quality of Life

1. Getting aerobic exercise — regular exercise can set the clock back twenty-five to forty-five years
2. Getting anaerobic exercise
3. Monitoring what and how you eat
4. Not smoking
5. Taking control of your blood pressure
6. Lowering your cholesterol (if it is too high)

7. Monitoring your blood sugar

8. Regularly having your vision and hearing checked

9. Limiting your consumption of alcohol

10. Participating in complex and intellectually stimulating activity

11. Participating in social activities

12. Turning off the television some of the time

13. Wearing your seatbelt

14. Wearing a helmet when you ski, ride, etc.

15. Having a purpose in life

16. Directing yourself toward personal growth

17. Accepting yourself

18. Living with a spouse, especially if you are male

19. Possessing a flexible lifestyle

20. Being resilient —maintaining a high degree of well-being despite set-
    backs

CHAPTER FIVE

Circumstances That Increase Forgetting

*"Our ability to create information and data has far exceeded our ability
to find, review, understand and recall information."*
(Richard Saul Wurman, 2001)

Although some theories have suggested that we remember everything we encounter in life, either consciously or unconsciously, *forgetting is actually a natural part of memory*. Even long-term memory is subject to change and forgetting, because it is a process where the brain reconstructs memory from kernels. The original memory is subject to change during the process of recall. (Hence the problem of false memories, like remembering abuse that didn't occur. As you may recall from the discussion of flashbulb memory, belief in the correctness of a memory does not assure its accuracy.)

Memory is not fixed. It is a flexible and variable warehouse of fragments (making up the gist, or essence) that is subject to transformation. For example, the reliability of an eyewitness's recall and testimony in legal proceedings may be controversial. Indeed, many envy those with super memories (hypermnesia). Ken Jennings, for instance, was a legend for the breadth of knowledge he displayed on *Jeopardy*. However, the process of forgetting may be as important to creative mental functions as is the process of remembering. The reasons behind this are because forgetting helps us to think more creatively and to allow us to synthesize information. Thus, our reconstructions may be more interesting than reality.

Russian psychologist A. R. Luria presented a classical case study of hypermnesia. "S" was a reporter for a newspaper in Moscow and had "too good" of a memory. His editor once reprimanded S for not taking notes during a meeting. However, S was able to recite back to his boss the precise contents of the meeting despite not taking notes. During several years of testing, Dr. Luria could not find any limits to S's capacity to recall detail. S was able to recall long tables of seemingly random numbers. He could repeat the contents of such tables within an hour and even years later and could reproduce the tables forward or backward from memory. S did not forget with either distraction or time.

Yet despite this remarkable ability, S was generally disorganized and without direction. His ability to recall everything came at the price of not being able to form general impressions or draw meaning from events. Thus, S's case demonstrated that, rather than a blessing, the ability *not* to forget could be a curse. Either extreme — remembering too much or remembering too little — presents limitations that have to be managed. S, in fact, spent much time and effort trying to forget!

THE "SINS" OF MEMORY

Most of us have memories that function at a level somewhere between those of HM and S. *We must deal with forgetting and the imperfections of memory.* Daniel Schacter suggested that memory has "seven sins" — transience, absentmindedness, blocking, misattribution, suggestibility, bias, and persistence — that illustrate the complex interaction between memory and forgetting. The first three of these sins, or what we might call simple memory flaws, are the ones that most of us struggle with on a conscious level in everyday life, and these sins increase as we age.

Transience, the first sin, refers to the fading of memory over time. Try to recall all of your grade-school teachers or high-school classmates by name. Details tend to fade over time. We usually store fragments, not details. Transience is a function of time and interference. The more we ponder or practice an experience, skill, or piece of information, the more resistant it becomes to transience. Hence, the **One-Minute Rule** strikes again. *Visit often those memories you want to preserve.*

Absentmindedness, the second sin, results from dividing our attention and is driven by the properties of primary, working, and prospective memory. We spend so much of our time on autopilot in order to carry out routines that we often forget what we are told or what we have to do. Distinctive cues (external memory aids that we will discuss later) reduce absentmindedness.

Blocking, the third sin, refers to the elusive name or word that will not come to mind when we want it (the tip-of-the-tongue experience), and it increases as we age. The best solutions to this frustration are time (if you wait, the word or name may come to you) or searching the alphabet for the first letter of the name or word you want.

The fourth memory sin is **misattribution**, which refers to our tendency to forget the source of a given memory. Misattribution also increases as we age. How many of the thoughts that we have are truly original? Numerous lawsuits have been filed in which someone wrote words that were the thoughts of someone else (a sin I hope I have been able to minimize here). As our memories age, we tend to forget their origin. Plagiarism is often not intentional but rather results from forgetting the source of our thoughts or ideas. This, too, may increase as a particular memory ages.

Another but more infrequent example of misattribution is the **experience of déjà vu**. This occurs because we often remember something that is familiar. Misattribution allows a con artist to engage in the "where's the check?" scam. Here, a contact is made, perhaps a phone call to gather information and to establish a sense of familiarity. After a short time, the person called forgets the details but experiences a sense of familiarity when the con artist calls back. At this point, the con artist makes a false claim, such as, "Our records indicate that you paid $160, leaving a balance of only $60. Please make out a check for $60 to clear the balance." See the movie *Cold Call* (currently on Acorn TV) for an example of this tactic.

Suggestibility, the fifth sin, is a process similar to misattribution but is not generally a problem encountered in everyday life. Rather, suggestibility is more likely to occur in legal and clinical contexts. Consider the difference of being asked the open-ended question, "What color was the car?" as opposed to the closed-ended question, "Was the car red?" Suggestibility creates complications in the legal processes of lineup identification, witness interrogation, and false confessions. Suggestibility also underlies many of the experiences that occur under hypnosis and the "false memory syndrome" where, for example, a person recovers "lost" memories of trauma.

The sixth sin of memory, **bias**, is when we reconstruct our memory to fit with our own biases, needs, and views of the world. For example, we may view the past as consistent with the present. If we are depressed, we may recall our failures rather than our successes. If we buy a car that is too expensive, we immediately engage in rationalizations to justify our spending more than we can afford. If we smoke, we create elaborate justifications for our behavior. Hindsight, egocentricity, and stereotypes create bias in our memories. This tendency to reconstruct memory to fit with our biases is the price we pay for being able to generalize and form schemas.

Finally, **persistence**, the seventh sin, is the opposite of transience. Persistence is often driven by disappointment, failure, or trauma. We experience persistence when we have a tune that we cannot get out of our head, or when we fall in love and cannot (and do not want to) get the person of our affections out of our head. Persistence produces the symptoms of grief and rumination. It underlies waking in the middle of the night to recall what we forgot to do (absentmindedness) earlier that day. Persistence can be the outcome of trauma, such as being robbed, assaulted, or abused (i.e., posttraumatic stress disorder, PTSD).

Persistence is driven by strong emotions that make certain experiences stand out from the background of life. These emotions take us immediately out of autopilot. The best treatment for dealing with persistence is to make ourselves aware of these feelings and allow ourselves to repeat them until they eventually diminish. This is what occurs among those of us who are normally bereaved — we have waves of sadness until acute pain subsides over a period of months to years.

FACTORS THAT LEAD US TO FORGET

Not Paying Attention

If you don't pay attention in the first place, you will forget. Take me, for example. I took copious notes in classes to help me recall lectures. Handwriting your notes produces better memory retention of the material than typing them into a computer (probably like a skilled transcriptionist who types fast and accurately but does not think about the content). Revising your notes shortly after taking them also enhances recall and recognition at a later time. You have to think about content if you write it down. It is sometimes challenging to take notes and listen carefully at the same time, but not taking notes increases the effect of transience.

Another situation that keeps you from paying attention is having someone next to you say something during a lecture or discussion. This breaks your concentration, making it harder for you to pay attention to the speaker.

Being ill, daydreaming, taking medications or drugs, or being tired also interfere with your attention, as does "pulling an all-nighter." Another practical example of not paying attention is when couples talk to each other while in different rooms. It would be much easier for them (and for their hearing and memory) to go to the same room, turn off the TV, and make eye contact with the other person. This way, each party can pay better attention to the communication.

You can also improve your ability to pay attention by getting enough rest and doing more mentally demanding activities when you are most alert. These strategies help you to improve your memory, because aging reduces the efficiency of processes such as attending to multiple tasks at the same time.

Distraction

It is easy to get distracted by thinking about things you have to do. As you are talking with someone, you may lose your train of thought (blocking) as you try to construct your arguments or think about what you are going to say rather than listening to what the other person is saying. Movement that you catch with the corner of your eye may distract your attention and cause you to lose track of what you're doing or where you're going. The radio or television in the background may distract you from reading. You may have trouble listening to the person sitting next to you in a restaurant because you are distracted by background conversations.

Distraction increases forgetting. Recall that primary, working, and short-term memory are subject to interference and distraction. Distractions can happen from a phone ringing, hearing a knock at the door, listening to a television show in the background, daydreaming, or having intrusive thoughts. Even playing the radio while driving slows your reaction times.

You can also be distracted by using too many notes as reminders. The multiple notes fight each other for attention. Clutter can distract. Working in a clean and organized environment usually improves mental efficiency. Sometimes, distraction and background noise produce stress. My wife and I once stayed in a lake cabin with no television or telephones. We also forgot the charger for the cell phone, so it quit working. It was such a treat, and a great stress reducer, to have the world of distractions minimized for a time.

Stress

Stress is another enemy of memory. The first time I tried to lecture, I worked very hard writing out the lecture in detail. I practiced and rehearsed the material so I could become comfortable with it. However, when I actually had to present the lecture to a live audience, my mind went blank, and I often lost my place in the written version of the lecture. As if this weren't enough, I completely lost my composure when someone asked a question.

To this day, I don't know how or why I finally mastered this terrible anxiety and became a lecturesr/speaker. Since then, I have learned how to organize information better, manage my feelings, and use stress as my ally rather than my adversary. However, it is interesting how well I recall the emotions from those early lecturing experiences, despite the fact that I don't recall the specific information. Managing emotions and stress can contribute to more efficient memory and will be discussed in Chapter 14.

Depression

Depression also distorts memory (can create bias and distraction) and may induce forgetting. In the extreme case, depression can make you so inner-focused on feelings of despair that you cannot manage pertinent information from your surroundings. Furthermore, depression does not allow you to focus on what is positive; instead, you tend to focus on your failings and all that is wrong. There is a complex relationship between depression and forgetting.

Many professionals still believe that it is important to differentiate depression from dementia. Depression is seen as a "treatable" cause of dementia for some. Thus, the term "pseudodementia" was coined to emphasize this distinction. The tendency of depressed persons with memory loss to report that all of their traits, including memory, are bad (the bias of negative self-image in depression) have led professionals in memory clinics to hypothesize that, if the depression were successfully treated, the memory loss would go away, especially in elderly patients.

Unfortunately, this does not seem to be the case. While some memory loss can be explained by depression (especially those with very severe depressions), it is much more likely that those who demonstrate objective memory loss and depression as they get older may show future *but not inevitable* mental decline. If you are depressed in middle age and beyond, it is wise to have your memory evaluated and managed early. This will be discussed in Chapter 11.

Loss and Grief

Loss and grief interfere with memory. One protective psychic mechanism that we use to manage extreme psychic pain is to become "numb." We seem to act without full awareness. This is a good defense to help keep us from immersing ourselves in persistent, extreme, unbearable emotions (a form of denial that can be good in the short run), but it destroys good memory operations because it interferes with attention and concentration.

When we are bereaved, we often do unusual things without apparent thinking and may make poor decisions, especially during the early stages. Once we have "recovered" from the loss, we are amazed when others reflect on our actions, decisions, and behaviors. Hence, it is important that we not make major decisions during the first year of bereavement. The image (memory) of the deceased typically changes during the course of grief. Part of the grieving process is reconstructing the memory of the deceased, often with idealization.

Grief is different from clinical depression. When we are bereaved, we do not experience loss of self-esteem (although we can be depressed and bereaved at the same time). Rather, we seem to "forget" the negative and remember the positive (bias) traits of the deceased. Thus, it is best not to do productive intellectual or mental work during the early stages.

Lack of Organization

A lack of organization in daily life is another major pitfall for good memory. I make *multiple* stacks of things that I feel I must remember to do. Often, I'm embarrassed to find a note buried under one of my stacks reminding me to make a phone call or respond to correspondence that I should have taken care of months earlier. Too many notes in too many places fight with each other for attention and thereby increase forgetting.

I once had to take a medication twice a day, one in the morning and one in the evening. I tied the morning medication to shaving, and this worked very well. However, rather than organizing a routine for taking the evening medication, I "tried" to remember to take it sometime before I went to bed. Needless to say, I forgot that medication often and had to devise a more organized plan for evenings (I tied it to brushing my teeth).

The solution is to organize and declutter. If you have not attended to an item in a stack during the first month, you will probably not get to it and have likely already forgotten it. As part of your reorganization, make priorities and use distinctive cues, takeaway spots, calendars, timers, and routines to combat prospective memory failures.

Illness

You're never at your best when you're ill or in pain. If you have a fever or a gastrointestinal bug, you'll have more trouble with your memory. If you suffer from sleep apnea, so will your memory. Don't count on your memory during times of illness or injury. The illness and/or the medications to treat the problem may cause you to forget (e.g., antibiotics can interfere with protein synthesis that is needed for storing memory and may induce forgetting because the "memory trace" is not being formed properly, contributing to transience; see more below under "Medications").

Don't do mentally demanding things when you are ill. Your memory will improve once you have recovered. For example, I evaluated a woman suffering with ovarian cancer. She was fearful that she was developing Alzheimer's disease, and test scores suggested Mild Cognitive Impairment (which in some is the early presentation of Alzheimer's disease). I am pleased to say that she made a full recovery from the cancer, and her evaluation scores had returned to normal eighteen months later.

Medications

Many types of medications can make our memory less efficient, and few make it better. For example, medications such as Valium, Klonopin, Ativan, or Xanax are good at inducing relaxation and reducing anxiety. However, they also cause subtle impairment in working and short-term memory, similar to the effects of alcohol intoxication. In other words, they can increase forgetting. Some antidepressant and pain medications also induce forgetting, as do over-the-counter sleep and allergy medications.

The effects of medications on mental operations are complicated by the fact that some of us are more susceptible to deleterious influences of medications than are others. Sex and age are not often considered in administration of drugs (many data used to inform drug treatments have often been based on white males) but are important variables in understanding the actions and side effects of medications. For example, alcohol has a greater effect on women than men as a result of differing body composition and in the concentration of a stomach enzyme that helps metabolize alcohol.

Further complicating the picture is that forgetfulness is tied to dosage, timing, and frequency of taking a medication. The effects of medications are also often magnified during the process of aging, when our liver, lungs, cardiovascular system, gastrointestinal system, and kidneys are altered in their efficiency. These changes influence the absorption, distribution, metabolism, and excretion of medications as well as other drugs. (This also applies to many herbs and supplements.) The bottom line is, we need to understand the trade-off between the benefits of a medication and the costs of side effects when it comes to our memory.

Poor Vision

Surprisingly, our eyesight can have a tremendous effect on our memory. If we do not see something in the first place, we will not remember it later. And it takes more effort to see, which comes at the cost of having fewer resources with which to remember. Therefore, we need to do our best to maximize our vision by getting regular eye exams and keeping our eyewear prescription current. We also need to do all we can to reduce the likelihood of developing glaucoma and macular degeneration. And, of course, we must wear eye protection when we are involved in any activity that may injure our eyes.

Poor Hearing

Just as we can't recall something we can't see, if we don't hear what someone tells us, we cannot recall it later. Furthermore, the effort to hear takes extra resources that we could better use to process memories. How will we know if our hearing is making it harder for us to participate in the world and to hear and recall what we want and need to? Psychologically, it is so much easier to have an eye examination and to wear corrective lenses than it is to have an audiology evaluation and to wear hearing aids. (Complicating the issue is that hearing aids are stigmatized, whereas eyewear is considered a fashion statement.) We should not wait to get a hearing evaluation until someone is constantly telling us that the television is too loud. And if we need to use hearing aids, we must wear them.

Alcohol

As discussed above, alcohol enhances forgetting. One area of my research was to evaluate the effects of alcohol on learning and memory in adults (young, healthy college students). Young adults who consumed alcohol clearly had poorer memory of newly learned information than did those who consumed a placebo. Interestingly, several participants were unable to reliably report whether they had consumed the beverage with alcohol or the placebo. The dose of alcohol used in the studies was below the legal limit of intoxication in most states. As the amount of alcohol we consume increases, so does the impairment of our memory.

If we enjoy a daily cocktail, beer, or wine, we must realize that it will impair our memory even if we do not feel the effects. Therefore, we should time our consumption of alcohol so that it does not interfere with any important functions that require motor skills, judgment, or memory. We also need to remember that aging and sex (women show a higher blood concentration of alcohol per volume than men) may cause alcohol to have a greater effect on mental and motor processes, just as do many other drugs and medications.

Malnutrition

Malnutrition makes mental operations less efficient and increases forgetting. Fortunately, I have not encountered this situation often in my work, other than some heavy users of alcohol who have needed dietary interventions. However, at times, depression and confusion can prevent us from managing proper nutrition. We need to address this, because better nutrition will often help those of us who are afflicted to think more clearly. The effects of diet on memory for those of us who have normal nutrition are not well understood at this time. This topic will be addressed in Chapter 12.

Fatigue

Fatigue contributes to forgetting. I have been a morning (but not too early morning) person in my adult life (interestingly, I have become an evening person since developing Parkinson's disease). This means that I will usually do better with all of my mental operations in the evening than in the morning. Others may be morning persons; still others may be neither. The bottom line: We must know our patterns and plan the more demanding mental activity during our peak times. If taking a nap revitalizes us, we should do so. Taking a walk can also break up our workday and make our mind more efficient and less fatigued.

Too Few Cues

As discussed above, clutter can inhibit memory and increase forgetting by adding interference (the enemy of primary and working memory). The inverse is also true. Having too few cues to trigger memory may cause us to have more instances of forgetting (transience and absentmindedness) that could have been avoided. As an example, just leaving the umbrella beside the door would have saved me the cost of many umbrellas when I was doing home visits after I moved to Florida. It is extremely useful for us to have an environment rich in reminders of important things to do or to recall. A great deal of forgetting can be reduced by using external memory aids such as calendars, timers, other people, smartphone apps, and trying recall to routine events (taking my morning medications when I shave). These aids will be discussed in Chapter 9.

* * *

Now that we better understand the naturalness and complexity of forgetting and memory distortion, we are ready to discuss how to manage memory. Our memory will never be perfect. Still, many factors that increase forgetting *are under our control*. It is important that we proactively expect and compensate for factors that lead to forgetting.

The most important strategy for managing and improving memory is the **One-Minute Rule**. Anything given less than one minute of thought will fade from our memory. How often do we think about where we are parked for one minute before going into the grocery store? How often do we forget names at a luncheon because we didn't take the time to write the names as a seating chart on our napkin? Spending the time to *plan how we will remember* is the foundation for improving our memory. This is the principle for mnemonics and strategies for improving memory that will be discussed in the next chapter.

CHAPTER SIX

What We Commonly Forget and Strategies To Help Us Remember

"When I was younger, I could remember anything, whether it had happened or not; but my faculties are decaying now and soon I shall be so I cannot remember any but the things that never happened. "
(Mark Twain, as quoted by David Shenk, 2001)

Now that we are familiar the concept of memory, the nature of changes in mental processes resulting from normal aging, and general factors that increase forgetting, it's time to focus on what we commonly forget and how we can improve our memory.

This chapter reviews several everyday examples of memory challenges. Anticipating these situations allows us to plan strategies and take the time to improve the strength of our memory. This is true for young adults with "normal" memory as well as adults who are experiencing the changes of aging. When you know about situations that are likely to challenge memory, you will better be able to plan for these events by developing *memory aids*.

The major difference between those with mild to moderate memory disorders and those with "normal" memory is a matter of degree rather than of kind. So if we can anticipate where we may have memory challenges, we can set up systems to compensate for changes in efficiency. It's like buying car insurance. We buy it before we have an accident and hope we'll never have to use it. The same is true for managing memory. *Good memory requires planning ahead.*

With this in mind, let's review some common scenarios that challenge memory. We should also consider having a consultation and evaluation by a memory expert if we have any concerns. This helps us to more efficiently develop plans based on our own strengths and weaknesses. These techniques are variants of the **One-Minute Rule: Anything given less than one minute of thought will fade from our memory**.

FORGETTING WHAT SOMEONE TELLS US

We often forget what someone tells us (spouses, friends, bosses, or colleagues). If we could recall everything we hear, we'd never have to take notes at lectures or seminars. Good note taking requires planning ahead. It improves memory because we spend more time and effort with the information as we think and write. This also gives us the chance to review our notes in the future.

Of course, both we and the speaker must decide in advance what is important to remember. This way, we can spend more time and effort concentrating on the important parts of the message. We also can make some notes or mentally rehearse what is felt to be important.

In my line of work, I must recall many details of what people tell me. I use notes to boost my recall, and rather than be annoyed with it, my clients feel that I am taking them more seriously. I also suggest to my clients that they record their sessions with me. When they choose to do this, I make sure that the machine is recording and place it on my lap or on a nearby table. They can then later review the recording to decide what is important for them to recall and make notes before erasing the audio. This way, clients can spend time with the more significant information and improve their recall of important points.

Be sure that you are in the same room during a conversation so that you can talk face-to-face. (This is especially important for me given my Parkinson's-induced soft voice and dysarthria [a speech disorder that weakens the muscles controlling speech].) I am especially careful to be in the same room with my wife Pamela or my close friends when discussing important matters. I then repeat back to them in my own words what I think they told me. (Paraphrasing is a very useful technique to improve understanding.) This way, I can clarify the communication, and it gives me more time (the **One-Minute Rule**) to develop my memory. This obviously makes me less likely to forget what is important for me to remember.

REMEMBERING DIRECTIONS

Remembering route directions can be challenging. It is a complicated mental task that requires listening, driving, and navigating. This is true of even relatively simple directions. Dealing with directions places a large burden on primary memory, working memory, and attention. So many variables can interfere with this process, and it's even more difficult if you are tired, stressed, or driving at night when landmarks used for navigation are limited. Personally, I am good for about two turns before I lose track if I try to retain directions in my mind. You can reduce a great deal of frustration and lost time by writing directions down or recording them on your smartphone.

PHONE MESSAGES

It's easy to forget phone messages because they also put a load on working memory. Don't rely on your ability to recall a message. *Write it down.* Use this skill at home as well as at work. Have a pencil and paper next to the phone for writing down information, or dictate messages to the "notes" app on your smartphone as they are being given. It's also a good idea to repeat the message, as this will reinforce your memory and make sure you've heard it correctly. And another benefit: You'll be able to replay the message whenever necessary.

REPEATING STORIES OR QUESTIONS

The longer I know someone, the more often I repeat the same story. As I get older, I occasionally have more trouble keeping my place in a conversation or knowing to whom I have said what. I also have more difficulty recalling whether I said something or if I just thought it (misattribution or failure of source memory). I most often have these lapses when I'm with my wife, friends, or colleagues with whom I spend a lot of time.

Furthermore, the content of the story may change (encouraging suggestibility and bias). Each time I recall and tell a story, I may add or subtract information *intentionally* (creative license) or *unintentionally*. I have not found a good strategy for managing this tendency. It is helpful if those listening to the story are patient with me. Telling stories is vital to our well-being (as will be discussed in the next chapter). It gives continuity to our life and allows us to enjoy the liberal use of long-term memory despite its tendency toward bias and distortion.

Living with individuals who have short-term memory loss (anterograde amnesia) is stressful and aggravating because of their often-repeated questions. They cannot monitor what they have asked or not asked. Each time they ask a question, *it is the first time for them.* If you are the one who is listening, you can keep track of these repeated questions, which helps you to be *aware* of what is being repeated. For example, I often encounter caregivers who are frustrated at being asked countless times every day what the date is or what has to be done at a certain time. In this case, a simple strategy can help. Simply have those with memory loss wear a watch that always has the date available, and direct them to look at it. Also, have them habitually carry with them a good, easy-to-read calendar. It can be prepared by or for them each morning. This will help them to monitor what has to be done and when and can dramatically reduce this repetition. A multitude of smartphone apps can help people to remember as long as they retain the ability to use such a device.

Difficulty Following Characters or Plots in a Novel or Movie

I recently had a lunch conversation with friends who were older than fifty and had good memory. One of the participants mentioned that they were having more difficulty now than they used to following characters in a novel. This is especially true of novels with many characters and complex plots. This can also happen with movies or TV shows that introduce new characters. Learning characters and plots (that is, new information) requires adequate short-term and working memory.

If you enjoy reading, managing these changes is much easier than if you enjoy movies or television, because you can go back to what you've forgotten in the text. You can also list new characters or important facts as they appear in the text. If you own the book, use the inside front cover or the margins of the book for your notes. Underlining can help as long as you reread, think about, and spend more time with the item or concept that you underlined. This way, you can more easily find the critical information for review at a later time. And if you do not own the book, you can use a "reading journal," where you can keep track of characters, plots, and main ideas.

It's a good idea to include *brief cues* and *page references* for ease in looking up characters or facts later. I have read many textbooks that are marked in the margins and front covers, because I developed this strategy to help my memory when I started college. This process is more active than just reading, and it helps me to focus on the important facts or concepts during review. And, my memory is strengthened while doing so. I continue to use this strategy today. I repeat: "Our ability to create information and data have far exceeded our ability to find, review, understand, and recall information" (Richard Saul Wurman, 2001). *We remember best that which we practice.*

Another good strategy is to *reread* books, novels, or articles in which the information is important. This allows you to work from long-term memory rather than just relying on short-term memory. This is a useful skill if you develop short-term memory loss.

I worked with a client who loved reading science fiction but was having some mild to moderate short-term memory loss. She was very aggravated, because she was struggling when reading new science fiction and was finding her favorite pastime frustrating rather than enjoyable and relaxing. She tried listing the characters as suggested above, but this no longer worked for her. As we discussed her frustrations, we decided to build on her strengths of long-term memory. She listed the science fiction works that she had on her bookshelves and wanted to reread sometime in the unplanned future. She then reread them and again enjoyed her favorite science fiction titles. This reduced her frustration and gave her more control. She is now marking the most enjoyable of her reread books so she can read them again if her memory worsens. The books she rereads will have the strongest memory traces and therefore be easier to follow, because she is strengthening her long-term memory in an area that will bring her joy for years to come.

This strategy is more difficult for movies or TV programs that are current, because they move rapidly; therefore, you can't take notes because it will interfere with continuity. Of course, you could record the show that you wish to remember and later stop and review parts of it as needed. Or you could buy a copy of the movie, then stop and take notes if you wish. However, it's probably better to just enjoy the movie again! Like the client who loved reading science fiction, if you develop short-term memory loss, you can focus your time on movies or TV shows that you enjoyed in the past. This process also takes advantage of your long-term memory. My wife and I watch DVDs of *Sid Caesar's Show of Shows*, *The Twilight Zone*, and *Frazier*, and they give us hours of enjoyment.

Game shows rely on long-term rather than short-term memory and can be enjoyed even by those who live with significant memory loss. Perhaps this is why the TV game shows like *Jeopardy* are so appealing. The same applies to group games such as hangman. Many who have short-term memory loss (even those with early and moderate Alzheimer's disease), if materials are well selected and do not require learning new information, can spend many pleasurable hours doing crossword puzzles, playing Scrabble, playing bridge, or watching old television shows that are now available as DVDs or through a streaming service.

FORGETTING NAMES

Forgetting people's names is the most common complaint about memory loss. I have never possessed a good memory for names, and I know that as I get older, this memory skill will not improve; in fact, it will probably decline. Struggling to learn new names is exasperating. Yet this ability tends to decrease as a result of aging. It also represents the weakening of our ability to bring to mind nouns.

One of the most common questions that people ask is how they can better recall names. This is true even for those who had a good memory for names earlier in their life. Names are especially problematic, because they have so few associations; they are not "connotative," as pointed out by John Stuart Mill more than a century ago. Names tell us little about a person's characteristics.

Consider what is called the Baker paradox. Think of someone named Mr. Baker. Now think of a person who works as a baker — an easy example. Although you can *try* thinking about someone who works as a baker to remember Mr. Baker's name, it's hard to actually find actual words to associate with the person. In other words, few or no connotative connections exist between the name and the person represented by the name. What if Mr. Baker is a banker? Instead, use your smartphone (if you have one) to take a picture of the person and record his or her name for later review. *It takes extra effort for most of us to learn new names.*

Finally, many (but not all) of us are good at forming visual images. If you are in this "good" category, you can learn and recall names somewhat easily. For example, my name is "Bill." You might recall my name more easily by picturing the bill you will receive for consulting with me, or you may imagine a duck's bill (the risk here is that you may call me Dr. Quack!). Of course, is it easier to conjure up images for names such as Cotton, Greenfield, and Redman than it is for names like Beckwith, Swenson, or Myers. The strategy of conjuring mental images to associate with names works much better when images are easy to come by.

Interestingly, we forgive others for forgetting *our* name but are *not* as good at forgiving *ourselves* when we fail to remember the names of others. *It is important to be as forgiving of yourself as you are of others.* One thought I have is, if we all could have our name tattooed above our eyes, we could instantly make eye contact and know the name of the other person. On a more practical side, we can use nametags whenever possible or construct a roster with pictures and some brief personal information on everyone who is important to us. This way, we can study and review using both language skills and images. We will be using multiple retrieval cues to our advantage when we next encounter these people.

FORGETTING WHERE THINGS ARE PLACED

Another exasperation that we all face is forgetting where things are placed (absentmindedness). (This, of course, does not apply to glasses. They have little hands and feet and crawl away when we are not looking.) We spend tremendous amounts of time hunting and gathering these items that we *know* we put *somewhere*. And we become even more flustered when we realize we could be spending that time in more enjoyable or productive pursuits. Forgetting where I placed my keys has cost me more time than I'd like to admit during my lifetime. It is also *not* a good idea to put things in a "special" but unique place; these items are often the ones we will most likely be unable to find when we want or need them. I was especially frustrated when I "lost" my wedding ring for three years by putting it in a special place rather than in its *assigned* location.

In principle, the solution for managing this failure of short-term memory is easy. Everything must have a place, and everything must be put in its place. The difficult part is that this includes the times when we are tired, busy, or preoccupied. Maybe we just don't feel like putting it away in its correct space. *This is an often-neglected skill that can save hours of time and frustration.* It means placing our glasses in the same place every time, even when we are tired or don't want to walk across the house to put them away. The rule also holds true for portable phones (fortunately, I can use my wife's smartphone to find mine when I violate this rule), remote controls, and/or hearing aids. In terms of organizing important papers, this means establishing and then sticking with a specific filing system. The time you spend developing these skills and organizing your things will save you hours of time later.

Difficulty Learning a New Language or Learning New Motor Skills

Aging slows not only the learning of semantics (concepts) but also the rate of learning a new language or motor skill. Language learning occurs without effort during the early years of life, as if we are born with a "language acquisition system" in the brain that only requires us to hear a language to master it. When I was in elementary school, it was not common practice for a second language to be taught. I also did not have the advantage of living near someone or having a relative who spoke a language other than English. I took three years of Latin in high school (though I can't recall *any* Latin). For my bachelor's degree, I was required to develop a reading knowledge of a foreign language. (I took one year of French and two years of German.) What I recall the most from six years of language study are some syntax and structures of these languages. I never mastered any of them. It would have been much easier to learn these languages as a child.

Another example of the ease of learning in childhood versus later in life is the development of motor skills. I did not learn to ski until I was in my thirties. It was exceedingly difficult for me to turn to the right (I am left- handed), and I had to spend much time and effort to master movements to my right. The children in ski school mastered skiing to either side without much difference in laterality. On the other hand, I was able to dribble and shoot a basketball using my right side because I learned this skill in grade school.

As we age, we need to put more time and effort into learning a new skill. It is useful to break down new skills into small steps, and it often helps to have coaching or lessons to help you master the activity. We also must be persistent, with frequent but short training sessions. These ideas have helped many clients in their seventies and eighties master the computer, which is another skill that is not intuitive unless we learn it when we are young.

Why is Returning to School a Challenge at the Age of Fifty?

A reader of a newspaper article that I wrote asked, "Would you be willing to tackle the issue of working memory? I returned to grad school at fifty, struggled mightily with learning a new language … and went through a battery of tests to figure out if it was an undiagnosed LD [learning disability] or cognitive decline. Interestingly my twenty-something peers were having no problems."

I commended her for seeking an objective memory assessment and was pleased that the problem was neither a learning disability nor cognitive decline. Whether similar concerns are the result of no longer being twenty or the early signs of memory loss can be difficult to determine without rigorous memory tests to rule out pathology. So why the "struggle?"

There are a number of contributing factors. First, there is the effect of normal aging. When twenty-year-olds are compared to fifty-year-olds for the speed and efficiency of memory skills, there is no contest. In general, as the brain ages, it slows, and after the age of about forty, minor errors/delays occur in word finding. This takes a toll on the speed of new learning.

To be fair, learning a new language as an adult, even for a twenty-year-old, is challenging for most. As discussed above, the easiest time to learn a new language is in the first few years of life when it seems to happen automatically. Learning a new vocabulary (almost like nonsense syllables in the beginning) is a highly demanding memory task. In addition, no formed associative networks exist in which to fit the learning. You must, at the same time, master a new vocabulary of grammar and syntax (which might not have the same alphabet). To add to the cognitive load, mastering written and spoken language takes yet a *different* set of memory and sensory circuits. It's no wonder that it is a struggle for some and that younger, faster brains that are practiced at studying learn faster with less effort. Learning a new language puts a significant strain on working memory.

As discussed earlier, at least two basic memory processes are involved in any new learning: working memory and short-term memory. Working memory is the brain's multitasking system. Think of the demands of a new language. You are constantly looking up new words that are not yet in your brain's lexicon, and at the same time you're incorporating pronunciation, mastering syntax and word order, translating (a native speaker thinks in the language and doesn't have to translate), and adjusting to unfamiliar word order (e.g., adjectives that follow nouns). It's amazing that you can master a new language at the age of twenty let alone at fifty! The fifty-year-old brain can't execute working memory as fast as it did previously and must compensate by expending more effort.

Short-term memory is the circuit that allows the brain to store new information, like the "save" command on a computer. However, moving information from short-term to long-term memory takes much practice and attention. This is especially difficult when rote and working memory loads are high. Short-term memory demands a great deal of repetition and practice over time, as few people, especially as they age, have a photographic memory.

Our memory is not like a computer or a photograph. The brain has astounding capacity; it does not fill up like a hard drive. Also, unlike a computer, the brain needs to exert greater effort and have more time as we age to store and recall/recognize information. But given the patience and dedication, it can master complex new information and retain profound competency as long as it remains healthy.

GETTING LOST

Getting lost can be very scary. Cities in coastal Florida (where I lived for twenty-five years) were especially challenging, because many rivers and canals posed challenges to route finding. It was very easy to get disoriented, especially when the city was new to me. I spent an inordinate amount of time driving around to regain my orientation in these cities. (I greatly appreciate the navigation system in my current vehicle.) I would have saved myself much time and stress if I had used a good map to plan routes and identify directions before departing.

Even though it's common to get lost in new places, it's not common to get lost in familiar places. This kind of getting lost or disoriented can be a sign of failing short-term memory or may be related to a neurological event such as a transient ischemic attack (a small or transient stroke). Routes and spatial maps are clearly stored differently by the brain than are oral directions. I do not have to "think" of the directions for most of my common destinations. I once had a client who could give detailed, accurate verbal directions to all locations within her community. She could give directions to the bank, the activity center, the beauty shop, and the restaurants. She could discuss in detail her life experiences and even compose music. However, she was unable to actually *find* any of the places she knew so well. She got lost on the way to the bank that she had used so often over the years. She even had difficulty getting off an elevator and leaving her room.

It is always useful to get a good map of the area that you want to navigate and to learn the major streets and landmarks. When you plan to travel, study the map before you depart. It may also help you to draw a schematic map of your route and carry it with you for reference. This extra time and effort of drawing your exact routes on a separate sheet of paper may even keep you from referring to the map itself during your journey. This opens up more time (the **One-Minute Rule**) for you to better reinforce the spatial map of your destination in your mind.

Be sure to study the map and make directions for your return, because the landmarks and turns are reversed and may confuse you. In fact, it's better to travel by day so you can more easily see the landmarks. You may also want a navigator with you. My wife Pamela is an excellent navigator, so she navigates while I drive. These efforts allow me to pay better attention to traffic, thereby making me a safer driver. Also, I don't have to use my attention looking at the navigation screen in my car. It's interesting that most states have laws forbidding the use of a handheld cell phone but ignore the impact of driver displays and apps that are standard in modern cars.

FORGETTING APPOINTMENTS, BIRTHDAYS, MEDICATIONS

Forgetting appointments, birthdays, anniversaries, and medications are frequent memory complaints. Interestingly, several clients who reported this to be frustrating said they do not keep a calendar anymore or never used a calendar in the past. They were concerned that they'd weaken their memory by using "crutches" and therefore felt that they were helping to "strengthen" their memory by *not* using a calendar. These same people may have used a calendar at work but not at home, because they were accustomed to knowing their appointments and when they needed to be places.

Despite the rationalization that you are forgetting because "your mind is full," you need to be practical about future appointments and important events (prospective memory). This means keeping a detailed calendar. Put things on your calendar that you enjoy, such as vacations or times when friends or relatives are visiting, or concerts you want to attend, as well as things you "need" to do, such as going to your dental or physician appointments. *Include appointments with yourself* so that you can spend more time on your favorite hobbies or pastimes, such as reading or bowling. Listing activities on your calendar that you enjoy makes it more likely that you will *do* them. This works best if you view it as a personal contract with yourself to add or increase the time you spend in reaching goals like exercising or spending more time reading for pleasure.

If you make it a habit to keep an accurate calendar, you can lead a relatively normal life *even with short-term memory loss*. As long as you refer to it often and use it as a personal contract for your time, you will improve your memory *and* your social life and your fitness.

Medications present another strain on your prospective memory. For example, I need to take medication for high blood pressure. Therefore, it's important for me to take this medication reliably. I've developed a routine of leaving the blood pressure medication next to my toothbrush, as I take it in the evening. This way I have direct contact with the medication each evening as I brush my teeth. However, for a time, I had to take the medication twice a day. It's amazing how much harder it was to remember to take the pills twice a day, and how often I forgot. I knew I'd forgotten because I counted my pills at the end of the month. I realized that "trying" to remember doesn't work. As we age, many of us need to take several medications, which increases the chances of forgetting or retaking medications.

The first step in remembering to take your medications is to *use a good pill organizer*. Put it in a place where you will reliably encounter it at the time of day that you need to take your medication. For example, if you need to take your medication at lunch, keep it where you eat lunch and make it stand out (e.g., put it next to your water glass). If you need to take your medication at a certain time of the day that does *not* have a natural marker, *use a timer*. Put the timer next to the medication container and use an alarm that you have to turn off and therefore will *not stop annoying you* until you see the container. To further ensure reliability, keep a checklist of the times you take your medications to monitor how well your system is working. This way, you can further refine your system to reduce failures.

FORGETTING THAT YOU FORGET

An irony of short-term memory loss (anterograde amnesia) is that *it causes you to forget that you forget*. This is both a blessing and a curse. It would be demoralizing to know all instances of forgetting. Forgetting that you forget is helpful if you have a memory disorder, because it can reduce frustration. However, you also have a more difficult time developing and recalling your strategies to manage memory loss. Furthermore, this phenomenon can create considerable stress if you *live* with a person suffering from significant anterograde amnesia. A recent case example illustrates this challenge.

Consider memory and driving a car. You reach a point where your level of forgetfulness makes it unsafe for you to drive. You may feel that you will *know* when your skills have deteriorated to the point where it is no longer safe to drive. Unfortunately, this is often not the way the situation unfolds.

A client with moderate short-term memory loss reached the point where her family became aware that she could no longer drive safely. They had a compassionate and lengthy discussion of her memory changes with her and made a plan for her to stop driving and sell her car. She agreed with the plan before retiring for the night. She had forgotten the discussion by the next morning.

We had to repeat this cycle most days. When we confronted her with selling the car, she became angry. She felt the decision was "out of the blue" and that her family was trying to sell the car for their own profit, despite the fact that she and her husband would receive all of the money from the sale. The situation was finally resolved but only after a great deal of anger and repeated discussions. She obviously continued for some time to forget that she had forgotten.

I have Parkinson's disease, and a time may come when I am no longer a safe driver. My strategy is to have my brother-in-law and wife periodically give me honest feedback on my driving. If they develop any concerns, I will stop driving. A more comprehensive discussion of issues surrounding driving will be covered in Chapter 14.

Interestingly, you might assume that having a poor short-term memory would make you more likely to be insecure about facts and details that you "recall." However, this is often not the case. As short-term memory loss increases and becomes more severe, forgetting that you forget protects you from knowing that you have a poor memory. You may be more likely to argue with others about incorrect facts that you clearly think are correct. If you can't find an item you have misplaced, you may assume that the item was stolen. It is important for you to attend to this aspect of memory loss *before* you actually need external memory supports. In other words, learn to use external memory aids *before* you need them. This will be discussed in more detail in Chapter 9.

* * *

I hope that I will anticipate my future memory needs as I grow older and that I'll continue to use many of the techniques from this chapter to make my memory better and reduce some of the frustrations. If I (or someone who knows me well) am concerned about my mental operations or short-term memory, I hope that I'll consult with a memory expert for an objective assessment of my memory. That feedback will help me, and those who live with me, to develop a plan and set up aids for managing my memory better. I'll also be able to monitor my memory over time and make progressive adjustments in the plan as needed.If my destiny is to develop dementia, I *must not be afraid of early detection of memory loss*. If I develop good memory strategies early in the course of memory loss rather than waiting until I am already disabled from it, I'll have the memory resources to do what is required. The major tools I will need are building on my long-term memory strengths, incorporating general rules of memory management, and developing my skills in using external memory supports. These tools are discussed in the next three chapters, beginning with a discussion of long-term and autobiographical memory.

As a parting reminder, don't forget the **One-Minute Rule**. Quit *trying* to remember. It doesn't work. *Make a plan for how you will remember.*

CHAPTER SEVEN

Who Am I? Autobiographical and Long-Term Memory

"We live life forward, unaware of outcomes, yet we are forced to understand events in reverse, working backward from outcomes to their supposed causes." (Robert McNamara, 2007, as originally proposed by Kierkegaard)

On a far-reaching level, the very *concept* of memory suggests that we are the sum (good and bad) of what we experience as the brain constructs itself throughout our contacts with the world, beginning before birth. We are the aggregate of our experiences, and each new experience alters the brain (neuroplasticity). The quote above is so true. When we have to live life forward but must understand events in the reverse, we experience a profound disconnect between lived experience and our understanding of that experience. We are always a few steps ahead of present awareness, as the brain operates by anticipation, which, in turn, arises from past experiences. In short, this is the function of long-term memory.

Our life of experiences, knowledge, skills, interests, and self are the essence of long-term memory. Short-term memory allows experiences and information to be recorded or consolidated, relying on the brain system that is necessary for new learning. If short-term memory declines, as it does in cases of traumatic brain injury, stroke, Mild Cognitive Impairment, or Alzheimer's disease, then we have increasing difficulty building long-term memory (in extreme cases even across a period of minutes to hours). Those with anterograde amnesia are stuck in the past. On the other hand, if short-term memory declines to the point that we develop anterograde amnesia, *long-term memory becomes our strength.* The good news is that this gives us a foundation upon which to build treatments. We retain our skills, knowledge, history, and our self. With the right planning, we can function well in the world even though we have a considerable decline in short-term memory. Therefore, *memory management must include an understanding of who we are, what we enjoy, what our skills and interests are, and what brings us joy.* In short, we move forward, whether we have excellent or poor short-term memory, by going backward through the process of life review.

In the early 1960s, Robert Butler, a well-known gerontologist, defined life review as a universal psychological process triggered by the increasing awareness of our mortality as we age. Life review is more than a closing of our life; it is a consequence of our life changes and transitions at *any point* in our life.

Life review is often activated by pivotal events ranging from graduating from school, falling in love, getting married, having children, moving, getting a job, changing jobs, or retiring from a job. Any life transition encourages us to review our life and redefine our sense of self. We are all prone to reexamine who we are and where we have been, so this process is not dependent upon becoming "elderly." Indeed, there are no significant differences between older and younger adults in frequency of reminiscing. Centenarians do not reminisce more often than adults in their sixties or eighties. Life review is not a sign of failing memory or health, although they may prompt it. Rather, life review is an adaptive response to life changes — it begins early and continues throughout life.

FUNCTIONS OF LIFE REVIEW

Life review helps us to develop and maintain our sense of identity. It encourages us to appreciate ourselves and to understand our uniqueness. It can provide guidance for living our life and empower our sense of continuity and purpose. Life review is an important component of our journey through life and relationships. It is especially important for anyone who is at risk of or has memory loss, because the past guides treatment in the present.

The skills and experiences that we store in long-term memory remain with us even as short-term memory loss progresses and new learning becomes more difficult. We often hear that, in Alzheimer's disease, we cannot remember the present (what I ate for breakfast), but memory-impaired individuals can often recall with great clarity the past (how I stuck Susie's pigtails in the inkwell in third grade in 1932). Short-term memory loss is a cardinal feature of Alzheimer's disease.

However, as the disease advances, progressive long-term memory loss does occur. Still, even in middle- and late-stage dementia, islands of skills may remain in long-term memory. For example, numerous persons with severe Alzheimer's-like symptoms who appear apathetic and disinterested in the world about them, may get up and dance or sing if they hear music that they have enjoyed and know well. They seem to gain a momentary connection with the outside world that surprises those who know them. Old pictures or movies may do the same thing. One of my clients was a writer, but he could no longer write coherently. Luckily, he was unaware that he couldn't write. Each day, he spent many enjoyable hours dictating his new book. It was then transcribed for him to edit. He never finished the book, but he and his wife benefitted enormously from the process.

Retelling our stories through life review is not always accurate, but *it doesn't need to be.* We all change the specifics of our stories as we tell them over and over again. (Recall that memory is reconstructive). We recall the gist of events and may or may not accurately recall the details. For example, I recall visiting St. Augustine, Florida, when I was a child. However, the details of the city became quite distorted in my memory. When I visited St. Augustine in my early fifties, I was stunned at how poorly I had visualized and remembered the city. What I recalled of St. Augustine was actually a melding of other places, both real and imagined. Memory transforms over time, which includes mixing the details of one story with another. This occurs frequently in persons with Alzheimer's disease. They are even more likely than someone with normal memory to forget the facts from the past but fill in details (confabulation) that sound plausible to them, or they may mix the details of different stories together. Of course, only someone who knows them well would know the inaccuracies of the story. In other contexts, we would refer to this transformation as creativity.

Even if stories become altered over time, we take for granted that we will be able to recall basic information, such as our birthdate, our husband's or wife's name, the names of our children, and the names of our grandchildren. However, those afflicted with advanced Alzheimer's disease become more vulnerable to forgetting their past and may even forget people who are extremely important to them. If they have resources like oral histories, video histories, photo albums, scrapbooks, and memorabilia, they can keep these memories alive for a much longer time and may be calmed when they become agitated. These materials also facilitate interactions with others, as they provide inducements for discussion. It is important to know that *these aids must be developed while long-term memory is still working fairly well.* The work involved in preparing these resources is enjoyable. It doesn't matter whether they are young or old, or whether they have good or poor memory. That's the force behind the multiple venues for exploring genealogy.

The best time to review the past is now. We do not recall events better with the passage of time (remember the sin of transience?), even those of us who have a normal memory. Although it is critical that those of us who have vulnerability to future memory loss (if we have relatives who had a dementia, or we are approaching our seventies and beyond) organize and recreate our past, we all benefit from the process of periodic life review. Recreating the past allows us to gain control of memory loss before it can occur and helps establish who we are and what is important to us, even if we cannot spontaneously discuss who we are. Life review concretely defines skills and events that may be exploited if our memory declines.

It is best for you to create your life story in a hard-copy format. You can do this by simply organizing photos into albums, putting memorabilia into scrapbooks, or creating digital slideshows/movies. Many books and apps are available that ask you questions for you to answer about your life. Or, you may hire a life historian to guide you through the process. If you are very ambitious and your memory works fairly well, you may wish to write your memoirs. The specific form for your memoirs is not important. Simple, brief, concrete formats are easier to create and to use.

PSYCHOLOGICAL BENEFITS OF LIFE REVIEW

Life stories provide many psychological benefits. If nothing else, creating a life history is enjoyable for most of us. Some of the clients with whom I worked were skeptical when I asked them to meet with a life historian to complete a guided life history. However, the intimidating visual or auditory recorder disappeared from their consciousness quickly. The self-consciousness also faded, and before long, participants became lost in the process. Many of them wrote thank-you notes to the historian for helping them to have such an enjoyable time. From their experience, these clients developed a better appreciation of who they are and what they've done with their life. And this was after spending only about ninety minutes with a guide and a tape recorder. (It's so much easier and less expensive in the digital age than it was five, ten, and twenty years ago.) Most of them have listened to the tapes again and again, and many have given them to their children (who were extremely pleased with both the process and the outcome). Even the most reluctant (who usually stated that their life was too uninteresting to review) were pleased once they completed this process. Most people like to talk about themselves.

Life stories and life reviews can be used clinically to ease depression, manage stress, calm agitation, and enhance self-esteem. Many of us are natural storytellers, even though we may not be aware of it. We create our histories based on the stories of our parents, relatives, and role models. We speculate about who they were and who we were at formative times in our lives. Life stories also can be used to stimulate thinking, enhance creativity, and re-create our interests or pleasures. We often get so involved in the routine of life — the errands, the work, keeping up the house — that we lose track of our interests.

Individuals with Alzheimer's disease (and other brain pathologies) may have the additional burden of losing initiation (losing the start button). They do not spontaneously engage in activity or socialization. They often appear withdrawn and depressed. When asked what they used to enjoy, they may not be able to respond because of the memory deficits. But if they have completed a life history that includes their unique interests, their present life can be built around their past interests, skills, and likes (called "biography-based programming"). This can be as simple as knowing that I love cats. Providing me with a cat can bring me endless hours of enjoyment. My cat will listen "attentively" to all of my repeated stories. My cat will never criticize or become frustrated with me. Knowing what music I like or dislike can also give me joy in the present, even if I develop a severe memory disorder.

Storytelling may even enhance the lives of those who already have moderate to severe memory loss. For example, my wife Pamela formed a unique support group for couples. One member of each couple was impaired by memory loss (ranging from very mild to moderate), and his or her spouse was the primary caregiver. This group stayed together for two years with various structured activities, including going on lunch outings, taking trips to museums, viewing videos, doing art projects, and playing games. As the group continued, it was clear that the impaired members showed progression of memory loss. All members of the group (those with normal as well as those with impaired memory) were asked to be videotaped individually while telling some aspect of their life that they chose in advance of the taping. Even those with seemingly little participation during general group discussions were able to present a meaningful five-minute review of an aspect of their life when prompted (such as showing them their wedding picture or asking about their career). Everyone had a wonderful time when the tape was replayed, and this stimulated further reflection and discussion in all group members.

About a year later, several in the group were often silent and rarely participated in usual discussions. When they did speak, it was repetitious. Then everyone was asked to bring in a photograph of a grandparent. This was a "key" that opened up even silent members. All of the participants showed expressions of joy as they described their grandparent and the time they spent together. There is often much more inside persons with memory loss than we know from the outside. We need to find the keys to unlock what is there, and *the keys are grounded in their histories.*

FORMAT AND STRUCTURES FOR LIFE REVIEW

Life reviews can take many forms. You can create an oral, pictorial, videotaped, or written document, or a combination of two or more of these. You can engage in storytelling to a trained biographer or use a myriad of books, apps, or websites that have questions to which a person can respond. This process can be undertaken alone or in a group. No matter what the form, you need to focus on a few essential elements when developing a personal history: birth, growing up, parents, siblings, school, work, marriage, children, and grandchildren. You can also include interests, favorite books, lullabies, music, poetry, art, pictures, and places where a person has traveled. All of these materials provide a rich and varied means (the keys) of providing comfort to anyone who completes the process, especially those with memory loss.

The more multidimensional and varied the format (e.g., use of words, imagess, photographs, creations) used in the re-creation of a personal life story, the more beneficial it will be. The more coordinated the appearance, the more available the information is for review. You can establish who you are, what you enjoy, and in what areas you are skillful. This will then be available to you and others should your long-term memory fail in the future. Planning ahead this way allows you to establish continuity in your life and relationships. Because long-term memory is reconstructive and fluid, tell your story now. This way, you will give yourself and others potential clinical memory aids. If you wait until you *need* this information, you may not be able to develop it. Additionally, re-creating your life story provides intellectual stimulation and entertainment, and it makes concrete the legacy that you pass on to your family.

Although many possible structures can be used for organizing your life story, the following presents an outline of how to get started and some things on which you may wish to focus. The specific form you use is a matter of personal choice, taste, and convenience. Choose a format that is easy for you.

Someone who is a skilled listener and knows when and where to ask questions can serve as a guide and help get you started. I have a professional life historian, Pamela, sit with my clients (those with good as well as those with poor memory) for about ninety minutes. During this time, she asks questions about their past, starting with their places of birth, parents, and grandparents. The particular facets of history that gain focus depend on the person telling the story. The entire session is recorded (either with audio or video), and the recording is given to the storyteller at the end of the session. This is an easy and enjoyable way to start the process. The product is a source of joy for the storyteller as well as for other family members.

You can review many varying topics. It is critical for those who may develop memory loss to include skills, talents, and interests as well as family members and important defining events in their lives. The following questions are a guide to help with this process. Be sure to include reflections on important transitions, such as childhood, adolescence, young adulthood, middle adulthood, school, college, military, marriage or primary relationships, role models, career, parenting, pets, or spirituality/religion.

Family Stories:

- What are the names of your grandparents?
- What was the country of origin of your grandparents?
- What are the names of your parents?
- What did your parents do for a living?
- What are the names of your siblings?
- What are the ages of your siblings?
- What was the birth order of the children in your family?

- Who are the important relatives who served as role models as you grew up?
- What are some of the earliest stories that you remember being told?
- What are your favorite family stories?
- What photographs or memorabilia best capture your family life?

School Stories:

- Who were your important teachers and mentors?
- What were your favorite subjects?
- What subjects did you excel at?
- What are the shaping experiences from your elementary school?
- What are the shaping experiences from your high school?
- Did you attend college?
- Why did you choose that college?
- What was your major?
- Did you attend graduate school?
- Why did you choose that school?
- What was your major?
- What was your highest degree?

Marriage Stories:

- How did you meet your spouse?
- What attracted you to him or her?
- How long did you date before you became engaged?
- What is the date of your wedding?
- Where did you get married?
- How many years have you been married?

Parenting Stories:

- If you have children, how soon after your marriage did you have your first child?
- How many children do you have?

- What is the name and date of birth of each of your children?
- Where do your children live?
- What kind of work do your children do?
- How often do you see your children?
- If you decided not to have children, how has this affected your life?
- If you decided not to have children, how has this affected your relationships?

Career Stories:
- What was your first full-time job?
- How did you get into your major life's work?
- What have been the ups and downs of your career?
- Is there another career that you wish you had pursued?
- How has retirement changed your life?

Pet Stories:

- Do you have a pet?
- What is your pet's name?
- What kind of pet do you have?
- What was your first pet?
- How does having a pet affect your life??

Stories of Special Times or Events:

- What is the role of music in your life?
- What is the role of art in your life?
- What is the role of literature in your life?
- What is the role of leisure and recreation in your life?
- What is the role of holidays and vacations in your life?
- What is the role of spirituality and religion in your life?
- What skills or things do you wish you would have learned?

- What was your highest degree?
- What do you do for exercise, and how often do you do it?

This list is not comprehensive, but it gives you an idea of the various topics you can cover for your life story. Be creative and think of questions that will remind you or your loved ones of days gone by that brought you joy, and even those that may have been painful.

CHAPTER EIGHT

Ten General Rules for Improving Memory

*"Anything given less than one minute of thought will fade
from your memory." (Douglas Herrmann, 1990)*

Before turning to specific techniques that help lessen the memory flaws of transience, absentmindedness, and blocking, here are some general rules that will help you understand and manage your memory. *These rules are not shortcuts to a better memory.* However, if you follow these principles, you will better manage your timing and efficiency as you take in and recall information. The next chapter shows you the specific techniques with which you can focus your efforts on remembering.

RULE 1: MEMORY LOSS CANNOT BE CURED

One issue that keeps coming up in both professional and popular media is whether or not "mental aerobics" or mental stimulation improves memory and/or prevents memory decline (clearly different issues). As discussed earlier, memory is a complex and varied set of skills. Therefore, you cannot logically ask the general question of whether mental exercises improve "memory." Instead, you need to ask the question relative to the *kind* of memory you wish to improve. The answer is different for sensory, primary, working/short-term, and procedural/long-term memory.

Does Practice or Mental Exercise Strengthen Sensory Memory?

Sensory memory, the system that persists for only a part of a second (the amount of time that you can hold the word you are currently reading before the next word displaces it), cannot be strengthened by exercises or types of stimulation.

Does Practice or Mental Exercise Strengthen Primary Memory?

Primary memory is what you use to remember a phone number before dialing it. It has an upper limit of information that can be held at any one time, which is usually about seven (+/- 2) pieces of information. Primary memory remains active as long as you continue to rehearse or repeat those seven bits of information.

However, primary memory is subject to interference, such as an intrusive thought or the phone ringing. *Practice and exercise cannot add capacity to this memory*. Nevertheless, you can *consolidate* information to increase the data in each of those seven spaces. "Chunking" information is one way to do this; to remember a phone number, for example, take advantage of common prefixes, such as remembering that all numbers at work start with the area code 912. This way, you use only one of the slots rather than seven, meaning, you can gain extra slots. Another way to consolidate information is to use *patterns* that will make your primary memory more efficient. Take the numbers 1234 and 2468. These are easier to recall than is the number 9253, because you can group them in a pattern and thereby open up more slots.

I am very lucky. A number of years ago when I purchased my first cellphone, I was assigned the number 851-1968. The last four digits are the year I graduated from college (if only remembering things were always so easy). In short, cleverness (or, in my case, random luck) can make more efficient use of the seven spaces, but exercise does not make primary memory stronger.

Does Practice or Mental Exercise Strengthen Working or Short-Term Memory?

This is the multitasking system that continually processes information like you are doing now by reading this book. It manages, sorts, and manipulates information and permits the consolidation or storage of information into long-term memory. This memory system is the one that is impaired in memory disorders like Mild Cognitive Impairment and Alzheimer's disease. As you learned in earlier chapters, weakness in short-term memory produces anterograde amnesia, making it difficult for you to learn new information.

Unfortunately, this memory system does not function like a muscle, which increases in strength with repetition or practice. Therefore, mental stimulation and mental exercises do not make short-term memory stronger. Many suggest that exercises, such as learning to write with your non-dominant hand or doing crossword puzzles, will improve your short-term memory or prevent or delay the onset of Alzheimer's disease. However, short-term memory does not respond to being exercised any more than you can strengthen your eyesight by not wearing your glasses or hear better by not using hearing aids.

Does Practice or Mental Exercise Strengthen Procedural/Long-Term Memory?

Yes! Mental exercises and stimulation *do* strengthen long-term memory. The "use it or lose it" principle clearly applies here. While short-term memory can't be improved, the good news is that it can be managed by using specific techniques (covered in the next chapter).

RULE 2: MAKE USE OF YOUR REMAINING SKILLS AND EXTERNAL MEMORY AIDS

If you feel that your memory — that is, your short-term memory — is not as good as it used to be, make use of other skills (good organization, like a detailed calendar habit). *Build your arsenal of memory supports early.* If you cannot keep track of the date and the day of the week reliably, use a digital watch or smartphone to compensate. If you forget what you are doing during the day, take a daily "to-do list" with you that reminds you of the activity and the time. You may also want to consult with a memory expert to determine the particular strengths and weaknesses of your memory. This will help you to make use of the best strategies for *you*.

Please understand that *external memory aids are not crutches*. Their purpose is to assist you in more efficiently using your remaining skills. I have been told by others that they do not want to use external memory aids (calendars, digital watches), because these "crutches" will further weaken their memory. *This is simply untrue.* I have used a calendar to track my time for years. This does not mean that I am weakening my memory; it means that I am trying to be clever in *managing my memory* so that I don't forget many things that are important to me. Building a good calendar habit clearly benefits my memory, but it does take more time and effort than merely "trying" to remember.

RULE 3: KEEP LEARNING SESSIONS SHORT AND FREQUENT

The best way to learn new information (things we want to or must remember) is to do it in small bits and repeat it often (ideally at unevenly spaced intervals). This is the same principle we all learned in school. Cramming for an exam is both inefficient and unreliable. Frequent, short, spaced study sessions build much stronger long-term memory. It is much easier to learn two new names than it is to learn ten. You can master the other eight (preferably a couple at a time) after you can recall the most important two reliably.

RULE 4: MANAGE STRESS

We all experience stress. So far, no one has found a way to eliminate it. Stress can be positive, like getting married or being promoted, or negative, like death or getting fired, but I'm not sure that completely eliminating stress would be as good for us as it sounds. Indeed, it may be that having no stress would reduce motivation, impair learning, and result in little need for memory. We may operate best under moderate levels of stress, which can add to motivation and effort. It is the high (panic) and low (nearly asleep) levels of stress that are disruptive to learning and memory. Techniques to manage stress are covered in Chapter 14.

RULE 5: REDUCE DISTRACTIONS

Make your environment work for you rather than against you. Turn off the television. Do the most demanding mental work when you are rested and efficient (which is the mornings for many but not for all of us). Turn off the ringer on the phone and let the machine take messages while you are working. If you want to better recall what someone is telling you, be in the same room, make eye contact, and repeat the message back in your own words.

RULE 6: SPEND MORE TIME AND EFFORT

The more time you spend with something, the better you learn and recall it. Old skills get "rusty." This is where "use it or lose it" works. You remember best the information with which you spend the most time. New information does not stick if you do not spend enough time and make an effort to learn.

RULE 7: REPEAT AND PRACTICE

Long-term memory, knowledge, and skills are built on repetition. This is a part of the effort that you must expend if you are to better manage your memory. You may not learn someone's name unless you repeat the name upon first meeting the person or see the same person in multiple situations.

Practice means building a routine to systematically repeat things you want to learn or to keep current information or skills that you want to retain. The more often you do something, the better you become at it as a result of better memory. Therefore, *schedule regular practice sessions* to keep your skills efficient. Great musicians and artists become great only by constant repetition and systematic practice. Their skills and memory fade if they do not put time into their craft.

RULE 8: MAKE ASSOCIATIONS

Memorizing by rote is very difficult. For example, if I ask you to remember three-letter sequences that are not real words, such as cqz or kyc, you'll find them very challenging to learn and recall. On the other hand, if I ask you to recall a sentence such as, "The hiker climbed the tree," you can use images or associations to help you learn and later recall. If you want to remember that last sentence, you might visualize a bear that chased a hiker to the tree, up which the hiker climbed for safety. It is much easier to recall the sentence later, because you spent more time and effort to learn the sentence in the first place *and* because you now have an association or cue to trigger the memory. Forming a visual image further increases your likelihood to recall it at a later time.

RULE 9: ORGANIZE

People who are well organized are much more likely to remember what needs to be done and when. As a result, they save time and expend less effort than those who have to look for things and decide to deal with them at some unidentified future time.

I admit that I am a "stacker." I have many piles of "stuff" that I know I must attend to eventually. I often let my piles accumulate over long periods of time, and each pile is somewhat eclectic. I don't allocate enough time to organize the items into files that I could use more easily. I do not keep a "to-do" list where I can realistically decide what can be done in a day and cross off items as they are completed, which would be a good reinforcer for me. I do not use my calendar to schedule time for necessary phone calls. In short, I am not a good organizer. I know I would "forget" fewer things and have to make many fewer apologies for not being timely if I spent more time and effort to get and stay organized. I have some work to do here.

RULE 10: ENGAGE IN RELAXATION AT LEAST ONE TIME EACH DAY

Spend at least some time each day in formal relaxation; it enhances performance on memory tests as you age. Relaxation therefore may enhance memory in everyday situations as well. Relaxation is one way to manage stress. It allows your emotions to "cool off" at least once a day. According to a friend, one of the most productive things he does each day at work is to take a short nap. Another friend turns off the phone, props up his legs, turns down the lights, and meditates each day after lunch. All of us could benefit from relaxation, whether it be improving our mental efficiency or reducing our stress.

You can engage in relaxation in multiple ways. Find apps for your smartphone, or locate some good relaxation tapes. You can work with a therapist who can train you in relaxation skills. In-person and online classes are available. You can practice meditation or yoga, both of which are great ways to induce a relaxed state. The important thing is that you (and I) need to organize our lives in such a way that we have a period of relaxation at least once a day.

Developing good habits that lead to memory retention is not something that comes naturally to many of us. Following the rules above will give you a good start toward organizing yourself for the future. The next chapter reviews many practical techniques for enhancing your memory.

CHAPTER NINE

Techniques That Enhance Memory

"Tell me and I forget,
Teach me and I remember,
Involve me and I learn." (Benjamin Franklin)

What can you do to improve your memory? By now, I'm sure you realize that this is not the right question. If you want to improve your short-term memory, you need to manage new information (associate with the familiar and common, use cues, arrange your environment), manage forgetting, and manage attention. If you want to improve your long-term memory, start by managing your short-term memory, then practice, rehearse, and review regularly. *Long-term memory accrues and is strengthened by exercise; short-term memory is not affected by mental exercise.*

Recall the extreme examples of short-term memory loss and hypermnesia revealed by the cases of HM and S. HM demonstrated severe short-term memory loss — anterograde amnesia. His memory loss was much more severe than in most cases of Alzheimer's disease. He could not learn new people, places, or events. Yet his long-term memory, prior to 1951, remained good. On the other hand, S could remember it all. He demonstrated what is called extreme hypermnesia. S's short-term memory was too good. Fortunately, most of us do not have to live with either of these memory extremes.

Short-term memory does not itself learn. Rather, it promotes learning by allowing consolidation to occur. Short-term memory — in coordination with working memory — allows sorting, selection, association, and rehearsal so that you can move information to long-term memory. Long-term memory is the reservoir of learning and is what most mean by the term "memory." Long-term memory consists of facts, skills, knowledge, and self. The challenge you face is *how to better manage short-term memory*. Long-term memory usually takes care of itself as long as you (1) manage your short-term and working memory and (2) revisit and review what you feel is important.

Many memory courses over the years have relied on training in techniques called *mnemonics*. These techniques date back to a time before writing was convenient (before the invention of printing presses, let alone computers). Mnemonics were designed for orators who passed on oral traditions that required memorizing extensive narrative.

An example of a mnemonic is the "peg" method (also known as paired associate learning). If you want to recall items to buy at the grocery store, for example, you associate them with a predetermined set of elements such as the clothing that you are wearing. To remember to buy bread, butter, eggs, and salmon, you might pair bread with your shirt, butter with your pants, eggs with your socks, and salmon with your shoes. This utilizes both long-term and short-term memory.

The problem with this and other classical mnemonic techniques is that few people use them spontaneously, and they are less likely to be used as we age. Even those trained in these methods don't often use them in everyday life. Persons with short-term memory loss cannot even learn the techniques, and those who already have learned them will probably quit being able to use such complex methods.

Still, a few mnemonic techniques (listed below) are simple enough to help you manage your short-term memory, whether you are five or 105. Choose the techniques that best suit your own memory needs. Some of these techniques, however, such as a good calendar habit, are essential to nearly all of us.

NAME BADGES

Recalling names is a challenge for short-term memory. Names are usually first presented in a single introduction and have few natural associations. If you are distracted, as may often be the case when meeting someone new, interference will remove the name from your primary memory even before it has a chance to get into your short-term memory. That's why it's a good idea to repeat the name during your greeting when you first meet someone new. Instead of saying, "It's nice to meet you," say, "It's nice to meet you, Bob." A simpler method is for everyone to wear a name badge, which helps you rehearse names easily and make multiple associations between their name and their face. Name badges are simple and reliable ways to learn names.

FLASH CARDS

Flash cards are a great technique used often in schools, but any information that must be learned (e.g., vocabulary words or names) can be organized onto flash cards for easy study and review. Even the act of making the cards helps you spend more time with the information so that you can build stronger memory traces from the start. Many of my students use flash cards to prepare and study for exams. I also provide each participant in my small-group classes with pictures and names of everyone so they can more easily study and learn names of other group members.

NOTEBOOKS

Notebooks are fundamental examples of the benefits of organization. The mere act of making the notebook utilizes short-term memory to promote rehearsal and facilitates review, thus allowing for stronger long-term memory. The act of making the notebook automatically makes you spend more time and effort with the information and often utilizes multisensory inputs (written words, pictures). I got through many years of education by making a notebook for each course I took. I kept notes from lectures and readings in notebooks organized by subject. I usually rewrote class notes the same day as the lecture, because it caused me to review information while it was fresh in my mind. This, in turn, helped me to better retain the information that would appear on a test.

Computers and smartphones make notebooks even easier to construct today (that is, if you are comfortable with computers). For important projects, I still take written notes and make notebooks to organize and review information.

A memory notebook is a specialized notebook for organizing into easily usable form what you might easily forget. Memory notebooks are especially useful if you have short-term memory loss. The notebook (which, of course, can be electronic rather than paper) may contain the medications that you take and your medical history. This can be useful when you visit your doctor, and especially when you see a new doctor. You can also use a memory notebook to track what you need or want to do, such as errands.

A memory notebook works best when it is organized and brief, when it focuses on currently important information, and when you carry it with you at all times. The information you include will depend on what you feel you need and want to remember. A memory notebook also helps you to facilitate your interactions with others, especially if you suffer from more severe memory loss.

JOURNALS

A journal is a narrative (which may also include photographs and drawings) record of events, transactions, and observations that you keep at frequent intervals. This is a wonderful memory aid for keeping track of your life. You may want to keep a journal(s) of vacations and trips. If you are a movie buff, you may keep a journal of movies that you have seen along with basic facts about them that you want to recall, such as the names of the movies and the actors in various roles. How often have you forgotten details of a trip or movie that you enjoyed and would like to recall? Another idea is to keep a journal on the places where you've lived during your life.

Reviewing your journals can bring back good memories. They also help sustain your long-term memory by providing easy review, promoting reminiscence, and serving as documentation of your interests and pleasures.

DIARIES

A diary is like a journal but usually contains more personal reflections or feelings about events, situations, people, and times. Of course, diaries may be combined with journals of important information, events, transactions, and observations. Journals and diaries take time and effort to create, but they are an excellent means of organizing information that you feel is important and are good source of review.

CALENDARS

Nearly everyone uses some kind of calendar to keep track of important events such as appointments. For most, this means having a *master calendar* at home that shows many details over weeks or months. However, the most detailed and wonderful calendar that is at *home* when you are *not* does you no good. To make your memory more reliable, carry a *daily calendar* with you.

The most useful daily calendars are organized into days that have time slots and enough space in which to write. (You can also do this on a smartphone calendar app.) In my case, I often wish I had my daily calendar "leashed" to myself so I would not misplace or forget it.

The effort you expend to construct a daily calendar or appointment book anew for each day helps you build a stronger memory of what you want to accomplish. You may not even have to refer to it (assuming you have an adequate short-term memory). The attention you give to writing a daily calendar reduces interference from what you did the day before or what you have to do tomorrow.

Include on both your master and daily calendars pleasant events and activities you want to do as well as things you "have" to do. Schedule time to listen to music, read, walk, and enjoy conversations and intimate time with your mate or close friends. Include the movies, concerts, or plays you want to see as well as important birthdays and anniversaries. Your exercise and stress-management routines are also important to write down. Or use your calendar to remind you to send flowers spontaneously to someone you love on a predetermined but frequent schedule.

One of my clients and her husband use her calendar quite creatively. She has mild short-term memory loss but a very good calendar habit that she developed before she began to experience significant memory loss. Her calendar was the blueprint for her to keep her life together as her short-term memory declined.

One of her difficulties with memory loss was doing laundry. This was an important activity to her, because it reflected her competence. She refused to have her husband take over this task and became angry with him if he tried. They both would run out of clothes before she'd remember to do the laundry again. If she started the laundry, she'd forget to move the clothes from the washer to the dryer. And the clothes might remain in the dryer for a week because she wouldn't remember to take them out. Her husband insisted that he help, but this caused conflict. She felt strongly that doing laundry was her job, and doing it made her feel good about herself.

After discussing her frustrations, we devised a plan where she would do laundry on Saturdays. She brought her master calendar and entered "put laundry in the washer" at 9:00 a.m., "put the clothes in the dryer" at 9:30 a.m., and "remove the clothes from the dryer" at 10:30 a.m. She added this to her schedule on the calendar for every Saturday for the rest of the year. This plan worked very well. She and her husband always had clean clothes, and they no longer argued.

ADDRESS BOOKS AND SMARTPHONE CONTACTS

An address book and/or contacts on your smartphone are other specialized journals for you to keep important phone numbers and addresses. Keep your address book up-to-date and neat for easier use. You may have trouble deciphering written entries when many of them have been crossed off or written over.

TO-DO LISTS

To-do lists force you to decide what is important to complete. They help you set goals and reinforce your efforts by allowing you to see your progress. Revise your to-do lists often, because, just like with address books, they work best when they are neat and organized. Too many crossed-off items and scribbles make you lose your focus, thus increasing rather than decreasing any memory failures.

Ideally, cross off items as you complete them, and make a new list every day. Have your goals be realistic and manageable in a short time, such as a day. You can break down larger goals into a series of brief sub-goals or steps. These lists help you remember what you want to accomplish, and you can better manage stress when you see yourself progress toward both your short- and long-term goals.

GROCERY LISTS

Grocery lists are specialized to-do lists. Although they can save a lot of time and aggravation, I don't often see people using them at the grocery store. I now use a list and am pleased at not having to make extra trips to the store because of items I forgot to buy when I didn't use a list. I can think of many other ways I'd rather spend my time. A grocery list saves time and makes you less likely to forget. The list works even better if you organize it by food categories and check off items as you put them in your cart. By the way, be sure that you make a plan to *remember to take the list with you*. I keep mine next to the car keys.

TAKING NOTES

We all have to master note taking to survive in school. If you take notes by hand rather than typing them into a computer, you'll enhance your later recall/recognition. This will support both your short- and long-term memory.

Writing down main ideas helps you review what you were told or what you read. It promotes *thinking* rather than just transcribing. Skilled transcriptionists usually do not know what they are typing, because it would slow them down. The *act of taking notes* makes you spend more time with new information and encourages you to ask questions when you may be unsure about something.

Although taking notes is an obvious way to recall phone messages and conversations, surprisingly few of the clients who come to me for advice about how to improve their memory have a notepad and pencil next to their phone. It is also helpful for you read back to the caller any important information that you noted to be sure it is correct. Reading back adds repetition, which builds long-term memory.

RECORDERS

Recorders, such as a smartphone, are a simple way to manage memory. If you take a recorder for your next visit to the doctor, you'll be able to recall what you are told, plus you can review any explanations, instructions, or changes that may be recommended. You can later transfer critical information to a journal organized around your medical information. You also may wish to record lectures or talks by others. You can later select and transfer this information to a more easily accessible format, such as a journal or notebook.

Many types of recorders are available for different purposes. One of my clients bought a small recorder (about the size of a half dollar) that she kept on a ring attached to her car keys. Whenever she parked her car, she recorded its location and saved herself hours of time and frustration looking for her car afterward. This clever system kept the recorder with her car keys as a cue for her to use it. Of course, if you are savvy about smartphones, you can use an app to find your car.

TIMERS

While many of us are accustomed to using an alarm clock (a timer) to get up in the morning, we are resistant to using it for other events during the day. (This is changing with the wide use of smartphones that have numerous reminder alarms.) You may "try" to remember to take your medications at specific times, to monitor your cooking while involved in other pursuits, or to remember to take the clothes out of the dryer. *Trying doesn't work well; timers do.* You can even use timers to remember to look at your calendar.

Timers are helpful in developing new routines such as exercising at a certain time or engaging in relaxation every day. They can remind you when to leave for a movie or a play so that you won't be late. You can even use them to prompt you to make phone calls. Timers are excellent for prospective recall, that is, recalling that you need to do something at a preselected time or interval.

CLOCKS AND WATCHES

We organize so much of our time by clocks that we take them for granted. Modern clocks can do much more than just tell time. If you are comfortable with smartphones (small but powerful computers with thousands of apps), use the clock as a timer to track medications, monitor your home, find your car, track your personal schedule, and a myriad of other functions.

If you are *not* comfortable with smartphones, use the alarm in a watch or clock to remind yourself to send flowers to someone you love or take a medication at critical times. If you've never mastered computers, you can find a digital clock to help you keep track of the date, the day of the week, the current month, and the year. This is most relevant if you are progressively declining, and using a higher-level technology like a smartphone may be beyond your grasp. Even if you possess the necessary technology skills, you might lose this ability. (Caregivers, however, can use computers in ever increasingly clever ways to provide safety, monitoring, care, and stimulation.)

You never have to be disoriented in relation to time as long as you have a good clock or watch that contains the information you need but does not require learning new skills and is easy to read. Some clocks are even updated for time and date every day as a satellite passes by and are therefore always accurate. I love my "atomic" clock in the bedroom. It is always accurate, and it is one less clock to reset when the time changes in the spring and fall. Digital clocks work from batteries, so they aren't influenced by interruptions in power. They can even indicate when the batteries need to be replaced. Some watches and clocks even give you the present time and date aloud. These were developed for those with failing vision but can be helpful to anyone who finds them convenient.

PILLBOXES

We have increasingly become a pill-taking culture. A normal part of aging in contemporary America involves taking medications. Many of them, such as cardiovascular and diabetic drugs, have significantly added years to a person's general life span and quality of life. *But the successful use of medications requires memory,* especially if you have to take multiple medications. The main tool for using medications reliably is a pillbox, and some of these have useful bells and whistles.

The most reliable and easy-to-use pillbox is one that sits in your house and is connected to a computer over your Internet service or that runs on a set program. Each time you need to take a medication, the pillbox sounds an alarm, which does not stop beeping until you open the compartment with the pill and take it out. If you fail to open the compartment within a certain time, you will receive a phone call reminding you to take the pill. This pillbox is an excellent choice if you have anterograde amnesia. While many pillboxes are much simpler and less expensive, the most helpful ones make a sound when you need to take the pill and do not stop making the sound until you open the pillbox.

It is also important for you to match medication times with events that you always complete and to keep the pill organizer *where* you complete those tasks. For example, if you wash your face at 8:00 each morning, keep your pillbox on your sink. If you brush your teeth each evening before going to bed, keep your evening pillbox by your toothbrush. You must be reliable in taking your medications; therefore, create a monitoring system (such as a checklist) as a backup reminder.

Handling Public Restroom Visits

If you or your spouse or companion experiences short-term memory loss, get a walkie-talkie (which is like a baby monitor) for when you need a bathroom break at a mall or an airport. It is easy to use and very convenient. I know of several instances where couples became separated, and the person with memory loss could not find his or her companion. Both individuals became fearful and full of anxiety. A walkie-talkie allows you to be in contact with the other person easily. Although cellular phones can also serve this function, they are more complicated to use, especially if you have memory loss and were not familiar with using cell phones before your decline.

And, if possible, try to use the same public restroom. Many places now have family restrooms, and all you need to do is get over any modesty issues.

Organized Workspace

Clutter interferes with attention and therefore with memory. Reducing clutter and organizing wsill help you better manage your memory. One important key to organizing a workspace is to *keep out only active projects*. Organize your other projects but keep them out of your active workspace. Another key to organization is to *establish your priorities and stick with them*. Eliminate things that you have not "gotten to" in weeks. If you have not gotten to something within six months, it most likely has a low priority. Keeping it around to worry about will simply interfere with other, more urgent projects and tasks.

One of the best techniques for organizing a workspace was that of a client who had suffered a traumatic brain injury. She loved to cook but found that, after the injury, she could no longer complete recipes without leaving out items. Her solution was to organize, on the counter, in the order she would use them, all items for the dish she was preparing. She then worked from one end of the counter to the other. If any interruption (phone ringing, knock on the door) occurred, she cleared the counter, set up all the items again, and completed her food prep. She was very pleased with this routine and said it saved her much frustration and put the joy of cooking back into her life.

ROUTINE PLACEMENT OF OBJECTS

Everything must have a place, and everything must always go in its place. This may sound obvious and simple, but it can be very difficult to follow. It takes good organization and planning, and you must spend time initially setting up places for your things. Routine placement of keys, glasses, hearing aids, and important papers saves even those with normal memory a great deal of time. Cellular phones (as long as my wife Pamela can find *her* phone, I can call myself when my phone slips between cushions on the sofa) and TV remote controls save me from spending so much search-and-find time.

If you want to manage this aspect of organization, you must put everything in its place no matter how inconvenient it is or how tired you may be. One of my clients was continually frustrated when she forgot her sunglasses. We decided to have her place a small shelf at eye level next to her exit door. She made a habit of placing her sunglasses on the shelf as she entered her apartment, and she never forgot to take her sunglasses with her again.

TAKEAWAY SPOTS

How can I remember to take everything I need each day when I leave my home? I've often gotten to work or the grocery store and left something behind. To compensate for this, I use a takeaway spot in the kitchen. I keep all items that need to go with me in a box in an assigned drawer. The takeaway spot is a specific example of the routine placement of objects.

Place items that need to go with you in your takeaway spot *as you think of them*: keys, wallet, purse, phone, etc. It is almost guaranteed that you will leave without an item you need if you delay in doing this. It may be inconvenient to go to your takeaway spot at the moment, or you are too tired to bother dealing with that item. But it's worth the effort to follow through as you are thinking about it.

I have even used this method with umbrellas. I often leave my umbrella on the door handle or next to the door if I am visiting someone. I haven't had to buy as many umbrellas as replacements. I also place my shopping list with my keys. This habit of having a takeaway spot is also essential for tracking eyeglasses or hearing aids.

TRAVEL SOUVENIRS

Travel souvenirs such as trinkets, art, postcards, photographs, slides, and refrigerator magnets are concrete objects that can supplement journals and diaries in keeping your memories of pleasing times. Refrigerator magnets are excellent ways to be reminded of your favorite places and trips. Souvenirs help keep valued experiences easily available for later recall, reminiscence, and enjoyment.

VISUAL IMAGERY

Visual imagery is a more complicated strategy for memory management. Some of us are naturals at visualizing, whereas others are not. We are better at recalling objects that can be transformed into an image. Some people can picture in their head what a room will look like painted a certain color or with a new sofa.

If you have this skill, exploit it by forming images of objects that you wish to remember. If you aren't skilled at drawing, making crude drawings (even poor ones — this is not an art project) enhances later recall (remember the **One-Minute Rule**). I was once testing the memory of a very clever artist by reading her a long list of words. She looked around the room and visualized objects that were on the list. This greatly enhanced her test score because she had many representations of words right there in my office (for example, the bookcase).

ELABORATION

Elaboration is another complicated strategy for enhancing memory that involves spending more time with important things that we want to learn or recall. For example, if you are trying to recall the names of several landmarks that allow you to travel a new route, you might list the landmarks and create a story that links them. The more time and effort you put into constructing the narrative, the better your recall will be.

RHYMES AND JINGLES

Rhymes are a specialized example of elaboration. Rhymes have been used as a mnemonic technique for as long as oral information has had to be recalled. Rhymes are a mainstay of advertising. For example, what comes to mind when you see a checkmark or hear the slogan "just do it?" If you are old enough, try to complete the following sentence, "See the USA in your _____________________" Again, this takes considerable effort and may not work well if you are experiencing short-term memory loss.

PQRST
(PREVIEW, QUESTION, READ, STATE, TEST/REVIEW)

This is another technique that you may have used in school, but it often won't apply to other parts of your life. This method takes much effort, and you need to spend considerable time to become competent at using it. It is usually applied to learning from textbooks but could be applied to any material that you wish to better retain. This is an *active* rather than a *passive* method of reading that helps you to build better long-term memory by incorporating repetition and review early in the learning process. Here's how it works:

- **Preview**. Before reading an article in a magazine, or a book, browse through it. Note the pictures, captions, bold items, subheadings, summaries, and abstracts. This starts to create a map in your mind of the information you will learn and begins to build your memory trace. In most textbooks, the chapters start with objectives. They liberally use pictures and graphs and end with summaries and terms. Then work through bold words, pictures, graphs, summaries, and terms.

- **Question**. Convert each objective or heading into a question that you write down. Then work through the bold words, pictures, graphs, summaries, and terms. This lays down a cognitive map of the material to guide your reading and warms up your brain.

- **Read**. Read chapters before lectures/discussions. Write down what you have learned by hand. This cements the information in your mind. Writing facilitates learning and memory. Make outlines and organize your notes. Compress the information into a short number of main points. Make flashcards for new terms.

- **State**. Answer the questions you prepared using your own words as you read the material.

- **Test/Rehearse.** Use the questions you created to later test your memory of what you've read and to show you facts or concepts that need greater attention. Practice, practice, practice. Build in booster and review sessions. Test yourself often. In fact, taking multiple-choice pretests can enhance your learning of new material before you read or hear it. Most courses come with practice items either in the text or in supplemental materials. Consider using this material as a pretest to improve your learning. Also, be sure to know what you do *not* know well, because this is where you need to spend more time. If you take notes, review and clarify them soon after your initial learning.

MASTERING NEW INFORMATION

Earlier, I discussed the trials and tribulations of my returning to school as an "older" student and competing with much younger students. The key to doing well in school or competing in an increasingly information-demanding workforce is *being efficient in your efforts and strategies, regardless of age*. In addition to using the PQRST method just discussed, follow these guidelines:

- **Don't multitask.** Your brain cannot do two things simultaneously without losing its efficiency or you losing your attention.
- **Make sure your study environment is neat and quiet.**
- **Take frequent breaks** to refresh your attention and concentration.
- **Take advantage of the time of day when you are most alert to study.**
- **Space your practice and review.** Progressively increase the retention interval between reviews. *Cramming doesn't enhance learning.*
- **Sleep on it.** Complete at least some of your study/review sessions just before going to sleep. Years of data indicate that sleep helps consolidate new memories.

In all of my years as a student and educator, I never found a shortcut. You use more than 10 percent of your brain all the time, and normal brains use both sides of the brain together. (These facts refute the 10 percent and lateralization myths.) There is no best learning style unless the learning is demanded by a task (you can't learn to shoot a basketball by reading about it), and playing games or doing "brain aerobics" will not make you smarter. *It's the time and effort that count.* You may or may not need to put in more time and effort than others, but regardless, competency is there for the taking. Don't forget the **One-Minute Rule** — anything given less than one minute of thought will fade from your memory.

Expanding Rehearsal

Expanding rehearsal is a simple yet effective way to learn small bits of new information. For example, if you want to learn a new word that is difficult for you to remember, you could use this technique.

Let's say the word you want to learn is "mnemonic" (a technique to assist with memory). Start by saying "mnemonic." Then wait thirty seconds and say "mnemonic" again from memory. Next, wait sixty seconds to repeat the same word. Double the retention interval each time you repeat the word until you can easily recall it (there's an app that sets up this interval for you). If you miss recalling the word at a certain interval, go back a few intervals and build the time between recalls without making a mistake again.

I had a client with short-term memory loss who kept forgetting the name of a grandchild who was getting married. It was important to him to attend the wedding and be able to recall his grandchild's name. He used this technique for two weeks before the wedding and successfully achieved his goal.

Expanding rehearsal is also useful for recalling new names or for learning vocabulary words in a foreign language. This technique requires considerable effort, but it can be a very effective way to build a new memory.

FADING

Fading is another technique for new learning that requires a great deal of effort but is very effective. To learn about this technique, try using the following strategy to help master the spelling and recall of the word "mnemonic." At each step, say the word out loud and spell it upon seeing the written-out visual cue. As you can see, each successive step presents less information (one less letter from the end of the word) to stimulate your memory of the word and how it is spelled. You could further reinforce learning the word by using the word in a sentence, which is the method of elaboration.

"Mnemonic"
"Mnemoni"
"Mnemon"
"Mnemo"
"Mnem"
"Mne"

"Mn"
"M"

SEARCH MNEMONICS

Search mnemonics are simple strategies that cue your memory when spontaneous recall fails. These techniques are especially useful for nouns/ names. Here are two strategies that may help:

1. **First Letter or Number**

   Try to think of the first letter of the name or noun, or the first number of a longer number, that you want to recall. This often primes your association networks and allows you to remember names and numbers.

For example, if I momentarily cannot think of my phone number, I might think that it starts with an eight, which might cue the prefix "851" along with the last four digits.

2. Alphabet Search

This is similar to the first-letter strategy but is more systematic. Start reciting the alphabet to try to come up with the first letter of a name you are trying to recall. My name comes quickly if this works — Bill. If my name were Zane, it would take much longer.

SMARTPHONES AND COMPUTERS

I have mentioned throughout this book that smartphones and computers can assist in many of the memory-enhancing ideas presented here. It seems peculiar in today's world, but my wife Pamela and I did not enter the smartphone age until 2010. She treated herself to an I-Phone and MacBook Pro computer. She instantly enlarged her memory by having access to the Internet, which allowed her to explore ideas, places, and events. She has access to applications ("apps") that allow her to calculate, argue, plan, and daydream. She can also use these devices as memory collaborators. She can track as well as have auditory reminders for appointments. She can pay bills, organize her life, and record events (pictures and videos) that we want to remember. She is delighted. Her I-Phone and computer work for her (in the words of David Chalmers) as an "extended mind." I joined the movement about a year later. I couldn't dream how much this has changed the world. We operate with memory systems that evolved to meet the demands of the prehistoric ages. It's no wonder that it's hard to cope with the demands that accompany the glut of information and the time we need to keep up with the modern world.

Smartphones and computers serve as memory collaborators for many individuals and organizations. Computers have taken over a multitude of previous jobs done by humans: manufacturing, answering phones, flying airplanes, helping us drive more safely, even in playing games.

There is an app to help you manage most of the techniques described here; for example, an app can manage your expanding rehearsals. On the one hand, smartphones (small portable computers) allow you to multitask better, such as tracking and taking your medications or other tasks that are a function of prospective memory. Multitasking was the Achilles' heel of memory before portable computers. (Did you remember to pick up milk on the way home from work tonight? Did you take your 9 a.m. medication?) With a smartphone, you can set a "chime" alarm to remind you. This is the upside of the technology.

However, smartphones may also add to your anxiety from overstimulation. It's challenging to be reminded constantly of a new e-mail or text, 24/7. Notifications interrupt your train of thought, interfere with sleep, and replace human interactions. Why has attention to notifications or keeping up with social media replaced face-to-face human contact? How does the ability to look up nearly everything influence your ability to remember? What are the consequences of not having to learn and recall things? I had a colleague who used the navigation system on her phone to travel anywhere she went. Without the phone, she could not find her way to the grocery store, her office, or back home.

Computers are thought by some to extend our working memory and thus to make our mind and memory more efficient. Maggie Jackson (*Distracted*, 2009) describes our working memory as similar to the news headline crawl, which is "constantly updated, never more than a snippet, and no looking back." But *memory is based on more than unlimited access to new information*. With the advent of computers and smartphones, we can now create and have instant access to information at a rate that far exceeds our ability to find, review, understand, and recall the information. We live in what Richard Wurtman (*Information Anxiety*, 2001) named the age of information anxiety.

As an "expert" on human memory, my concern is that the newly developing technology presents a risk. Human memory evolved thousands of years ago and is not structured around information technology. Maggie Jackson stated my fear best. "The way we live is eroding our capacity for deep, sustained, perceptive attention — the building block of intimacy, wisdom, and cultural progress." Let's not forget a corollary — the **One-Minute Rule** — that underlies human memory: Anything given less than at least one minute of *focused thought* will fade from memory. Smartphones help you look things up; they don't improve memory. Indeed, smartphones sometimes get in the way of learning, because you don't have to recall phone numbers. You just press the name or picture in your contact app. Of course, this depends on how you want to spend your time. If you like memorizing phone numbers, go for it.

DOES GOOGLE IMPROVE MEMORY?

How does Google influence memory? Before trying to answer this question, let me briefly review the practical dynamics of memory. Recall that *memory is not a unified skill but rather a large number of processes*. First, *sensory memory* registers sound, touch, images, etc. Although the information in sensory memory holds considerable detail, it lasts only part of a second. Second, *working memory* constantly surveys, attends, decodes, and decides meanings and actions. Working memory functions best when you are doing one thing at a time (e.g., your brain does *not* parallel process very well when you are driving and texting at the same time). Third, short-term memory is not a time but rather the process whereby the brain learns or "consolidates" new information and skills into long-term memory. This is enhanced when you take notes, rehearse, and practice. Fourth, *long-term memory* is the ability to access information at a later time from which it was originally encountered. Long-term memory is our knowledge, autobiography, and skills.

Human memory systems did not evolve with computers and Google in mind. We have an impressive and creative history of inventing tools to extend our limits. For example, we have cars that move us further and faster than walking. We have telescopes and microscopes to extend vision. We have books, Post-It notes, journals, recorders, timers, smartphones, and computers to augment our longer-term and working memory. The complication is that technology has vastly expanded our ability to create information and data, but it has not helped us understand, contemplate, and recall information — all of which are necessary for adaptability.

Human memory creates a bottleneck that does not exist for computers. We can take in, at best, about seven new pieces or chunks of information at a time. Furthermore, there are limits on our attentional resources. We can only bring in new information at a fixed and finite rate, which may change as we tire or become bored. Multitasking distracts us. For example, we remember 10 percent fewer facts from a news story if a scrawl is at the bottom of the screen. Finally, recall takes more effort than recognition. That's why many prefer multiple-choice to essay tests.

To answer the initial question, Google is a wonderful tool for finding massive amounts of information quickly; it is faster than thumbing through resource books or going to the library. However, the actual process of integrating and remembering information takes time and effort (you have heard this often enough by now that you'll remember it well). When we convert information to drawings, or write rather than transcribe, we better recall that information. As Nicholas Carr (*The Shallows*, 2010) put it: "The problem today is that we're losing our ability to strike a balance between these two very different states of mind," one of which is *finding information* and the other one *pondering it*. Memory needs time for us to understand and reflect. Has Google caused us to develop a technologically driven attention deficit disorder as it interferes with understanding and contemplation?

OTHER PEOPLE

Other people are very good memory aids as long as they don't become frustrated with your asking them for help remembering. This is a very good method for couples. For example, Pamela often recalls certain things better than I do, such as routes. I can rely on her navigational skills and memory when I am driving new places, which allows me to better concentrate on my driving. Of course, this often means that I need to take more time to learn the route if I have to travel it alone.

As a matter of "family engineering," one member of a family often does the checkbook. Both members of the couple rely on the memory of that person to pay bills on time and to remember to balance the checkbook. Other family members may be called on to remember when to wash clothing or to take out the garbage and recycling on the day the truck comes. People who live with others often use a team effort to remember critical aspects of what needs to be done. And who hasn't had a partner help you find that word that was on the tip of your tongue?

* * *

The many methods reviewed above work very well to help us manage normal forgetting or compensate for the loss of efficiency in memory as we age. However, these techniques are also useful for anyone who has mild short-term memory loss. The one caveat is that *a technique must be mastered early in the course of any progressive memory loss*. The bottom line is that you need to quit trying to remember and *start planning how you will remember*. If you wait until you need a skill, you may not be able to learn it. In the next two chapters, you'll learn about clinical memory loss — specifically, Mild Cognitive Impairment and Alzheimer's disease.

PART II

WHAT IS
MEMORY LOSS?

Introduction to Part II

So far, you've mostly learned about challenges to memory — no matter how old you are. Moreover, *aging does not make you lose memory but rather makes your memory less efficient.* You've also discovered the multitude of memory systems and their functions.

It is clear that *not all memory systems work like muscles.* You can "exercise" your long-term memory and make it bigger and stronger. You cannot exercise your short-term memory, but you can find strategies for managing it. *Better memory takes time and effort.* The principles and strategies discussed will work for you if you are struggling with the demands of work or education, or if you are still young and/or you are managing normal changes associated with growing older. If you want a better memory, don't try to remember. *Plan your strategies in advance.*

Part II of this book changes the focus of the book to memory *disorders.* Chapter 10 discusses Mild Cognitive Impairment (MCI), a disorder that lies between normal short-term memory and dementia. Chapter 11 describes dementias, a disorder in which you can no longer live independently. Alzheimer's disease will be the main neurodegenerative disease discussed, because it is the one that provokes the greatest fear and is by far the most prevalent diagnosis underlying dementia.

We do not know what causes Alzheimer's disease. It is diagnosed based on the density of plaques (caused by abnormal amyloid protein buildup) and tangles (caused by abnormal processing of tau proteins) that are found in the brain on autopsy. Recent technological advances have allowed measurement of amyloid and tau in living human beings using imaging techniques and tracers.

The predominant theory to date is that amyloids (plaques) in the brain are the main culprit. Simply, if amyloid-induced plaques cause Alzheimer's disease, then reducing the amyloid load in the brain should improve the thinking and behavioral characteristic of the disease. However, this strategy has not produced a successful treatment, as hundreds of drug trials have failed over the past two decades. More recent attention has turned to tau (tangles) with the development of a reliable tracer for tau, allowing its distribution in the brain to be mapped through imaging. Adding to the complexity of finding a medical treatment is the fact that it is not known whether the plaques and tangles are the result or the cause of Alzheimer's disease (chicken and egg problem).

It is uncertain whether Alzheimer's disease is a single entity, several distinct disorders, or a spectrum disorder. Further, what is the sequence of biological events underlying the degeneration that takes place over at least a couple of decades before symptoms occur? How do strokes and inflammation fit in? What triggers the disease process? How does insulin, so-called "diabetes type 3," contribute to the disease process? Why do many have the pathology without symptoms? The fact is, many practical treatments do not require knowing the molecular biology of the disorder.

*The key to managing memory disorders is to catch them early and to create and implement strategies for managing memory **before** you need them.* Although the word "Alzheimer's" strikes fear in everyone, the actual disease unfolds over several decades and typically progresses very slowly (Alzheimer's disease never has a sudden onset). This slow, progressive unfolding gives you the opportunity to control and manage your own future if you start early in the course of memory loss and make a family plan for dealing with possible changes before they occur. Detecting and monitoring the early signs of possible future progressive decline also gives researchers an opportunity to discover and develop techniques for slowing the course of the disease.

Early detection of vulnerability or potential for memory loss is more likely if you become familiar with the risk factors associated with conditions like Alzheimer's disease. You must also be open to professional assessment (including a neuropsychological evaluation) before decline challenges your independence or becomes more than just memory loss (e.g., compromises judgment, reasoning, doing the checkbook). Mild

Cognitive Impairment appears to be an early stage for many, but not everyone will later be diagnosed with Alzheimer's disease (some recover normal memory; others never progress to more serious cognitive decline). Therefore, Mild Cognitive Impairment will be our entry into the world of memory disorders.

CHAPTER TEN

Mild Cognitive Impairment

"Our memory is both fragile and resilient at the same time. It does not take much to throw it out of gear. A small blood clot, a shortage of oxygen, an infarction of the cerebral membrane — the slightest organic defect can cause irreparable damage. Yet even in the most drastic forms of memory loss, much is left intact." (Draaisma, 2004, p. 226)

OVERVIEW OF MILD COGNITIVE IMPAIRMENT

Mild Cognitive Impairment is the earliest characterized stage of memory loss. For some individuals, it may be a transitional state to Alzheimer's disease. Three subtypes of Mild Cognitive Impairment have been identified: amnestic; having a decline within a mental function other than memory; and a mixed type.

The amnestic type of Mild Cognitive Impairment is the most studied and discussed. It is characterized by a person demonstrating a greater than expected decline in memory performance on demanding memory tests when compared with his or her peers (see Table 10.1). Individuals who are affected by Mild Cognitive Impairment are not demented. They are independent. Persons with Mild Cognitive Impairment of the amnestic type have deficient short-term memory leading to difficulty with learning new information and recalling recent events. But they have good intellectual skills and are able to compensate for their memory loss well despite its inconvenience. If followed without treatment for six years, about 50 percent of individuals with this form of Mild Cognitive Impairment achieve a diagnosis of Alzheimer's disease (meaning that there are changes in mental functions in addition to decline of short-term memory).

Formal criteria for the diagnosis of the amnestic form of Mild Cognitive Impairment are evolving, but we can consider the following as a working definition. First, there must be a complaint about short-term memory (they must not forget that they forget). Second, an informant, such as a spouse or other family member, or a close friend, should corroborate the short-term memory loss. However, I have evaluated many persons over the years who were rightly concerned about their own short-term memory despite the lack of concern by others, including their spouse and children.

It is often difficult to differentiate simple "senior moments" from actual mild short-term memory loss. Indeed, during the early stages of memory decline, you may be the best judge of your own weaknesses. You may have a feeling that your short-term memory is not quite right, because you are having failures in skills that you feel should work better, such as doing your finances, reasoning, worrying about your memory despite reassurances from others, or making poor decisions that are not characteristic of you. *It is important for you to seek an assessment by someone trained in memory evaluation.*

A second form of Mild Cognitive Impairment occurs in which the person afflicted has adequate memory but displays a decline within a domain of mental function other than memory. For example, the person may display impairment in judgment, changes in personality, or decline in reasoning but have adequate to good short-term memory. One client of mine who fit this subtype believed that he had won the Publisher's Clearinghouse Sweepstakes prize, despite having a good short- and long-term memory. He even bought airplane tickets for another state to pick up his believed winnings. He did not win but was never persuaded otherwise and believed he would eventually receive the money (sort of like the movie *Nebraska*).

The third type of Mild Cognitive Impairment is the mixed type, which is marked by multiple small changes in mental functions including remembering, decision-making, and judgment.

TABLE 10.1

MILD COGNITIVE IMPAIRMENT OF THE AMNESTIC TYPE

Criteria for Mild Cognitive Impairment of the Amnestic Type

- Memory complaint
- Intellectual functioning consistent with history
- Normal self-care
- Short-term memory deficit on rigorous memory test for age and education
- Not demented
- Speed of mental operations may be slower than normal
- Mental flexibility may be reduced

Some Facts About Mild Cognitive Impairment of the Amnestic Type

- 10–15% convert to Alzheimer's diagnosis per year (normal conversion is 1–2%)
- 50% convert within 6 years without treatment
- Conversion may speed up with advancing age
- May exist in 20% of persons older than 75
- May be a transition state to Alzheimer's disease for some
- No differences for sex
- Some show improved memory over time
- Alzheimer's disease is not inevitable for those diagnosed with Mild Cognitive Impairment of the amnestic type

---

If you are over the age of sixty, I encourage you to have a baseline "demanding" memory evaluation. You can repeat this every couple of years to determine the trajectory of your short-term memory. *Do not rely on brief memory screenings.* By the time you are identified as impaired by current screenings, you would have lost several years of setting up a needed compensation program that uses many of the strategies described in this book. If you wait too long, you may not be able to learn and master the compensation strategies. *You have to incorporate the techniques into your lifestyle. Include this as part of your wellness program.*

Another criterion for the amnestic type of Mild Cognitive Impairment is that formal testing reveals good intellectual ability consistent with the person's life history and accomplishments. In addition, the person can clearly care for all personal needs without assistance or prompting. Nor is the individual demented, which means that he or she can independently carry out all social, recreational, and vocational functions. One of the most important professional lessons that I learned is that no one can identify those with Mild Cognitive Impairment by just talking with a client, by doing a brief exam of the client's mental state, or even by doing a thorough clinical interview. Many who show clear decline in thorough evaluations pass all of these hurdles with flying colors.

THE IMPORTANCE OF EARLY DETECTION OF MILD COGNITIVE IMPAIRMENT

The current interest in Mild Cognitive Impairment reflects our understanding of the need to detect Alzheimer's disease in its earliest stages. This is also true for conditions such as vascular dementia, Lewy body dementia, frontotemporal dementia, primary progressive aphasia, or other progressive conditions that may first be diagnosed as Mild Cognitive Impairment.

One of the most essential aspects of managing short-term memory loss is establishing compensation strategies before they are needed. Many clients have assured me in all sincerity that they will learn the skill(s) (for example, using a personal calendar) or make the appropriate change(s) (such as no longer driving) when they must. But this is exactly the rub for short-term memory loss: *As memory loss progresses, many lose awareness of their mistakes.* One of my clients had five documented car accidents in the previous month but thought she had a perfect driving record because she could not recall any of the incidents. Despite the intuitive belief that we should become *less* convinced of our convictions as memory loss *increases,* those of us who *forget* that we forget are often more convinced of the *reliability* of our memory.

The habits you build today protect your tomorrow. If you have Mild Cognitive Impairment, you need to establish your future plan, or "safety net," immediately in case you experience further decline over time. Involve family members and/or friends in your safety net. Specific elements of this planning will be discussed in Chapter 14. If you have Mild Cognitive Impairment, you can still comprehend and master strategies, such as those discussed in earlier chapters, to manage your short-term memory loss. However, self-management becomes increasingly difficult to master as your memory declines and your ability for complex thinking and planning becomes compromised. Thus, as short-term memory declines, you will increasingly become reliant on the routines, memory aids, and skills that you have already developed.

At some point in the progression of Alzheimer's disease, new learning becomes nearly impossible. Furthermore, as short-term memory declines in Alzheimer's disease, other mental skills increasingly decay as well, including insight, planning, judgment, and reasoning. The bottom line here is to *act early*. Don't be afraid of Mild Cognitive Impairment. It is the opportunity to take control of your future.

A multitude of studies are underway to better determine the underlying changes in brain function/anatomy and cognition that occur with Mild Cognitive Impairment. Additionally, numerous studies are being done to determine which treatments may slow the "conversion" of Mild Cognitive Impairment to Alzheimer's disease. Trials have included use of agents such as Aricept and Exelon in addition to vitamin E, anti-inflammatory agents, and Ginkgo Biloba. The number of support groups and workshops that help persons with Mild Cognitive Impairment to gain better control over their future are also increasing.

HOW DO PROFESSIONALS DETECT MILD COGNITIVE IMPAIRMENT?

Formal memory tests like the California Verbal Learning Test or the Wechsler Memory Scale are the "gold standard" for early detection of both Mild Cognitive Impairment and Alzheimer's disease (which, by definition, requires the loss of short-term memory). A memory test must evaluate both immediate and delayed recall and should be challenging. If you desire a thorough evaluation, make sure that it assesses not only your memory but also other mental operations, such as intelligence, reasoning, attention, constructive skills, and language.

Formal testing can be used for monitoring the course of and response to treatments if you have Mild Cognitive Impairment, Alzheimer's disease, or other progressive conditions. It allows you, as well as those who care about you, to track your course and to plan ahead. Wellness programs do not wait for an illness before evaluation, and they use established metrics to assess and monitor your progress.

MILD COGNITIVE IMPAIRMENT AS A POSSIBLE TRANSITIONAL STATE FOR ALZHEIMER'S DISEASE

As mentioned above, Mild Cognitive Impairment may be a transitional condition between normal mental functioning and Alzheimer's disease. Alzheimer's disease is chronic and starts in a very mild form. You do not suddenly wake up with Alzheimer's disease out of nowhere. Noticeable mental decline appears at least two to four years before a diagnosis of dementia can be made, and a "preclinical state" characterized by very mild deficits may extend for as many as ten, twenty, or more years before the disease can be clearly diagnosed. A decline in short-term memory (the kind of memory needed for development of new learning) is especially predictive of Alzheimer's disease.

At some point in the natural history of Alzheimer's disease, many patients display a more rapid decline in skills. This is the time when most seek medical diagnosis and treatment. I can do much more for those who come to me with Mild Cognitive Impairment than I can for those who already have Alzheimer's disease.

You will experience a transition in progressive dementia from caring for yourself to someone caring for you. *The time to start treatment is when you can intervene for yourself* rather than when the plan is executed for you. This is why it is essential for you to not to put off a professional consultation if you are concerned about your memory well before this transition occurs.

SIGNS OF POSSIBLE MILD COGNITIVE IMPAIRMENT

At the earliest onset of Mild Cognitive Impairment, you will probably experience a growing awareness that something is wrong, but friends and relatives are likely to suggest that the symptoms are the "same as we all experience as we age." They are simply "senior moments." In addition to concerns about short-term memory, you may also exhibit changes in behavior (such as depression or unusual irritability) that are often inexplicable at the time.

One of my clients who detected a problem at a very early stage first became concerned that something was wrong with her when she was driving back to her home from a visit with her daughter. She had driven this same route of about fifteen miles hundreds of times before, but when she suddenly could not recall how to get home, it caught her attention. She was clever and stopped at a restaurant to have coffee. After a short time, she recalled the route she needed to take. She was also proactive in that she called for an assessment the following day. We established a family program for her based on her retained skills to better her future, whether or not she would experience progressive cognitive decline. Changes, such as those described in Table 10.2 may go on for many years before you seek a diagnosis. But the earlier you get evaluated, the better your outcome will be in learning how to manage the changes.

AN ARGUMENT FOR EARLY ASSESSMENT

Ron Reagan revealed in his book, *My Father at 100*, that his father was thrown from his horse six months after leaving office during July 1989. He sustained a closed-head injury and needed neurosurgery to relieve the pressure from a hematoma (bleeding) in his brain. The surgeons discovered that he already had the neurological changes of Alzheimer's disease.

TABLE 10.2

CHANGES THAT MAY BE A SIGN OF COGNITIVE DECLINE
(Indicate a need for professional evaluation)

Mental Changes That Are Not Characteristic

- Concerns about short-term memory and new learning
- Inability to follow through on projects
- Difficulty following a train of thought
- Difficulty with work
- Trouble holding a thought or idea, no matter how often others explain
- Gaps in logic that cannot be closed, no matter what

Behavioral Changes

- Later-life onset of depression
- Uncharacteristic outbursts of irrational rage
- Intense suspicion or fear of others
- Hostile responses for no apparent reason
- Unbelievable stories of bad things done by others
- Sudden onset of drinking alcohol in someone who doesn't drink
  with Mild Cognitive Impairment of the amnestic type

This raised two interesting issues about memory. First, there is debate about whether President Reagan showed signs of Alzheimer's disease while he was in office. Second, John McCain would have been the oldest elected president of the United States, if elected. In 2020, the two men running for President were in their mid to late seventies and displayed memory and word-finding errors. Were these minor errors from aging? Were their errors signs of early Alzheimer's disease? How can we know?

First, consider age. Although we don't have a standard of how old is too old to be President of the United States, a number of prejudices prevail about age and competence. Should there be an age for mandatory retirement? Should there be an age for mandatory surrender of the privilege of driving?

On the one hand, mental processes clearly change in their efficiency as we age. Our thinking slows. We have more struggles in finding words. Our reaction time slows. We have a more difficult time multitasking. On the other hand, we are very good at compensating for the changes in mental efficiency that accompanies aging. Also, knowledge and problem-solving experience improve with age as long as our mind stays "sharp." More importantly, the clearest finding from research on cognitive aging is that there is great variability. This means that some function very well into their ninth decade and beyond and others don't. Therefore, it doesn't seem fair to make an arbitrary decision based on age alone.

Second, consider the chance of someone developing a progressive dementia such as Alzheimer's disease. This unfolds over decades, and the early signs are very difficult to differentiate from normal aging. The greatest risk factor for developing Alzheimer's disease is age. According to some, nearly 50 percent of those who live to be eight-five to ninety will receive a diagnosis of Alzheimer's disease. Again, age does not determine who may be capable and who is not. The converse of the statistic is that 50 percent of those aged eighty-five to ninety is cognitively able.

So how do we determine the cognitive capacity of our leaders? *It comes down to understanding what will happen early in the course of Alzheimer's disease.* The first sign usually is subtle short-term memory loss. This will affect new learning as well as complex decision-making. However, in the very early stages, just listening to someone or administering a Mini-Mental State Exam (or other screening or imaging technique) cannot detect *subtle* memory loss. The only practical and fair way is to provide a challenging evaluation of short-term memory and other cognitive skills as compared to peers and past abilities. I propose that the only way to adequately assess whether a person is cognitively able to be President is to have him or her undergo a thorough memory evaluation, not a quick screening. We raise the issues of physical health of the president (present or future) and can reassure ourselves by thorough evaluation. I recommend adding rigorous memory assessment for evaluating those running for political office *with full disclosure.*

But why just pick on those who are in their seventies, or only presidential or elected candidates? It is time for all candidates for public office to undergo appropriate cognitive testing. This also applies to doctors, teachers, lawyers, and accountants, especially if they are older than fifty. Standard cognitive evaluations are being provided for players in the NFL in the age of CTE to track their cognitive skills. Why not do the same for those in public office or professional positions that influence the lives of others? Furthermore, why not for the rest of us?

CHAPTER ELEVEN

Alzheimer's Disease and Dementias

"Americans fear getting Alzheimer's disease more than heart disease, stroke or diabetes." (Metlife Foundation Alzheimer's Survey)

Knowing that you have cancer gives you only the most general information about your condition — you may have a serious and sometimes a fatal illness. Your eventual outcome depends, in part, on the type of cancer you have. Many cancers exist (e.g., lung, prostate, breast, bone, pancreatic, basal cell, melanoma, glioma, meningioma, etc.), each having different dynamics and protocols. Pancreatic cancer is more lethal than many skin cancers. The four stages of cancer (I, II, III, and IV) indicate the severity of the disease. The cancer is more serious, with a greater degree of spread (metastasis), when the number is higher. Four factors are therefore needed to better understand a diagnosed victim: Is the tumor benign or malignant? What type of cancer is it? What organ system is affected? What stage is it?

The concept of dementia, just like with cancer, is complex and not simply "you have it or you don't." A widespread misconception about "dementia" exists in the minds of those who do not really understand it. Diagnosing someone with dementia provides little useful information, because it is actually a broad term for a number of disorders. Many of my clients have expressed relief because someone, sometimes a professional, told them that they have "dementia" and therefore do not have Alzheimer's disease. I also had clients who were told by professionals that they are "too old" to get Alzheimer's disease. *These statements stem from a confusion of terminology.* The terms "cancer" and "dementia" both represent superordinate categories that subsume many specific disorders, *each with a unique cause and prognosis.*

There are many types or causes/etiologies of dementia. For example, it may include not only Alzheimer's disease but also a closed head injury, stroke, Pick's disease, Lewy body disease, infection with viruses, Parkinson's disease, and AIDS, to name a few. Alzheimer's disease is the most common cause of dementia.

Dementia is a syndrome (a constellation of signs and features) that requires systematic evaluation to determine the cause. *Alzheimer's disease is a specific form of dementia* that is caused by plaques and tangles (although many are now questioning the role of amyloid plaques and, indeed, if Alzheimer's disease is a unitary entity) in the neurons of the brain. *Vascular dementia* (discussed below) is another specific form of dementia caused by multiple small strokes. The former typically develops slowly over years, whereas the latter often arrives as sudden changes or small discrete steps, depending on the volume of tissue injured. Diffuse Lewy (the name of the physician who identified these features in the brain) body disease is a dementia caused by the pathologic changes in brain structure known as Lewy bodies. These and other specific names of dementias refer to the presumptive cause of the damage to neurons in the brain. Most simply, *dementia is an irreversible, progressive or sudden adult-onset deterioration of mental and adaptive functions that interferes with your ability to live independently.*

DEMENTIA OR ALZHEIMER'S DISEASE?

Among the most frequent questions I am asked is, "What is the difference between Alzheimer's disease and dementia?" Dementia refers to mental deterioration to the point that you can no longer do higher-level mental tasks like balancing a checkbook, using a computer, or preparing a meal — the so-called Independent Activities of Daily Living (IADLs). In more severe forms of dementia, you may no longer be able to tend to personal needs such as bathing, toileting, or dressing — considered Activities of Daily Living. In other words, dementia refers to mental decline where you are disabled (i.e., you need at least some level of external care) as a result of cognitive decline from a higher level of ability. The term "dementia" designates a level of *severity* of the mental deterioration.

The most common type of dementia is seen in individuals who have a heavy burden of aberrant proteins identified as amyloid (i.e., plaques) and tau (i.e., tangles) that interfere with brain functions. When these proteins are pervasively present in the brain, the decline is diagnosed as Alzheimer's disease. Dementia is the general term for decline, and Alzheimer's disease is but one of many possible causes of decline.

Dementia (as mentioned earlier) has many causes other than Alzheimer's disease. When stroke or multiple mini-strokes cause the decline, the diagnosis would be vascular dementia. When a head injury causes the decline, the diagnosis would be dementia due to traumatic brain injury. If the frontal lobes (the part of the brain that plans and makes judgments, causes you to act in socially appropriate ways, and generates expressive language) decline, the diagnosis would be frontotemporal dementia. Progressive loss of expressive language is diagnosed as a primary progressive aphasia. A progressive dementia occurs in many people with Parkinson's disease. Another rather common progressive dementia is caused by Lewy bodies and is called diffuse Lewy body disease. These conditions (as well as others) are all *irreversible* declines in ability. Some dementias are *progressive* (meaning they get worse over time, usually several years or decades), whereas others may develop suddenly, then stabilize or even improve over time (such as those caused by a stroke or a brain injury).

Adding confusion to the situation are the so-called "treatable dementias." This is a poor choice of words. The term "dementia" should refer to *irreversible* conditions. Some medical conditions may cause only temporary mental deterioration. With appropriate treatment or over time, you may recover to your normal or near-normal state. Medical conditions such as thyroid disorder, metabolic disorders, certain vitamin deficiencies, tumors, severe depression, normal pressure hydrocephalus (if discovered and treated early enough), reactions to medications, untreated sleep apnea, "brain fog" from chemotherapy, and acute illnesses (e.g., urinary tract infections, high fever) may cause a temporary (may last hours to days to weeks) inability to function and may be more appropriately called *delirium*. These possibilities must be evaluated in anyone thought to be showing decline.

In summary, dementia is an *irreversible* and *severe* decline of mental abilities that interferes with independence. Alzheimer's disease is one of several possible causes of dementia.

DEFINITIONS AND CAUSES OF DEMENTIA

Two general technical sets of criteria are used by professionals to define/diagnose dementia. These are drawn from professional sources such as the *International Classification of Disease* (ICD) and the *Diagnostic and Statistical Manual V* (DSM 5) of the American Psychiatric Association (although the DSM 5 dropped the term "dementia" in favor of "neurocognitive disorders"). However, I prefer to use the term "dementia." It is so widely used and I'd rather not complicate the topic by introducing new terminology.

For you to be diagnosed with dementia, you must exhibit a persistent decline in at least three of five major mental domains: *language* (difficulty expressing yourself with words, difficulty comprehending language); *memory* (difficulty learning new information or skills, recalling past information); *visuospatial* (illusions, hallucinations, neglect, lack of object recognition) along with visuoconstructive abilities (problems with navigation or route-finding, difficulty with drawing); *executive functions* (deficits in judgment, reasoning, abstraction); and *praxis* (difficulty dressing, using utensils to eat) and/or personality (becoming more passive or irritable).

A more restrictive definition (see Table 11.1) requires impaired short-term memory accompanied by decline in at least one other mental domain that impairs occupational, social, or interpersonal functioning. The essential difference between these definitions is that the latter restricts the term to disorders that include memory loss, such as Alzheimer's disease, whereas the former does not make memory loss necessary for a diagnosis of dementia.

TABLE 11.1

COMMONLY USED CRITERIA FOR DIAGNOSING
DEMENTIA OF THE ALZHEIMER'S TYPE

Impaired short-term memory **and** one or more of the following:

- Difficulty with reasoning
- Difficulty with language
- Disorientation
- Poor concentration
- Difficulty with spatial relationships
- Poor judgment
- Change in personality
- Changes in sexuality
- Delusional thinking
- Diminished coordination
- Diminished or lost sense of taste and/or smell
- Lowered IQ

Alzheimer's disease is the model for the second definition and has gained so much attention because it is clearly the main cause of dementia as we age. Nearly 60 percent of cases of dementia are correlated with plaques and tangles — hence the name Alzheimer's disease. About 14 percent of the remaining cases are a result of vascular processes, whereas Parkinson's disease and/or Lewy body disease account for about 10 percent. Frontotemporal diseases cause about 8 percent of dementias. The remaining 12 percent are triggered by multiple factors or other causes.

The projected number of persons who will develop Alzheimer's disease over the course of the next fifty years is staggering. About 4 million cases of Alzheimer's disease were diagnosed in 2000 in the United States, and by 2050, about 16 million Americans may be affected by it.

Table 11.2 lists several causes of dementia, each of which is believed to have a different underlying cause even though the external manifesta-

---

TABLE 11.2

**MAJOR TYPES OF DEMENTIA
(DIFFERING ETIOLOGIES; NOT EXHAUSTIVE)**

- Alzheimer's disease
- Pick's disease
- Frontotemporal dementia
- Vascular dementia
  - Lacunar state
  - Binswanger's disease
- Lewy body dementia
- Parkinson's dementia
- Supranuclear palsy
- Huntington's disease
- Infections
  - General paresis
  - Slow virus infections
  - Creutzfeldt-Jacob disease
- Hydrocephalis
- HIV encephalopathy
- Primary progressive aphasia
- Semantic dementia
- Dementia resulting from a head injury (CTE)
- Neoplastic disease

---

tions can be very similar. This is because the specific deficits and severities of cognitive changes are a function of location and volume of the damage in the brain. Keep in mind that real life is never as simple as our schemas. *Many dementias are of mixed causes.*

Although much of this discussion focuses on Alzheimer's disease, let's begin with primary *progressive aphasia* and *chronic traumatic encephalopathy (CTE),* as these disorders are often *misdiagnosed* as Alzheimer's disease.

PRIMARY PROGRESSIVE DEMENTIA

As you learned earlier, normal aging produces frustrations in word finding that are often referred to as tip-of-the-tongue phenomena. Nouns and names are particularly troublesome. Everyone experiences these changes as a normal part of aging. However, some people have *changes in expressive language* that go beyond normal aging. Some show decline that may include:

- poor understanding of the meaning of words,
- pronounced struggles with finding words,
- very halting speech that lacks normal rhythm or melody,
- difficulty articulating words,
- reduced output of words,
- circumlocutions (saying "that thing that tells time" for "watch"),
- using word substitutions,
- mispronouncing words,
- not being able to use pronouns, or often saying "these" and "that" with no clear referent,
- and the inability to name common objects (looking at a lamp but being unable to say the name yet able to pantomime its function).

These changes in expressive language are often accompanied by good language comprehension in the early stages.

This cluster of struggles with expressive language is called *primary progressive aphasia*. The changes do not result from any obvious brain pathology such as a stroke, tumor, or head injury. Language changes are often the only initial problem, because short-term memory is intact. This differentiates primary progressive aphasia from Alzheimer's disease, which also can be accompanied by changes in expressive speech. The disorder is progressive, and the changes in the patient's language become more generalized (e.g., extending to writing as well as speaking). Those with primary progressive aphasia experience declining language comprehension, a severe reduction in their verbal output, and mutism in the most severe cases. Eventually, the deficits may affect other cognitive functions and lead to dementia (i.e., loss of ability to function independently).

These clients struggle to give their history. Their partners/friends often help them with words, but the clients are independent early in the course of their decline. When they are tested, they struggle with information. For instance, when they are asked who wrote *King Lear,* they say, "I don't know," but if they are given "William," they quickly say "Shakespeare." If they are asked to name pictures of common objects, they often gesture how the object is used (like an accordion) but cannot say the name of it. When asked to list as many animals as fast as they can in one minute (a fluency test), they may be able to come up with only ten animals rather than at least twenty or more animals. (Try it yourself by writing down as many animals as you can in one minute.) But again, this is different from Alzheimer's disease in that their short-term memory is often good.

As with all progressive brain diseases, early identification is essential. Sometimes speech therapy helps. Partners, friends, and family members need to understand the problem and learn communication skills (such as prompts and gesturing) to help when the person's language is no longer clear. Some individuals can be helped for a time by Alzheimer's disease medications. The main treatment goal is to support the patient and make sure that a proactive approach is being taken to keep the person engaged in life despite increasing struggles with self-expression. There is so much of life that we experience without speaking.

As an interesting aside, I evaluated a client who had recovered from a stroke that left her with no meaningful expressive language. She wanted to return to living independently, and I was asked to determine whether she was capable of living alone or whether she had become demented from the stroke. This was an interesting challenge because she had no expressive speech. Her son participated in the evaluation and verified her answers. The first item assessed was if she could reliably answer yes and no questions. She could. The focus then turned to practical adaptive skills. Could she dress, shower, prepare meals, balance her checkbook, shop, drive, do laundry, etc.? The answer was yes. The prognosis: She could not produce intelligible expressive speech, but she was not demented.

HEAD INJURIES AND CTE

It all started as a typical Monday. Pamela and I rise at about 6 a.m. and greet Gracie and Vanna, our lovely cats. We have coffee and conversation to start the day. Rain was in the forecast. We were doing some upgrades on our home and needed to pick up supplies at Home Depot — our home away from home. Pamela also volunteered at the library on Mondays and needed to arrive by 1:00 p.m.

My normal Monday routine is to drop Pamela at the library and go for a walk/run. The course is wonderful with streams, wildlife, and a small lake. It circles a reservoir in the mountains and is a rough hiking trail in the forest. The terrain is challenging, with a change in elevation of about 700-plus feet and a distance of three-plus miles. I had completed this course at least twice a week for the past several months and had improved my time to less than an hour.

I dropped Pamela off at about 1:00 after a light lunch. She had reservations about my run that day, as the weather was threatening — as you might expect, wives have more sense than husbands. I reassured her that I would be fine.

I actually don't remember most of this beyond a vague sense of the morning, and I do not recall dropping Pamela off with a promise that I would pick her up by 3:00. Jump forward to about 7:00 p.m. I became aware that I was in a hospital bed with an IV — my first ever hospital stay — and was quite confused. I had a number of painful abrasions and bruises on my legs, arms, hands, and back. I surmised I had fallen on a very steep part of the course.

Pamela filled me in on the details, which I still can't recall. I did not pick her up at 3 or even 3:30. She got a ride with a friend to the reservoir and found the car but not me. After awhile and a lot of worry, she saw someone emerge from the end of the trail and asked if he had seen anyone else on the way. He had seen me looking for my car keys and agreed to go back to retrieve me.

I was a sight, with bloodied, torn clothes, and I was svery confused. It was a good thing I'd lost my keys, because my cell phone was destroyed. Over the next several hours, I was unable to recall where I lived, the name of the President, and even Pamela's name. I was repetitive. "I didn't pick you up at the library, did I?" "I am so sorry." "Did I fall?" "Did I have a concussion?" "Can I go home?" Pamela repeatedly answered these questions for about three hours. Not only was she scared but also a little crazy from my repetition and confusion. I had tests in the ER — a CT scan and heart tests to rule out a stroke or heart attack.

About three months later, I still couldn't recall any details — the fall, the morning, or the afternoon. I had experienced a temporary loss of short-term memory and will never have firsthand knowledge from those several hours. I am fine now but have promised myself never to *run* this course again. However, I will never see other victims of memory loss — either the forgetful ones or those who live with them — in the same way. I have dedicated about twenty-five years to the study of memory loss. In an afternoon, I had gained more personal understanding than I have from my entire past career.

Obviously, I had a concussion (the incident happened about five years ago, and I still don't remember that day before my awareness returned). Let's review the issues of concussion and chronic traumatic encephalopathy (CTE). Estimates are that as many as 4 million athletes in the United States experience sports-related concussions each year, and the incidence of subconcussive trauma is far more extensive. One study reported that high-school football players average 652 blows to the head each year. CTE pathology has been found in athletes as young as age seventeen.

The possible long-term effects of concussion was discussed as far back as 1928, when Martland (*Journal of the American Medical Association*) used the term "punch drunk" to describe boxers who experienced long-lasting consequences of repeated blows to the head. Subsequently, the condition was variously named traumatic encephalopathy of pugilists, traumatic encephalitis, cumulative encephalopathy of boxers, chronic boxer's encephalopathy, and chronic progressive encephalopathy. The later was shortened to chronic traumatic encephalopathy, or CTE, because progression of this condition is possible.

CTE was mainly thought to be the result of boxing injuries until 2005. At that time, Omalu (see Will Smith's movie *Concussion* from 2015) described the first case of CTE in a professional football player. In boxing, as well as in football, the time between the end of exposure to repetitive head trauma and the development of clinical signs and symptoms is often several years. It is also interesting that boxers are more likely to show cerebellar pathology than football players. CTE has also been observed in other sports like ice hockey, soccer, and wrestling. Furthermore, the neuropathology has been described in non-athletes like epileptics, self-injurious head bangers among developmentally delayed individuals, victims of physical abuse, and soldiers with a history of repeated head injuries.

CTE neuropathology is diagnosed by means of a PET scan using selective binders for tau proteins that are associated with neuritic tangles (also found in Alzheimer's disease). It differs neuropathologically from Alzheimer's disease (in CTE the tangles do not co-occur with amyloid plaques), frontotemporal dementia, MS, frontal lobe tumors, and Parkinson's disease. CTE appears to begin in the cerebral sulci before spreading to the medial temporal lobes, frontal lobes, diencephalon, and brainstem.

It remains unclear whether all neuropathological confirmed cases of CTE will eventually have a progressive course. Even a single head trauma may initiate the processes underlying CTE. Head impact is necessary but not sufficient to initiate the cascading pathologic processes. The risk factors for CTE remain unknown (studies are exploring factors such as number of impacts, severity of impact, duration of exposure to the impact, age, lifestyle, and genetic susceptibility).

Five basic clinical patterns mark the first signs of CTE:

1. Behavior that is marked by explosiveness, verbal and physical violence, impulsiveness, aggressive rage, and being out of control.

2. Mood that is marked by depression, anxiety, hopelessness, suicidal thoughts, apathy, fearfulness, fatigue, and irritability.

3. Mixed mood and behavioral changes.

4. Cognition that is marked by memory impairment, executive dysfunction, poor attention and concentration, poor insight, perseveration, language dysfunction, and visuospatial difficulties.

5. Motor skills. Parkinson's features occur in less than one-third of cases so far observed.

CTE is a poorly understood complication of head trauma. It is not just a problem for boxers, football players, the NFL, or athletes. Leisure sports requiring a helmet or high-risk fall activities (e.g., bicycling, rollerblading, skiing, surfing) may also cause CTE. CTE may not increase the risk for Alzheimer's disease (despite CTE victims often being misdiagnosed with Alzheimer's disease), but recent studies suggest CTE may also play a role in idiopathic Parkinson's disease.

A multitude of issues and questions still need to be resolved. Who is susceptible to progression? What level of risk is there from playing contact sports early in life? How do we make those who want to play contact sports safer? What reduces the risk of progression? Are present-day concussion protocols adequate? How many are falsely diagnosed with Alzheimer's disease who actually have CTE?

DIAGNOSING DEMENTIA

The process of diagnosing a dementia, such as Alzheimer's disease, may take several years. The beginning of the disease is often subtle and variable in its time course as well as in symptoms. Many persons who will later develop Alzheimer's disease are first diagnosed with depression. No specific threshold exists for calling a decline in abilities a dementia, or for changing the diagnosis from Mild Cognitive Impairment to Alzheimer's disease. *Diagnosis is a complex clinical judgment.* In Alzheimer's disease, a several-year period of memory loss may occur along with language loss that begins with Mild Cognitive Impairment (which itself may have a several-year course). The early stages of Alzheimer's disease will not be severe enough to label the disease a dementia. Evaluation and ultimate diagnosis take time and may require complex and repeated assessment over time.

RISK FACTORS FOR ALZHEIMER'S DISEASE

Currently, about 5.5 million people in the United States have Alzheimer's disease. Of these, 3.5 million are older than age sixty-five. If the prevalence rate remains as it is today, 16 million people in the United States will have Alzheimer's by 2050. If we can develop a medication that slows the progress of the disease by five years, we can cut the prevalence in half, to about 8 million cases in the United States by 2050.

Epidemiological studies suggest that the greatest risk factor for developing Alzheimer's disease is age. Persons who live to be between eighty-five and ninety years of age have nearly a 50 percent chance of developing Alzheimer's disease, and those living beyond age ninety-five have about a 60 percent chance. Add to this the fact that about 50 to 60 percent of persons with short-term memory loss but otherwise having intact mental skills (that is, with Mild Cognitive Impairment) will be diagnosed with Alzheimer's disease after about five years if no treatments are provided. Clearly, the risk is greatest for those who are aging and who already experience significant short-term memory loss (with no apparent complications like stroke, head injury, or encephalitis) when compared with their peers. But be aware that the outcome is not nearly 100 percent. Neither aging nor short-term memory loss condemns anyone to eventually developing Alzheimer's disease or becoming demented.

Several other risk factors add vulnerability for development of Alzheimer's disease, but none of them are as strongly associated with the disease as are age or short-term memory loss. Having a first- degree relative (parent or sibling) with Alzheimer's disease increases the risk of developing this disease, but *the relationship of genetics and Alzheimer's disease is complex.* Most clients whom I have assessed did *not* have a primary relative with Alzheimer's disease. One client was a terrified woman in her sixties. Her identical twin was in a nursing home with Alzheimer's. Fortunately, she had a superb memory and mental skills — no hint of Alzheimer's disease.

The risk is increased when multiple family members experience memory loss late in life. For example, a physician in his seventies asked me to assess his memory because he was one of seven children in his family, and all of his siblings had a diagnosis of Alzheimer's disease. (A small number of families have a dramatic risk of developing Alzheimer's disease, usually relatively early in their life.) His assessment showed that he had Mild Cognitive Impairment and a high risk of becoming demented. We developed a proactive treatment plan, because he could still function independently, and our goal was to stay ahead of changes that might occur. Still, in most cases, family history is less than perfect in predicting Alzheimer's disease and has less impact on risk than do age and Mild Cognitive Impairment.

Another genetic factor to consider is the presence of apolipoprotein E4 (a gene that modulates cholesterol metabolism and may also have a role in cardiovascular disease). There are three forms of apolipoprotein (coded on chromosome 19) known as E2, E3, and E4. You receive one of these genes from each parent, leading to combinations such as E2 – E2, E2 – E4, etc. Anyone with an E4 is at somewhat higher risk of developing Alzheimer's disease, and anyone with an E2 is less likely to develop it. Again, the relationship is complicated and *not diagnostic* in that many individuals with E4 do *not* develop Alzheimer's disease and some with E2 do.

Other risk factors for developing Alzheimer's disease include having sustained a closed head injury (or series of head injuries) at some point in life. Note the more recent concerns of those who play contact sports and the rise of chronic traumatic encephalopathy (CTE). Incidentally, the prevalence of Parkinson's disease also is higher for those in contact sports (e.g., Muhammad Ali). Recent head trauma in the elderly may also increase risk (wear a helmet for cycling, skiing, surfing, etc.). I have seen a number of persons in their sixties and seventies whose first concerns began after what appeared to be a mild head trauma. However, I have also seen a number of persons with a past history of head trauma who did *not* develop Alzheimer's disease. A history of depression in later life is also associated with increased risk for the developing Alzheimer's disease. Many who have depression have structural changes in their brains, as determined by imaging studies such as the MRI.

Women are slightly more likely to develop Alzheimer's disease than men, but this advantage for men is small and may disappear for those who are older than age eighty-five. Also, persons with lower educational attainment (probably having less than a ninth-grade education) are more vulnerable. The modest protective effect of education appears to be a benefit at the beginning of "old age" (the exact age has not yet been defined). Education does not prevent possible rapid decline once clinical symptoms appear and may not slow cognitive decline resulting from age. The more interesting question here may be the association of "brightness" with Alzheimer's disease. Do those who start out brighter have more "mental reserve" and therefore more ability to fend off the impact of Alzheimer's disease longer? Can mental stimulation increase mental reserve? What is the age limit for gaining an educational boost? This is an area where we have personal control to foster better cognitive health. *It makes a strong case for spending time doing things that you enjoy and challenging your thinking, starting in at least "middle age.*

Cardiovascular disease presents yet another increased vulnerability for developing Alzheimer's disease. Along with mental reserve discussed above, lifestyle may influence the onset of Alzheimer's disease. To repeat, *you have a choice of the lifestyle you pursue.* Therefore, it is critical to maximize your brain health to manage hypertension (especially systolic hypertension), cholesterol, and diabetes. Do not smoke, and limit your alcohol consumption to two drinks per day for men and one drink per day for women. Exercise and eat a predominately "Mediterranean"-style diet. This is especially important given the findings that those with the greatest mental impairment appear to have both the plaques and tangles of Alzheimer's disease combined with small strokes that represent the damage from cardiovascular disease. Apparently, the extra burden of cerebrovascular disease, added to plaques and tangles, is critical in determining the severity of impairment. *As the heart goes, so goes the brain.* This may also explain why, on the one hand, a sedentary lifestyle increases risk while exercise may be neuroprotective.

If you know the risk factors, you can control them. If you have several risk factors, assess the lifestyle choices you are making and plan ahead. Consider seeking guidance from a memory expert, especially if you have concerns about either your memory or your mental skills. Knowing the risk factors also helps researchers identify those who are more vulnerable. This leads to them devising and testing substances (medications, vitamins, herbs) and lifestyle changes that can potentially slow or prevent the progression of Alzheimer's disease. The discovery of a large group of persons with Mild Cognitive Impairment led to strategies that allowed some control over the course of memory loss and Alzheimer's disease. It also allowed high-risk individuals to gain early intervention. Ongoing clinical trials will help to determine what works and what doesn't work to slow or prevent progression.

A Metric for Understanding and Tracking the Changes in Progressive Dementias

To better understand the complex nature of the changes that may define the course of Alzheimer's disease, let's review the stages of the Global Deterioration Scale (devised by Reisberg, Ferris, de Leon, and Crook in 1982). The Global Deterioration Scale is a seven-point rating system for staging the severity of changes in mental and functional capacity that begins with forgetfulness and ends in severe Alzheimer's disease.

The changes represented by this scale are very gross generalizations that allow rough judgments to be made of progression of the disease, and specific movement through the stages is inexact. However, this scale helps us view the natural history of Alzheimer's disease that may unfold anywhere from three to twenty years after diagnosis.

Normal

The first stage in this scale is the one in which we all aspire to remain for the duration of our life. This includes the changes in mental efficiency that are associated with *normal aging*. In this stage, there are no complaints of memory loss by self or others. Furthermore, no objective evidence exists of memory loss from either a clinical interview or an objective assessment.

Forgetfulness

In the second stage, a person presents with subjective complaints about short-term memory loss but does not appear to *show* memory loss either during casual observation or during a careful clinical interview. Forgetful persons do well on screening tests and can only be identified through well-constructed memory testing.

Forgetfulness may be the earliest presentation of the amnestic variant of Mild Cognitive Impairment, and individuals in this stage are appropriately concerned about changes in their memory. Others may rationalize these changes as "senior moments," but in reality, the person is experiencing genuine changes. The instances of forgetting are often exaggerations of normal memory failures, such as forgetting where things are placed or forgetting names that are known well. These are things we all do occasionally. A thorough memory evaluation is recommended so that future changes can be tracked. Individuals in this stage set and implement their treatment plan in coordination with family. Many do not progress from this stage, and some improve on sequential evaluations.

Confusional States

The next two stages are known as the "Early Confusional State" and the "Late Confusional State," respectively. A person in the Early Confusional State may sometimes get lost when traveling in familiar locations. Also, spouses or friends may become concerned about deficits in skills and/or in word and name finding. The person with memory loss may not be as aware as are others of the changes, and typical clinical interviews and screening tests are not able to detect the changes in memory. As the disease progresses into a Late Confusional State, the person has a decline in knowledge of current and recent events. He or she may not be able to travel independently and to handle finances. Deficits are now clear in interviews and screening tests. The person may be quite befuddled but can usually survive on his or her own.

During the evolution of confusional states, progressive changes occur in a person's communication patterns that are typical of the early stages of Alzheimer's disease. My cat functions very well in her world despite the fact that she cannot speak a human word. But human beings are bound by language. Although we all know much more than we can say, degradation in language and communication brought on by the progression of Alzheimer's disease profoundly affects both the person with the disease and the receivers of the communication.

We all spend more time searching for words as we age. However, in Alzheimer's disease, the problem goes beyond the normal frustrations of word finding. As Alzheimer's disease progresses, our vocabulary shrinks and we often substitute simpler, more general words for specific terms. In other words, we are more likely to refer to "stuff" or "thing" rather than to say "fork" or "cat." The "clock" becomes "the thing that tells time" as function words (called *circumlocutions*) replace nouns. These changes in language lead us to become increasingly quiet, especially in lengthier conversations or in groups, because we cannot find words fast enough to keep up with the flow of conversation. Also, we are more quiet because we are struggling to remember what has just been said by either ourselves or someone else.

If we are in the early stages of Alzheimer's disease, the cohesiveness of our speech begins to deteriorate, and we overuse pronouns. We are confused by jokes and sarcasm due to a reduction of our executive functions (abstraction, reasoning). Our reading comprehension declines, and in combination with increased short-term memory loss, we become less interested in reading. Despite these changes, our mechanics of writing tend to be good. However, the combination of memory loss and poor initiation makes writing increasingly difficult. This causes our ability to correspond, make notes for ourselves, and use e-mail or smartphones to deteriorate.

Early Dementia Stage

The "Early Dementia Stage" may last as long as five years. People in this stage cannot recall major personal information, such as their phone number or address of many years. They often forget the names of their grandchildren or the name of the high school or college from which they graduated. Time disorientation (such as claiming that the current year is 2000 or not knowing the month) may occur. Confusion about place is also possible (reporting that they are in Michigan when they are in Florida, or not being able to recall the town in which they currently reside). Persons in the Early Dementia Stage do not need assistance with personal care such as using the toilet or dressing, but they cannot survive without some assistance or a companion. During this stage, a person can clearly do well with supervision and support from a partner or caretaker.

Language skills further erode during the Early Dementia Stage. Language is often reduced to the level of a five- to seven-year-old. Reading aloud is spared, as are the mechanics of writing, but initiation and memory loss make it unlikely that these skills will be displayed unless prompted by others. Persons in early dementia can retain automatic and social phrases. However, they have less to say and use more words to communicate fewer ideas. The content of their speech is shorter and less complex. This kind of speech is labeled as "empty;" it makes their conversations disjointed and difficult to follow.

Increasing memory loss and the struggle with self-monitoring (tracking what they have just said) causes those in this stage to frequently repeat ideas as if they are being said for the first time. As the disease progresses, comprehension of spoken and written language declines, and interpretations become literal and concrete. For example, I asked a person during a memory screening to spell the word "world" backwards. She proceeded to turn her back to me and said "w-o-r-l-d." She then turned back to me and asked, "How did I do?" Communication for those in the Early Dementia

Stage becomes more dependent upon context, intonation, gestures, and behavior. First languages are better retained than second languages. Often, prompting and modeling are better forms of communication than is speech. In short, Alzheimer's disease is accompanied by progressive aphasia, making communication via speech to and by persons with Alzheimer's disease increasingly difficult.

Middle Dementia Stage

The last two stages (Middle and Late Dementia) are the ones that most of us fear. Indeed, these are the stages described in a headline in the *New York Times* (November 11, 2002): "More than death, many elderly fear dementia." These are the stages where disability rather than annoyance and inconvenience take over. The earlier of these two last stages is called "Middle Dementia Stage." Here, individuals may not always know the name of their spouse or children. They will be unaware of recent events and experiences, because they are facing an increasing toll from *anterograde amnesia*. Their knowledge of the past becomes sketchy due to the progressive erosion of their remote memory (called *retrograde amnesia*).

I recall my surprise when a woman whom I was interviewing had completely forgotten the mastectomy she had undergone a month earlier. In the Middle Dementia Stage, individuals will have increasing difficulty with personal care, such as knowing when to change clothing or how often, and how to shower. Personality and emotional changes (such as increased passivity or irritability) are also likely to occur, and those who are afflicted need considerable guidance and environmental support to engage even in pleasing activities.

Late Dementia Stage

Some are unfortunate enough to arrive at "Late Stage Dementia." In this stage, all verbal skills are lost, and the individuals are largely mute and in need of total care. Their brain has lost its ability to engage in the basic skills we all take for granted, such as being able to walk, talk, and eat.

Fortunately, most of those with Alzheimer's disease do not live to this stage.

AN APPROACH TO MANAGING DEMENTIAS: THE MONTESSORI MODEL

The educational philosophy known as the Montessori method (named after its founder) has increasingly been applied to Alzheimer's disease. This model was originally formulated as an alternative to traditional childhood education and was based on human development. It had the advantage (and still does) that it was more pragmatic (applied) than descriptive. In addition, its roots are in learning and teaching and do not arise from a medical model. Nor is the model pathology based. It is possible to develop treatment programs for persons with dementia based on Montessori principles.

The basic rule of thumb to apply the Montessori model for Alzheimer's disease is that, *as skills decline, they disappear in the reverse order of their initial appearance.* In short, "first in, last out." Thus, the higher-level skills are the first to decline. As the disease progresses, skills involved in doing taxes, balancing the checkbook, or using the computer may break down. With further progression, persons tend to lose their ability to travel independently or pick out appropriate clothes to wear. It is only later in the evolution of the disease that their abilities to tend to personal needs and to use language regress.

Montessori principles guide the development and implementation of self-correcting activities that focus *on participation and retained skills* rather than on *correctness.* For example, producing speech is more important than being correct with it. If those with dementia tell a story wrong, don't correct them. The goal for them is to interact with the world, not be competent in it. This is because self-initiation in these individuals is replaced by apathy. As the decline progresses, caregivers (intimates as well as professionals) need to arrange activities that are designed around *automatic behaviors* (e.g., petting a dog, singing a song, playing catch) and *environmental cues* (throwing a ball softly to these persons so they can catch it, or going into a pool with them so they will swim). The idea is that *production is more important than competence.* This approach adds to self-esteem rather than defeating it.

Whether you are more comfortable with a clinical model (such as the one reflected in the Global Deterioration Scale) or an educational model (such as the one discussed in the Montessori model), you will need to talk less and use more demonstration, imitation, and prompting as changes occur in the course of a progressive dementia. *You need to shift from "doing for" to "being with."* This general approach to management of memory disorders increases the self-esteem and self-respect of a person with dementia. Said another way, *we need to think in terms of adapting the environment to the person rather than adapting the person to the environment.* We shall return to a discussion of these principles in Chapter 13.

EVALUATION FOR ALZHEIMER'S DISEASE

The tools used to evaluate and diagnose Mild Cognitive Impairment and Alzheimer's disease have greatly improved over the past decade. The recommended evaluation involves gathering a detailed history from the affected individual and from a family member or companion who is well acquainted with the person being evaluated. The evaluation should contain a standardized mental-status exam (such as the Mini-Mental State Exam), a general neurological exam, and laboratory tests (chemistry, B12, thyroid, etc.). Neuroimaging studies such as a Magnetic Resonance Imaging (MRI) or Computerized Tomography (CT) scan are also recommended. In addition, a neuropsychological evaluation is strongly recommended to provide a description of the client's strengths and weaknesses. This information will provide a baseline to evaluate treatments and to monitor changes over time. A neuropsychological evaluation consists of a challenging and standardized memory test as well as an assessment of other mental skills such as intellectual ability, construction, language, and problem solving.

Many studies are underway to determine the presence of accurate and reliable biological markers for Alzheimer's disease. So far, no clear biological markers have been established (we still don't definitively know the cause or causes of Alzheimer's disease, which limits the development of definitive markers).

A Handy Self-Assessment

A thorough memory evaluation (see next few pages) needs to address our abilities to perform "instrumental and adaptive skills of daily living." These are everyday skills that we take for granted, like preparing a meal, managing a checkbook, and dressing. As part of my assessment protocol, I created a qualitative checklist to cover a number of these skills. This is not a psychometrically valid scale. However, it was very useful for me, and for my clients, over the years.

As you can see, a number of adaptive skills are covered. There is no cutoff for the numbers, but the greater the number of "yes" responses, the more likely the client will need external care. I suggest you take it yourself, then have a partner or family member complete it *about you*. I feel that the scale is fairly intuitive.

You can complete the checklist as often as you like. I use it for myself, as I have Parkinson's disease and want to have an objective way to see how I am doing. Fortunately, I only score yeses on items of balance and motor skills so far. Over the years, when my clients scored above 10 (depending on the item), it indicated some degree of difficulty. As the score (60 items total) increased, the client needed increasing external support.

What Is Early-Onset Dementia?

Terminology in medicine is constantly changing. In many older references, we find the dichotomy of "senile" versus "presenile" dementia. The definitions are simple. *Senile dementia* refers to any case that has an onset

YOUR HANDY SELF-ASSESSMENT

LEARNING AND RETAINING NEW INFORMATION

1.	Is repetitive	**Yes**	No
2.	Trouble remembering recent conversations	**Yes**	No
3.	Forgets what he/she starts to say	**Yes**	No
4.	Trouble remembering recent events	**Yes**	No
5.	Trouble remembering appointments	**Yes**	No
6.	Frequently misplaces objects	**Yes**	No
7.	Trouble doing chores without reminders	**Yes**	No
8.	Trouble shopping	**Yes**	No
9.	Trouble managing his/her own medications	**Yes**	No
10.	Change in sense of smell or taste	**Yes**	No
11.	Trouble discussing current events or areas of interest	**Yes**	No

HANDLING COMPLEX TASKS

12.	Trouble following a complex train of thought	**Yes**	No
13.	Trouble performing tasks that require many steps, such as balancing a checkbook or cooking a meal	**Yes**	No
14.	Trouble organizing objects around the house	**Yes**	No
15.	Trouble paying bills	**Yes**	No
16.	Trouble writing checks	**Yes**	No

17. Trouble balancing the checkbook **Yes** No

18. Trouble managing finances/taxes **Yes** No

19. Trouble doing calculations **Yes** No

20. Trouble using money **Yes** No

21. Trouble making tips **Yes** No

22. Trouble obtaining a cold beverage **Yes** No

23. Trouble obtaining a hot beverage **Yes** No

24. Trouble making a snack **Yes** No

25. Trouble making a meal **Yes** No

REASONING ABILITY

26. Unable to respond with a reasonable plan for problems at work or at home, such as knowing what to do if the bathroom is flooded **Yes** No

27. Shows uncharacteristic disregard for rules of social conduct **Yes** No

SPACIAL ABILITY AND ORIENTATION

28. Trouble driving **Yes** No

29. Trouble finding his/her way around familiar places **Yes** No

30. Trouble finding his/her way around unfamiliar places **Yes** No

LANGUAGE

31. Increasing difficulty with finding the words to express what he/she wants to say **Yes** No

32. Uses words or syntax that do not make sense	**Yes**	No
33. Trouble writing	**Yes**	No
34. Trouble following conversations	**Yes**	No
35. Trouble following directions/instructions presented verbally	**Yes**	No
36. Trouble reading a magazine or book	**Yes**	No
37. Trouble following a movie or TV show	**Yes**	No
38. Trouble paying attention in conversation	**Yes**	No

USE OF APPLIANCES

39. Trouble using a computer	**Yes**	No
40. Trouble using a telephone	**Yes**	No
41. Trouble using the TV remote	**Yes**	No
42. Trouble using the microwave	**Yes**	No
43. Trouble using the stove	**Yes**	No
44. Trouble using a washer and dryer	**Yes**	No
45. Trouble doing housework	**Yes**	No
46. Trouble doing handiwork	**Yes**	No

BEHAVIOR

47. Changes in personality	**Yes**	No
48. Appears more passive and less responsive	**Yes**	No
49. No longer engages in pastime, hobby, or games	**Yes**	No
50. More irritable than usual	**Yes**	No

51. More suspicious than usual	**Yes**	No
52. Misinterprets visual or auditory stimuli	**Yes**	No
53. Changes in standards of dress and/or grooming	**Yes**	No
54. Needs help with dressing	**Yes**	No
55. Needs help with grooming	**Yes**	No
56. Unstable balance/gait	**Yes**	No
57. Trouble controlling bladder	**Yes**	No
58. Trouble controlling bowel	**Yes**	No
59. A family member expresses concern	**Yes**	No
60. Worried about own memory	**Yes**	No

TOTAL SCORE OF BOLD ITEMS: _____________________

---

of age sixty-five and older. *Presenile dementia* is any case where the age of onset is less than sixty-five.

Recently, new terminology applies the labels "young-onset dementia" and "late-onset dementia." Early-onset dementia is when the condition is diagnosed before the age of sixty-five. Why sixty-five? No biological reason has been established for this distinction. This age is arbitrary, just as it is for qualifying for Medicare. It is a cultural definition for being classified as elderly based on tradition rather than being a biologic entity (see Draper and Withall, 2016, in the journal articles for a good review of this literature).

The main point to keep in mind is that Alzheimer's disease occurs more frequently with advancing age. Therefore, as you might have guessed, the symptoms at presentation for evaluation are the same for both categories, but the distribution of etiologies differs. Alzheimer's disease is more often the "cause" of disability in the old-onset (50–70 percent of cases) than in the young-onset dementia (15–40 percent of cases). Most cases of young-onset Alzheimer's disease are due to an autosomal familial gene (like for Huntington's disease) that runs in very few families.

The most common causes for young-onset dementia include fronto-temporal disease, Huntington's disease, Lewy Body disease, Parkinson's disease, alcohol-related dementia, traumatic brain injury, HIV infection, multiple sclerosis, vascular disease, and other much less common diseases. A number of other conditions have been labeled by various terms, such as "pseudodementias," "treatable causes" of dementia, or, more recently, "secondary" dementias. This terminology is confusing to me. By definition, a dementia is a condition that is irreversible. Therefore, if a treatment is found that *resolves* the presenting problems, the condition was not a dementia and should not be labeled as such (given the implications of this diagnosis). Illnesses that may present with symptoms similar to those manifested in dementias include metabolic disorders, infections, diabetes, neoplasms, stroke, autoimmune diseases (e.g., lupus), and substance-misuse disorders (e.g., chronic misuse of alcohol, opioids, or benzodiazepines). In short, unlike in Alzheimer's disease, where the root cause is unknown, the underlying cause can be directly addressed.

The presenting range of neurologic symptoms varies for both younger and older groups and stems from the main brain areas (i.e., skills) that are affected. For clients younger than age sixty-five, dementias are less likely to be considered initially as a likely diagnosis than for those over age sixty-five. *The focus of evaluation for young-onset dementia is to first consider factors such as marital discord, alcohol abuse, menopause, and/or occupational stress.* Although this slows the final diagnosis (it may take years for younger cases to get a final explanation), it adds to the distress of those affected. Treatment strategies are the same for dementias in both younger and older cases.

If you or someone you care about who is in the younger classification displays any of the following problems (especially if these behaviors are not typical in the client), I strongly suggest you obtain a thorough dementia evaluation:

- Changes in behavior or personality, especially in frontotemporal disease or alcohol-related disease (for example, apathy, social withdrawal, sexual inappropriateness, disinhibition, uncharacteristic irritability, loss of empathy, selfishness, and lack of insight.
- Draper and Withall (2016) suggest that a complete dementia evaluation be conducted in the following scenarios.
  - Treatment-resistant depression or anxiety, especially when accompanied by cognitive concerns.
  - Persistent memory concerns, especially given a positive family history.
  - Concerns of close family or friends.
- Change in behavior that is inconsistent with the person's past behavior.
  - Heavy alcohol or substance abuse over a long period of time.
  - HIV positive.
  - Family history of dementia, with young-onset dementia in close relatives.
  - Chronic systemic diseases, such as diabetes, lupus, thyroid disorder, and cancers accompanied by concerns about memory and thinking.

Does Retiring Speed Up Dementia?

There are retirement stories that fall both ways. Some people have a long and rewarding retirement. Others seem to decline either physically or mentally shortly after retirement. The fear is that by retiring, you become disengaged and cognitive impairment sets in. After all, educational attainment, social engagement, exercise, challenging work, and bilingualism are "neuroprotective, so they are thought by some to decrease the risk" of problems like Alzheimer's disease. Of course, the conundrum is that the cause cannot be determined, because no study had been done that disentangles whether the *time* of retirement is a result or cause of cognitive decline. The facts that Alzheimer's disease unfolds over decades and has a subtle onset further complicate the situation.

A methodological note: We have to accept *correlational data* for us to understand dementia and to create evaluation and treatment options. We cannot use *definitive studies* that involve the random assignment of who retires when. Furthermore, many findings are based on use of the means (averages) that obscure details from data, such as individual differences (e.g., amount of education, sex, age, cohort, personality style, expertise, reason for retirement, and more). In addition, some data sets are enormous, thereby generating trivial findings. Does a treatment that improves recall by 2/16 words that is statistically significant really change your life? This is true of many of the studies that guide our healthcare decisions. This is not a criticism of many excellent studies but reflects the complexity of the issues studied and multifactorial nature of causation in biological systems.

With that caveat in mind, what does the research tell us about retirement and cognitive decline? A few studies indicate that a correlation — an association — does exist between retirement and the risk of "developing dementia." The favored conclusion is that a delay in onset of Alzheimer's disease occurs for each year retirement is delayed. One study suggested a delay of 0.13 years for each year that retirement is put off. This begs several questions, like are we talking delays after the age of sixty-five? Sixty? One widely cited and ambitious study was conducted in connection with the European Alzheimer's initiative ("Retirement Age and the Age of Onset of Alzheimer's Disease," *PloS One*, 2015). The conclusions were based on an epidemiological study in Europe of 815 patients with Alzheimer's. The database included age at retirement and age of onset (better thought of as "age diagnosed" because the disease comes on so slowly) of Alzheimer's. Both the age of the individual's symptom onset (best guess) and age of diagnosis were considered. Several possible confounding factors were utilized in the analysis: sex, level of education, income, complexity of job, and medical variables like hypertension, diabetes, depression, and stroke. The average age of retirement in this study was about sixty-one.

Overall, a later retirement age was associated with both delays in the age of the person for the *onset* of symptoms (average = 74.9) and that person's age at *diagnosis* (average = 77.1). This association held, even when considering only those who retired before age sixty-five. However, no significant association was noted for those who retired *before* age sixty-five *and* developed Alzheimer's disease ten years or more after retirement. This result indicated that some of those who retired early did so *because of symptoms interfering with their work performance.* The results were not associated with gender, income, medical conditions, occupation, or education.

The takeaway? An association does exist between the age of retirement and the age of onset of Alzheimer's disease, suggesting that some patients retired because their symptoms compromised their work performance. On the other hand, those who retired later obviously did not display changes in work performance and therefore were presumed to be free of Alzheimer's disease when they retired.

The question of whether early retirement speeds up the onset of Alzheimer's disease remains unresolved. It is clear that developing cognitive impairment can speed up the age of retirement, but it is not clear whether retirement speeds up the onset of Alzheimer's disease in those who retire with intact cognitive and memory skills. This is reassuring to people like me who were successfully able to put off retirement beyond age sixty-five. However, it does not indicate that I will not become demented *during* retirement (so far, so good).

WARNING SIGNS

There are warning signs that should lead you to seek professional evaluation for Alzheimer's disease. If you notice any of the changes described in Table 11.3 (next page) in yourself or in others you care about, take action early.

WHAT ABOUT ME? THERE IS ALZHEIMER'S/DEMENTIA IN MY FAMILY

I was facilitating a support group for families who were caring for a parent or sibling with Alzheimer's disease. One of the participants was sixty years old, and after some discussion of her mother, she turned and asked:

TABLE 11.3

SIGNS OF POSSIBLE EARLY-STAGE DEMENTIA

Mental Changes

- Overall inability to function as well as in the past
- Difficulty performing a familiar task
- Unable to think of simple words
- Getting lost in time or place
- Making poor judgments
- Trouble with abstract reasoning
- Trouble with arithmetic
- Misplacing things
- Putting things in odd places
- Difficulty with household bills and documents
- Domestic accidents
- Leaving appliances on
- Leaving pots burning on the stove
- Getting lost in the car
- Unaccounted-for accidents in the car
- Struggling with daily activities
- Inconsistent memory and/or behavior

Behavioral Changes

- Rapid mood changes for no apparent reason
- Sudden or dramatic changes in personality
- Loss of initiative
- Loss of interest in normal pursuits
- Deteriorating appearance
- Changes in grooming and dress
- Odd combinations of clothing
- Decline in personal hygiene
- Dropping old friendships
- Inappropriate social patterns
- Becoming more dependent
- Avoiding contact with close family

TABLE 11.3 (continued)

SIGNS OF POSSIBLE EARLY-STAGE DEMENTIA

Behavioral Changes (continued)

* Staying in bed for long periods without a reason
* Relating strange events
* Summoning police with no legitimate reason
* Changes in sleep patterns
* Little or no food in refrigerator and cupboards
* Spoiled or expired food in refrigerator and cupboards
* Hoarding
* Mood changes that don't seem related to external events

"What about me?" She was noticing changes in her memory and was concerned, as was her thirty-nine-year-old daughter sitting next to her. She reported no clear memory deficits but was worrying about her future and whether her current memory concerns were normal for her age, a result of the stress of caregiving, or signs that she may one day develop Alzheimer's disease.

Clearly, your risk for developing Alzheimer's disease increases if someone in your immediate family was diagnosed with the disease. I recall a retired physician (discussed earlier) who sought evaluation, because he was one of seven children, and each of his siblings had Alzheimer's disease. He was having clear decline in his short-term memory but otherwise was doing well cognitively. We put together a proactive plan to protect his future.

However, the genetic link is not always this clear. There is no established genetic test for Alzheimer's disease. Furthermore, *most of those diagnosed with Alzheimer's do not have a family history of the disease*. To make things even muddier, I once assessed a sixty-five-year-old identical twin whose sister was in a skilled nursing home with Alzheimer's disease. After a thorough evaluation, the well sister had excellent memory and other cognitive skills. If the assessment had been based strictly on genetics, she would be in the bed next to her sister. Despite all of the advances in genetics, the greatest risk factor for developing Alzheimer's disease remains age.

Remember that Alzheimer's disease takes at least fifteen to twenty years to unfold. You have lots of time to plan for how you will handle possible changes *if* they occur sometime in the future. You need to write down this plan and include it as part of your advanced directives. Make certain that your plan covers anticipated needs and decisions like driving, assisted living, and transfer of financial decision-making. Additionally, start lifestyle enhancements but realize there are no guarantees. The clearest directive is to exercise; don't smoke; drink alcohol in moderation; eat a diet that is heavy in fruits, vegetables, vegetable oils, and fish; and stay intellectually and socially engaged.

The other good news is that Alzheimer's disease starts with a reduction in short-term memory — the ability to learn and retain *new* information. These changes progress slowly and begin years before a diagnosis of Alzheimer's disease can be made. You have many options to deal with your short–term memory loss if you get a baseline memory evaluation early (at least at age fifty) and continue to track your memory every few years. That's the best way to see where you are, especially if you have a positive family history of Alzheimer's disease.

Not everyone with poor short-term memory will develop Alzheimer's disease, but the risk is considerably higher for those that do. We think nothing of routine medical evaluations for various diseases like diabetes, cancer, hypertension, heart disease, and thyroid disease, but we fail to consider having routine memory evaluations (screenings are insensitive to early, mild changes in memory). You can do so much to help yourself if you know you are vulnerable. If you have a family history of Alzheimer's, start with a thorough memory evaluation that allows you to plan and be proactive with your memory and life style.

***

In summary, it is in your own best interests to identify and treat Mild Cognitive Impairment early rather than waiting to see if it progresses into Alzheimer's disease. It is wise to get an assessment and create interventions before symptoms appear. Even better, you should get a good baseline assessment, even if your memory is fine. This gives you that baseline for future reference. *The best way to manage Alzheimer's disease is early detection and proactive planning.*

PART III

WHAT CAN YOU DO TO PROTECT YOURSELF?

Introduction to Part III

Now that you better understand memory and its disorders, let's turn to ways you can protect yourself. What can you control? You cannot control genes, family history, or the life you have already lived. But some factors you *can* control. These include lifestyle, diet, and mental stimulation. A few choices in lifestyle that you make *now* may improve your odds of aging more successfully.

Unfortunately, making these choices is not a guarantee. Current studies suggesting what to eat or what supplements to take are not always clear and are sometimes contradictory. *I have approached the task of recommending what to do as a consumer.* In short, what do you want to know about medications, supplements, foods, and lifestyle?

The treatment of memory loss has been so "medicalized" that many are waiting for cures for chronic and disabling diseases like Alzheimer's to come from medicine. Many await the "magic bullet" that will make cancers, heart disease, diabetes, emotional pain, and neurological disorders go away. This belief, in part, stems from the expectation resulting from the development of antibiotics that can cure bacterial infections. (Viral infections are another issue, as can be attested to by anyone who has had shingles or dealt with the pandemic coronavirus.) We also rely on immunizations for diseases such as polio and smallpox. Somehow we have come to believe that molecular biology is the foundation for understanding and treating Alzheimer's disease.

However, no single drug or supplement exists that has a dramatic impact for treating Alzheimer's disease. Biological systems are profoundly complex. A multitude of variables determine the effect of any administered pharmaceutical, supplement, or food on function (e.g., time of day, sex, age, other drugs used, and a myriad of other factors). To add to the complexity, the systems are not independent.

As more research is completed, advice evolves as knowledge increases. If you carefully review the existent data on individual substances, you'll find that clear summaries are hard to find. Nor is there clear guidance for who benefits from what intervention and under what circumstances. *There are no definitive guidelines.* So take the following with some skepticism. Also beware of anecdotal data and testimonials. Which paths you should follow is a personal decision best made in collaboration with a trusted memory expert.

As I search my memory for true cures for diseases during my lifetime, I find very few. We did not find a cure for polio or for smallpox; rather, we found a way via immunization to keep them from developing in the first place. We were hopeful that the discovery of insulin would cure diabetes mellitus. It did not. Insulin clearly helps manage the disease and slow its progression, but simply using insulin does not cure diabetes. We hoped to cure Parkinson's disease with the discovery of ways to increase dopamine in the brain (a chemical messenger that is deficient in those who develop Parkinson's). But again, this was not a cure. We can better manage Parkinson's disease with current dopamine-enhancing medications, but we have not cured this neurological disease. We cannot reliably cure cancers, although modern treatments improve survival in many and do cure cancers in some.

Given this history, why do we have such high hopes that a medical cure for Alzheimer's disease, a complex and progressive disease of the brain, will be found? We now have medications that help with *managing* the disease. But if we rely only on medications, we fall short of helping those with Alzheimer's disease to have a better life.

The best paradigm for understanding how to manage Mild Cognitive Impairment and Alzheimer's disease is our understanding of how to manage diabetes mellitus and Parkinson's disease. We must detect our vulnerability to these diseases early and *manage lifestyle as well as medications.* Early interventions with lifestyle are critical in managing later stages of these diseases and in modifying their course. *Management is a lifelong commitment.*

Similarly, factors in early, middle, and later life can influence the course of many memory disorders. Early strategies require us to modify our lifestyle and environment as we develop and when we reach early adulthood. Middle-life strategies involve further lifestyle management, such as protection of the cardiovascular system and the brain. These strategies must carry into our later life and, hopefully, provide benefits whether or not it is our destiny to develop a dementia.

This and the next three chapters address elements that you can control or for which you can plan. Some of the factors discussed improve mental efficiency or reduce damage to the cerebrovascular system and therefore may help memory and mental functions in healthy adults as well as those at risk of cognitive decline. Other factors to be covered can help memory and mental functions in those who are vulnerable to memory decline or already have memory or mental decline. Good memory hygiene suggests that we pay attention to improving our odds as we age and to planning ahead for the inevitable changes in efficiency and possible decline. Obviously, we hope that memory problems will never happen to either us or to those we love. These strategies take time and effort, but the benefits will be felt for years and decades to come.

CHAPTER TWELVE

Managing Your Biology: Medications, Supplements, Foods, and Exercise

*"Grant me the serenity to accept the things I cannot change,
the courage to change the things I can,
and the wisdom to know the difference."*
(Reinhold Niebuhr, 1950)

MEDICATIONS FOR MILD COGNITIVE IMPAIRMENT AND DEMENTIAS LIKE ALZHEIMER'S DISEASE

Cholinesterase Inhibitors

The first medication to be approved to treat Alzheimer's disease was Cognex (tacrine). (Trade names are outside of parentheses, and generic names are inside parentheses.) Cognex belongs to a class of drugs called *cholinesterase inhibitors* (see Table 12.1 on the next page), which was introduced in the United States in the early 1990s as a treatment for Alzheimer's disease.

This class of medications was based on the discovery that a neurotransmitter (chemical messenger) called acetylcholine was deficient in the brains of persons with Alzheimer's disease. Reasoning from the logic for treating diabetes (e.g., insulin) and Parkinson's disease (e.g., carbidopa/levodopa), where successful treatments resulted from replacement of deficient substances, it was hoped that replacement of acetylcholine would

---

TABLE 12.1

FDA-APPROVED MEDICATIONS FOR ALZHEIMER'S DISEASE

Cholinesterase Inhibitors

- Cognex (tacrine)
- Aricept (donepezil)
- Exelon (rivastigmine)
- Reminyl (galantamine)

NMDA Receptor Antagonists

- Namenda (memantine)
- Namenda ER

Dual Action

- Namzaric (Aricept and Namenda ER combined in one pill)

Amyloid Cleaner

- Aduhelm

---

restore mental functions and memory in patients with Alzheimer's disease. Cholinesterase inhibitors make more acetylcholine available by deactivating the enzyme in synapses (gaps between neurons), thereby making more acetylcholine available to compensate for the loss due to disease processes.

The initial enthusiasm for Cognex was tempered by its side effects. Cognex produced changes in liver function, which meant that everyone on the medication needed to undergo frequent liver tests, and, if there were changes in liver function, they had to stop treatment before permanent damage was done. Cognex also produced a high incidence of adverse effects (e.g., nausea, vomiting, diarrhea) that made it intolerable to many patients who took it. Finally, Cognex had to be taken four times a day, and building up to a therapeutic dose of Cognex was a long and complicated process that was more likely to produce side effects than a treatment response.

Fortunately, the FDA approved a second cholinesterase inhibitor, Aricept (donepezil), in 1996. Aricept does not have the incidence of side effects of Cognex, and it does not cause liver toxicity. It is also easier to use, as it is administered once a day rather than four times a day, and only one increase in dose (from 5 to 10 mg) is required after four to six weeks on the medication.

More recently, two newer cholinesterase inhibitors have been introduced into the market in the United States. Exelon (rivastigmine) is similar to Aricept in action, but the original formulation must be taken twice a day. Higher doses of Exelon are more effective than lower doses, but these higher doses also produce more severe side effects. Reminyl (galantamine) was the last of these medications to be introduced. It also must be taken twice a day and has an incidence of side effects similar to that of Aricept.

The improvements from these medications are usually quite modest, and some recipients do not display any apparent effects from them. Some clients and their caregivers wonder if the medication is doing any good, and they may stop taking it. However, those who stop taking it often show a drop in functioning, and reinstating the medication does not reverse these changes to the level before they stopped taking the medication. Therefore, once a cholinesterase inhibitor has been started, it must be taken continuously unless the side effects are intolerable, another medical condition conflicts with use of the drug (e.g., ulcers, low heart rate [also known as bradycardia]), or the person reaches the end stage of Alzheimer's disease and receives no benefits from medical treatments.

Treatment Effects of Cholinesterase Inhibitors

Cholinesterase inhibitors do not cure or prevent Alzheimer's disease. They address only one of many possible neurochemical changes found in Alzheimer's disease — decreased cholinergic activity. They do not return the user to "normal" mental or memory functioning. Rather, these medications improve cognitive functions in some and may preserve the ability to do self-care for a longer time when compared to a placebo.

Cholinesterase inhibitors, in my experience, do not appear to have much direct effect on short-term memory. However, they do make the user more likely to interact with the world. They also preserve some of the patients' mental and personal care abilities. For example, individuals may be more likely to enter into a conversation or pick up and read a magazine. Furthermore, when persons on these medications are observed over the course of a year, they score higher on cognitive tests and on tests of instrumental activities (using the telephone, handling mail, preparing food) and basic activities (dressing, eating, using the toilet) of daily living than those given a placebo. Cholinesterase inhibitors also may reduce the time caregivers need to provide care and may reduce problematic behaviors such as delusions, agitation, anxiety, and disinhibition in some clients.

As an example, Marilyn Truscott was diagnosed with Alzheimer's disease in the late 1990s. After being placed on a cholinesterase inhibitor, she writes: "Thank heaven for the new Alzheimer medications now available. I could hold on to thoughts and words better when I read them or heard them spoken. I could understand information and instructions better. I had vastly more mental stamina to carry out activities and social conversations. My brain wouldn't tire out so quickly" (Truscott, 2003, p. 12).

In short, these medications appear to improve mental skills and behavior in persons with Alzheimer's disease when compared to those who are treated with a placebo. Early initiation of treatment with a cholinesterase inhibitor may be associated with greater benefits when compared with later initiation. These medications may improve mental functioning in persons with Mild Cognitive Impairment, and, in an interesting study of airline pilots, treatment with Aricept improved judgments made by airline pilots (who had normal memory and mental abilities) in a flight simulator. Presumably, if the medication were used earlier in the course of mental decline in Alzheimer's disease, or, better yet, if it were begun while the person was in the stage of Mild Cognitive Impairment or earlier, treatment would have a greater benefit and improve quality of life when compared to those who do not take one of these medications. However, remember that these drugs are not magic bullets.

Side Effects of Cholinesterase Inhibitors

The most common side effects of cholinesterase inhibitors are fatigue, diarrhea, nausea, vomiting, anorexia (loss of appetite and weight), muscle cramps, dizziness, and rhinitis (inflammation of the nasal mucosa that leads to congestion and increased secretion of mucus). These medications can also induce vivid dreams and/or nightmares and fainting in some. Side effects vary with the dose. That is, the higher the dose, the greater incidence of side effects, and side effects are more likely to occur when the dose of the medication is increased. The drugs may also reduce heart rate to the point that a pacemaker is necessary or contribute to some people developing ulcers.

Although few studies have compared cholinesterase inhibitors in a head-to-head clinical trial, there is no clinically significant advantage in taking one of the drugs compared to the others. Therefore, the most important determinants of which medication to use are the side effects and the ease of use. If someone is intolerant of one medication, another can be tried and may be tolerated.

It is also important to note that cholinesterase inhibitors are effective for both Alzheimer's and vascular dementias and may have benefits for those with other forms of dementia such as Lewy body disease. Caveat: The effects are small, and these drugs do not keep the disease from progressing.

NMDA Receptor Antagonists: Namenda and Namenda ER (Memantine and Memantine ER)

Namenda (memantine) is in a different class of medication that was first used in Germany to treat Alzheimer's disease. It affects a different neurotransmitter system — glutamate (an excitatory neurotransmitter whose effect is believed to be mediated by blocking the N-methyl-D-aspartate or NMDA receptors). It has been used for persons with moderate to severe Alzheimer's disease as well as in patients with pain syndromes because it also has an analgesic action. Aricept and Namenda work conjointly to improve the functioning of persons with severe Alzheimer's disease.

The FDA recently approved an extended-release form of Namenda (Namenda ER) that is administered once a day rather than twice a day. Interestingly, the patent for the original formulation of Namenda expired in 2015, and the manufacturer, Forrest Pharmaceuticals, planned to discontinue Namenda and only produce Namenda ER (patent to expire in 2029). Of course, this strategy would leave only the more expensive version of the medication available. Fortunately, a lawsuit stopped the company from discontinuing Namenda, so both forms remain available.

Dual-Action Drugs

I recently saw an advertisement on TV for what I thought was a new drug treatment for Alzheimer's disease. As I looked up the medication, it became apparent that Namzaric is not new (developed in 2014) but a combination of two existing FDA-approved drugs: donepezil and Namenda ER. Further research has demonstrated that combining these two classes of medication produces modestly better benefits (the effects are additive) for those with moderate to severe Alzheimer's disease. Therefore, the standard of care for moderate to severe Alzheimer's disease is combination therapy, which can be managed by taking generics for both donepezil and Namenda.

Namzaric combines 10 mg of donepezil and 7, 14, 21, or 28 mg of Namenda ER (it can be titrated up to the recommended dose of 28 mg over the course of four weeks). In 2016, the FDA approved Namzaric for those already stabilized on donepezil.

Here's a good question: Should persons with moderate to severe Alzheimer's disease replace donepezil and Namenda (three pills daily) with Namzaric (one pill daily)? According to Deardoff and Grossberg (2016), "There does not appear to be compelling evidence that Namzaric (with 10 mg of donepezil and 28 mg of Namenda ER) would substantially improve clinical outcome over lower-cost regimes such as generic donepezil and memantine ER."

Amyloid Cleaner: Aduhelm

Aduhelm (aducanumab) is the first drug developed to reverse an underlying disease "process" in Alzheimer's disease that has been approved by the FDA (the first new drug in almost twenty years, since 2003). Aduhelm was created (by Biogen and Eisai) to reverse the accumulation of amyloid in the brain. The hope is that Aduhelm will slow or reverse the rate of decline in Alzheimer's disease as it reduces amyloid plaques in the brain. Despite decades of failure of amyloid blockers to reliably treat Alzheimer's disease, Aduhelm was "fast tracked" for FDA approval.

Aduhelm is administered by intravenous infusion given every four weeks. The hope is that treatment with Aduhelm will reduce plaques in those with early-stage disease (this begs the question of how to identify "early-stage" individuals).

However, the approval is quite controversial. First, the evidence from clinical trials offered to gain approval for Aduhelm in slowing mental decline is mixed. In some of the trials, the medication had no effect on cognitive skills. Second, there are serious potential adverse effects: headaches, dizziness, and (more seriously) allergic reactions, brain swelling from accumulation of fluid in the brain, and brain "bleeds." Third, there is the high cost of the medication. The initial cost was $56,000 per year. Although Biogen lowered the price to $26,200 (makes me wonder how new drugs are priced), the medication is still beyond the budget of most that have the need for it. Fourth, Medicare does not cover the drug because of lingering doubts. If Medicare does cover Aduhelm (other insurers typically decide on whether to cover a drug and then follow suit after Medicare's decision), it will only pay for patients with mild cognitive problems related to Alzheimer's disease who are participating in clinical trials. And fifth, it is not a cure for Alzheimer's disease.

It will take time to determine whether Aduhelm is effective, safe, and (if it is effective) make it affordable to all who would benefit from the treatment.

Supplements

Vitamin E

Supplementation with vitamin E may slow the progression of Alzheimer's disease. These results come from a major clinical trial demonstrating that administration of a high dose of vitamin E (1,000 international units [IU] two times per day) slowed the progression of Alzheimer's disease. Persons already afflicted by Alzheimer's disease who were treated with vitamin E took several months longer to decline to the point where they needed placement in a skilled nursing facility, and they did not die as soon as those in the study who received the placebo. The same effect was also found with selegiline (trade names for selegiline are Eldepryl and Deprenyl). However, vitamin E is preferred clinically as it has fewer side effects and is cheaper than selegiline.

Another study demonstrated that a high intake of vitamin E via diet correlated with higher mental function in men and women between the ages of 65 and 100 who did *not* have Alzheimer's disease when compared to those who did not ingest foods high in vitamin E. The same researchers showed a similar effect in persons with diagnosed Alzheimer's disease.

However, even if these findings hold up, consumption of vitamin E, especially at high doses, may produce serious side effects. Vitamin E can cause anticoagulants (blood thinners) such as aspirin or Coumadin to have a greater effect, which may promote bruising and bleeding. Although vitamin E may improve immune function in lower doses, it may suppress immune function when taken at doses above 1,500 IUs. A study of institutionalized elderly people in the Netherlands suggested that use of vitamin E was correlated with slower resolution of acute respiratory tract infections as well as the production of more symptoms per episode. Supplementation with vitamin E did not affect the incidence of the infections or the severity of symptoms experienced by those who developed the respiratory infection.

Given the risks of using high doses of vitamin E, some physicians recommend that only those with definitely diagnosed Alzheimer's disease should take 2,000 IUs. Others, such as those with Mild Cognitive Impairment, should not take doses above 1,500 IUs. Higher doses of vitamin E than those recommended in the standard Recommended Daily (or Dietary) Allowance (RDA) should not be taken without a physician's supervision.

There is more to the story of vitamin E as an antioxidant therapy. Presumably, vitamin E is administered to those with Alzheimer's disease to modify lipoproteins, which are thought to be pathogenic to the disease. However, vitamin E alone does not curtail the oxidation of lipoproteins in cerebrospinal fluid (an index of activity of substances in the central nervous system). Retrospective studies suggest that persons taking vitamins E and C together have better memory performance and less mental decline than those who take either vitamin alone. Therefore, it may be advisable to take vitamin E and vitamin C together. So far, it is not clear what the optimal dose of vitamin C is, but some physicians seem to favor 500 mg per day.

Vitamin B

Among the various kinds of B vitamins, it appears that folate (or folic acid) and vitamin B12 may be important for those trying to protect their memory. These vitamins are critical in the formation of RNA and DNA, the building blocks of cells, including neurons. One step in the synthesis of RNA and DNA is the conversion of an amino acid named homocysteine into an amino acid named methionine. Vitamin B12 and folate enable this conversion, and when the amounts of these vitamins in your system are low, homocysteine builds up. Increased plasma concentrations of homocysteine are associated with increased risk of cardiovascular disease and progression of dementia. Low levels of vitamin B12 are associated with anemia, memory loss, and nerve damage. Low levels of folate are associated with cardiovascular disease. Supplementation of these vitamins may also slow mental decline, and dietary folate has been shown to cut the risk of stroke.

Given these relationships, some physicians are evaluating the concentration of homocysteine in blood tests during physicals. This may be even more critical for persons with Alzheimer's or vascular disease or those who may be vulnerable to these conditions. Some physicians recommend consumption of 1.0 micrograms of vitamin B12 and 400 micrograms of folate per day.

Other Antioxidants

Many other antioxidants, in addition to vitamins E and C, may protect your memory and mental function. For example, lycopene is an antioxidant found in tomatoes. Catechin is an antioxidant found in green and black teas. Tumeric is an antioxidant found in curry powder and mustards (especially yellow mustard). Vitamin E can be increased in your diet by eating nuts and oils. You can obtain vitamin C and other antioxidants by ingesting foods such as strawberries, blueberries, melons, spinach, brussel sprouts, and tomato juice. One cup of orange juice per day provides 100 percent of the RDA of vitamin C for men and for women. My take from this is: You may do yourself good by structuring your diet around fruits and vegetables (e.g., the "Mediterranean" diet). Consuming these antioxidants in food may be more effective than taking supplements, especially for those who do not have a specific vitamin deficiency.

Ginkgo biloba, a derivative of an Asiatic tree leaf, has antioxidant properties and also may improve cerebral circulation. Ginkgo is currently available as a treatment for dementia in Germany and is available in the United States as an herbal supplement. A 1997 study in the United States suggested a modest improvement in *people with dementia* who took Ginkgo biloba. The finding that Ginkgo has a beneficial action has not always been replicated, however. For example, supplementation with 40 mg of Ginkgo three times per day for six weeks in healthy older adults did not improve their learning, memory, or attention when compared to treatment with a placebo.

Despite some failures to find treatment effects for Ginkgo, millions of Americans take this herb in the hope that Ginkgo will either improve their memory or treat/delay the onset of Alzheimer's disease. Be aware that the brands of Ginkgo biloba sold in the United States show considerable variation in quality and consistency. They are not classified as drugs and, therefore, are not subject to strict regulation, as are pharmaceuticals. Do you really think there is a One-A-Day vitamin that improves memory?

A study by the World Health Organization demonstrated that few of the brands it tested actually contained Ginkgo at the dose labeled on the bottles. As with many other "natural" substances, Ginkgo has potential side effects, including nausea, heartburn, headache, dizziness, excessive bleeding or bruising, and lowering of blood pressure. Beware that Gingko has anticoagulant properties, thereby making the actions of blood-thinning drugs such as aspirin and Coumadin more pronounced. Furthermore, Ginkgo can influence the secretion of insulin, making it risky for diabetics. Just because something is labeled "natural" or considered a food or supplement does not mean that it is harmless. If you feel that you want to take Ginkgo, or other supplements, consult with your physician.

Omega-3 Fatty Acids

High-caloric and high-fat content in your diet, especially in midlife, may be a risk factor for developing Alzheimer's disease later in life. Conversely, a diet containing low levels of saturated fats and cholesterol has been associated with a lower risk of mental decline. These and similar findings suggest that a low-fat, low-cholesterol diet may protect memory and mental functions.

But the story is complicated. Omega-3 fatty acids (docosahexaenoic acid, or DHA) may increase acetylcholine, and consumption of omega-3-rich fish oil may boost mood and memory. Omega-3 fatty acids are referred to as the "good fats" whereas omega-6 fatty acids (found in steaks and other "nonfish" animal fats) are referred to as the "bad fats." Given this distinction, it may be farsighted to eat at least two servings a week of fish such as tuna, salmon, sole, and cod. The takeaway is to supplement your fruits and vegetables with fish that are rich in omega-3 fatty acids as another possible way to reduce your vulnerability to memory and mental decline.

Statins

An intriguing finding is that the use of medications (statins) is associated with decreased prevalence of Alzheimer's disease. Statins are widely used to reduce high cholesterol (hypercholesterolemia). Statins include medications such as Zocor, Lipitor, and Pravachol. Whether the benefit from taking statins results from a general lowering of vascular disease or is specific to Alzheimer's disease (perhaps by modifying amyloid, the protein that is found in plaques) is unknown. However, some evidence indicates that maintaining aggressive control of cholesterol may be an important component in warding off unwanted vascular disease and possibly in altering the course of dementia.

However, statins may also induce confusion or memory loss in some individuals. Let me give you an idea of how strange this adverse reaction may show itself. I had a client who tried taking statins (as advised by her physician) to lower her cholesterol. Without the statin, she was able to automatically climb stairs without thought. However, when taking statin drugs, she could no longer automatically climb stairs. Instead, she had to think of where to place her feet.

Whether synthesized in the lab or "natural," foods, herbs, and pharmaceuticals may produce unwanted adverse reactions on their own or by interaction with other things we consume.

HYPERTENSION AND DIABETES

Hypertension and diabetes are common disorders over which you have some control with both medications and lifestyle choices. These diseases affect cardiovascular and cerebrovascular functions (what hurts the heart can hurt the brain), and they also impact your memory function and the possible course of Alzheimer's disease and vascular dementia.

Hypertension is associated with increased risk for stroke and heart attacks. Upwards of 60 percent of people over the age of sixty-five have hypertension. Furthermore, chronic uncontrolled hypertension while in your forties and fifties creates a risk for memory decline in later life, and many patients with Alzheimer's disease also have cerebrovascular disease. The evidence is mixed regarding a direct link between hypertension and Alzheimer's disease. Hypertension can be managed through medications as well as through exercise, weight control, diet, and not smoking.

Diabetes also adds to your risk of memory loss and mental functioning. Small increases in blood sugar, as well as the timing of your meals, have been shown to improve learning and memory in unimpaired adults. Chronically high levels of blood sugar are associated with lower memory and intellectual function. Diabetics have increased risk for developing memory loss as well as Alzheimer's disease and vascular dementia. This is another factor that you can manage by combining appropriate medications with maintaining a healthy diet and exercising. Following this plan, you can lower your risk of developing type 2 diabetes. It is important to be evaluated regularly for diabetes, especially if you have a family history of the disease, and to treat high blood sugars and diabetes aggressively to further protect your memory and other mental functions.

ANTI-INFLAMMATORY AGENTS

Anti-inflammatory agents may also play a role in protecting you against Alzheimer's disease but may not help after the disease is clearly established. A large study by the National Institute of Aging between 1955 and 1994 demonstrated that people who regularly used nonsteroidal anti-inflammatory drugs (NSAIDs) (such as ibuprofen, naproxen sodium, and indomethacin) had a lower risk of developing Alzheimer's disease during the course of the study than did persons taking nothing or only taking acetaminophen. However, trials of prednisone (a potent steroidal anti-inflammatory agent), naproxen, and rofecoxib did not improve memory or functional ability in patients who already had Alzheimer's disease. Current trials are underway to determine if anti-inflammatory agents change the course of Mild Cognitive Impairment. However, *chronic use* of NSAIDs is not recommended as a routine practice. These medications have side effects such as stomach irritation, ulcers, and possible kidney problems that make them poorly tolerated in some and potentially dangerous.

SEX HORMONES

Many studies have been done on the effects of sex hormones, especially hormone replacement therapy (HRT) in women, on the risk of developing Alzheimer's disease as well as the effect of replacement in those who already have Alzheimer's disease. Several early epidemiologic studies suggested that hormone replacement therapy in postmenopausal women reduced the risk of Alzheimer's disease, even if the replacement therapy was continued for as short a period as one year. Estrogen (several other hormones are involved in reproductive cycles, all of which may play a role in cognition) has drawn interest in that it has been shown to promote neuronal sprouting, enhance cholinergic activity in the brain, have anti-inflammatory and anti-oxidative properties, increase cerebral blood flow, enhance glucose metabolism, and lower apolipoprotein levels (all potentially helpful actions).

In short, the final role for estrogens, progestins, and hormone replacement therapy in cognition and Alzheimer's disease is not yet known. The findings are correlational, not causal (as is the case for much of the research underlying the causes and treatment of neurological disease). Sex hormones appear to influence the development of dementias in complex ways. It is still unclear if you should take hormone replacement therapy, but it appears that timing is important when you consider your risk for developing Alzheimer's disease

Hormone replacement therapy in men is also controversial. Starting in their forties, men have a progressive decline in testosterone. This led some to propose a condition known as andropause, or testosterone deficiency (analogous to menopause in women). The symptoms of andropause include decreased libido, lack of energy, height loss, irritability, sadness, and decreased strength.

Few studies have been conducted of the effects of androgens (e.g., testosterone, but note that testosterone is converted to estrogen in the brain) on the brain. Some have speculated that androgens may be neuroprotective in men and may explain the lessened prevalence of Alzheimer's disease in men when compared with women before the age of eighty-four (after which the incidence appears the same).

Does testosterone supplementation improve cognitive function? As men age, their serum concentration of testosterone declines beginning at age forty, and 30 percent of men have below-normal levels by age seventy. Some research findings regarding testosterone suggest that this change may contribute to the cognitive complaints that accompany getting older. For example, men with low testosterone perform worse on tests of verbal fluency, visuospatial ability, memory, executive function, and attention than men who retain normal levels of testosterone (compared to the general population of younger men). However, the question of whether testosterone supplementation will help cognitive skills in men as they age does not have a definitive answer.

Testosterone can be administered orally, but only rarely, because it produces more side effects and has only weak positive effects. It can also be injected intramuscularly, sprayed intranasally, implanted as pellets, or applied to the skin as a patch or a gel. Each form or route of administration has its tradeoffs.

The complexity of performing adequate studies is reflected in a review by Hua, Hildreth, and Pelak (2016). This group identified 865 research studies of the effects of testosterone on cognition. Out of these studies, 804 were too poorly conducted to pass the initial screening. Of the remainder, only twenty-nine were strong enough to be included in the review. Their conclusion: "In summary, the overall quality-controlled studies published as of February 2016 and included in our review are not adequate to provide recommendations and clinical guidelines for T (testosterone) supplementation to preserve or improve cognitive performance" (p. 1135).

Should I Take "Smart" Drugs?

The demands of the workforce and education have dramatically changed since the early 1900s, when equal numbers of workers were employed in manufacturing and services. Today, fewer than 10 percent of workers in industrialized nations are employed in manufacturing, agriculture, and fishing. (For a good review of these issues, read "Drugs, Games, and Devices For Enhancing Cognition: Implications For Work and Society," 2016, April 4, *Annals of The New York Academy of Sciences*.) Added to these pressures is the explosive expansion of digital technology, which further lessens the need for humans in manufacturing and retail.

Consider the impact of amazon.com on the retail industry. How often do you have a human being answer your calls? How often do you use the convenience of ordering online? E-commerce is available 24/7. These forces have shifted the demands of work to the mind rather than the back. "White collar" workers spend more than forty-eight hours per week working and don't even get away from work at home or during weekends thanks to modern electronic devices like smartphones, tablets, and computers.

The increased demands take a toll on today's workers with consequences such as subjective fatigue, poorer quality and quantity of sleep, increased anxiety and depression, increased risk of gastrointestinal problems, metabolic syndrome, higher incidence of accidents, and errors. These transformations, combined with an aging population, have created demand for improving brain function as a focus for both the government and educational systems.

Increased demands for mental work, beginning with entry into formal education, have given rise to strategies beyond caffeine and nicotine. Pharmacological solutions include the development of "smart drugs" and "neuroenhancers" to reduce fatigue and improve mental efficiency, mood, and memory. Nonpharmacological strategies include physical exercise, diet, sleep, meditation, and brain training. Technological solutions include computer games, apps, and even transcortical stimulation. All have one goal: boosting brain function and mood.

There is a growing trend (for some an alarming movement) toward using prescription drugs such as antidepressants, stimulants, "anti-dementia" drugs, and beta-blockers to reduce fatigue and enhance endurance and cognition. Traditionally, these medications have been used to treat neuropsychiatric conditions; now many are seeking these same medications to improve mental function in healthy people. This creates a medical dilemma: Requests center on subjective "deficits" rather than objective deficits, such as those following head injury, stroke, attention deficit disorder, anxiety, and depression. The shift is from treatment for restoration to treatment for enhancement. This puts medical providers in a new role. Does this give an unfair advantage to those who are willing to take smart drugs over those who are unwilling? This issue needs continued debate, discussion, objective evaluation, and development of ethical guidelines.

I don't have the answer for whether or not to use smart drugs. However, I am not yet convinced that the drugs make you smarter or more productive in the long run. Taking drugs may make you feel more focused, creative, productive, or invincible, but the reality is, for most, drugs impair performance and cognitive processing. And you may interpret your outcome from taking the drug as positive because you want to justify yourself in taking it.

Many questions remain unanswered, and good data that these drugs improve performance in "normal" human beings are thin. Do these drugs only work for those who are overly fatigued? Do they benefit those with poorer as well as better cognitive skills to start? Do they actually improve performance? And under what conditions? What mental processes do the drugs target: memory, attention, decision-making, or reasoning? Who benefits and who doesn't? What doses are effective for whom? Do the drugs work best when taken as needed, or as a daily medication? What are the long-term side effects and adverse events?

Until these questions can be answered (especially those concerning adverse events), nonpharmacological approaches may be the best choice. Even here, the benefits are overstated in the name of making a buck, as has been demonstrated by the government crackdowns on marketing claims made by computer-based brain-training programs such as Lumosity.

Strategies such as notebooks, timers, reducing multi-tasking, meditation, exercise, and getting better sleep probably don't produce adverse events and are easy to use, available to all, and inexpensive. Don't expect miracles from either drugs or supplements. Cognitive improvement takes time and effort, and as you age, you need to increase both your time and effort. *There are no magic bullets.*

IF YOU DO ONLY ONE PROACTIVE THING, MAKE IT EXERCISE

You are most likely searching for the elixir of wellness. You read and hear promises every day about what you can buy that will guarantee youth (or your money back), improve vigor, and improve memory. Everyone seems to have something to sell. Fortunately, the best remedy for protecting your future is free: exercise. A sampling of studies reinforces this point.

An early study (November 5, 2012, in *Archives of Neurology*) addressed the effects of exercising on gait speed, cardiovascular fitness, and muscle strength. Sixty-nine participants (aged forty-two to eighty-six, with a mean age of sixty-six) who were diagnosed with mild to moderate gait or balance impairment were recruited for this research. They were randomly assigned to one of three groups: high-intensity treadmill, low-intensity treadmill, or stretching and resistance training (leg press, leg extension, and curls with two sets of ten for all exercises). Exercises were performed three times a week for three months (thirty-six sessions in total).

Lower-intensity treadmill exercise (fifty minutes at 40–50 percent heart rate) and stretching/resistance training both improved gait speed. Only stretching/resistance training improved strength, and only treadmill training improved cardiovascular fitness. Unexpectedly, higher-intensity treadmill training (thirty minutes at 70–80 percent heart rate) did *not* improve gait speed. The exercise regimes improved mood, reduced fatigue, reduced falls, or improved quality of life, but the duration of the study was short. A major limitation of this study was that amount of exercise was assessed by self-report and subject to distortions in recall (i.e., transience, social desirability in responding, and self-bias).

In another study (November 1, 2012, in "Stroke"), a multinational European prospective study on physical activity demonstrated that progression was slowed for cognitive decline and dementia in elderly persons with small-vessel white-matter brain changes. This advantage was present even after adjusting for diabetes, stroke, severity of white-matter changes, age, and temporal lobe atrophy. However, physical activity did *not* reduce the risk for Alzheimer's disease in this study — not surprising, because Alzheimer's takes decades to unfold, and the study was monitored for only three years. This study's major limitation was that amount of exercise was also obtained by self-report and was subject to distortions in recall (i.e., transience, social desirability in responding, and self-bias).

On the other hand, a prospective study (part of the Rush Memory and Aging Project) of 700 elders (average age was eighty) showed that vigorous exercise lowered the risk of development of Alzheimer's disease and slowed cognitive decline. Participants in this study were enrolled and followed forward and was the first to objectively measure the amount of exercise. Data were analyzed after three and a half years.

Another study (Exercise for Cognition and Everyday Living) demonstrated that resistance training twice a week for six months and twelve months improved executive function (planning, reasoning, and judgment) and memory function in women seventy to eighty years of age with Mild Cognitive Impairment.

There is good news for those with Parkinson's disease. Vigorous resistance training reduces the effects of the disease. Participants in this study averaged fifty-nine years of age and had been diagnosed with Parkinson's disease for an average of seven years. They engaged in either resistance training or a traditional fitness program focusing on balance, flexibility, and strength. Weight training produced improved scores on a Parkinson's rating scale. Apparently, challenge to the neuromuscular system improves function in Parkinson's disease.

Finally, the Cooper Center Longitudinal Study published findings from study enrollees who were prospectively followed over the course of several decades (nearly twenty-five years on the average). Fitness was measured objectively, with a treadmill test, not by self-report. This 1971 study included 19,458 men and women who, in 1971, were on average in midlife (average age was 49.8). Fitness level was measured by the maximum time on a treadmill test. Dementia was determined from Medicare records for participants who were sixty-five and older by December 2009; 1,659 cases of dementia were included in this study. Fitness at midlife was associated with a lower risk of dementia from all causes (e.g., Alzheimer's, vascular disease).

Physical fitness therefore has many possible benefits for brain fitness. First, high levels of fitness are associated with reduced effects of the wear-and-tear of aging on the brain (i.e., shrinkage and white- matter disease). Second, maintaining higher levels of fitness reduces the risk of diabetes and hypertension that contribute to decline with aging. Third, exercise may improve hippocampal (the short-term memory structure) function and induce the release of brain growth factors, which increases neuroplasticity.

Even if you are older than fifty, *it's not too late*. The best way to protect the future of your brain is through physical exercise. It is estimated that fewer than 10 percent of the U.S. population reaches the minimal goal of at least 2.5 hours of moderate exercise per week. All you need are a good pair of comfortable exercise shoes and comfortable clothing. Start slowly and gradually and work toward consistency.

The Physical Activity Guidelines for Americans affirms this conclusion. Avoid inactivity. Some physical activity is better than none. Both physical and cognitive health benefits occur with physical activity, and greater benefits derive from increasing the intensity and duration of physical exercise. The minimal recommended activity is 150 to 300 minutes per week of endurance exercise at a moderate level of activity (twenty to thirty minutes per day for at least ten minutes at a time), along with resistance training two days a week. For those at risk for falls, balance training, yoga, or tai chi is also an essential part of exercising. Positive results from endurance or aerobic exercise include:

- Improvement in cardiovascular reserve
- Improvement in skeletal muscle adaptations
- Reduction in age-associated central body fat, which, in turn, protects the heart
- May counteract the age-associated decrease in bone mineral density in post-menopausal women
- May lower the risk for clinical depression
- May lower the risk of cognitive decline
- Improvement in some aspects of quality of life

Positive results from resistance training include:

- An increase in muscle mass and a decrease in fat mass
- An increase in bone mineral density
- An increase in strength
- At a higher intensity, may improve endurance
- An improvement in walking, chair stand, and balance
- The combined effects of endurance and resistance training may have greater benefits for cognitive functioning than either form of exercise alone.
- May be helpful in treating depression.
- High-intensity exercise is more effective than lower-intensity levels for managing type 2 diabetes, clinical depression, osteopenia, sarcopenia (loss of muscle mass), and muscle weakness.

Tips for Starting or Expanding An Exercise Plan

Consult your physician to determine if the plan you desire is safe for you. The basic equipment you need is a pedometer (a smartphone or Fitbit if you are more into technology), good walking or running shoes, and comfortable clothing that can be layered for varying weather conditions.

Aim for a minimum of 300 minutes of moderate-intensity endurance exercise per week, but start small and move forward in small, incremental steps, whether you are starting from scratch or adding to an already-

---

TABLE 12.2

**CALORIC VALUE OF COMMON ACTIVITIES FOR
DURATION OF ACTIVITY**

	30 minutes	60 minutes
Biking (12 mph)	300	600
Circuit training with weights	400	800
Aerobic dancing	350	700
Golfing without cart	175	350
Running (12-minute mile)	300	600
Free-style swim (35 yards per minute)	275	550
Tennis (singles)	230	450
Tennis (doubles)	100	200
Walking (3 mph)	120	240

---

existing exercise regime. Start slowly. Record the distance you walk each week. Track the distance (and or time) on your calendar so you can measure progress (smartphones and other fitness devices can do this for you). *Aim for consistency rather than distance and intensity to start.* Once you get comfortable with meeting your consistency goals, you can work slowly on increasing intensity and adding resistance training.

Below is a sample program:

Beginning
- Become more active than you are currently (ten minutes on each walk)
- Aim for thirty minutes in a given day

- Increase your time until you can walk thirty consecutive minutes three times per week.
- Add time or days until you hit your goal of 300 minutes each week.

Intermediate
- Add brief intervals of aerobic walking (brisk pace but able to converse)
- Begin to add resistance training. See a physical therapist or trainer to set up a personal program for you. Add two sessions per week to your exercise program.
- Consider starting a tai chi class

Advanced
- Increase either intensity or duration of your endurance training, but do so slowly. *Don't overdo it.*
- Step up aerobic intervals
- Continue to do resistance training two to three times per week. Set small, progressive goals.

COMBINE EXERCISE WITH EATING SMART 80 PERCENT OF THE TIME

Ways to make your exercise become even more effective by eating smart include:

- Reduce your intake of processed foods
- Reduce your intake of dietary trans- and saturated fats
- Limit your alcohol intake to four ounces or less per day; alcohol acts as a depressant, it impairs normal thought process and body control, and worsens your mental and physical performance
- Minimize your intake of high-caloric food
- Eat more fruits and vegetables
- Eat fish at least three times a week and try to follow a Mediterranean diet: olive oil, avocados, fruits, vegetables, nuts, beans, whole grains,

and red wine (you may get similar antioxidant value from purple grape juice than you do with wine)

- Consume foods lower in glycemic value
- Eat foods high in folate
- Monitor how many calories you need each day
- Eat five or six small meals
- Consume five or six servings of fruits and vegetables per day
- Switch to whole grains
- Eliminate refined carbohydrates such as sugar and white bread
- Eliminate sugary drinks and fruit juices
- Carry healthy snacks with you
- Allow yourself a treat; I love ice cream, strawberry shortcake (especially from the Cheesecake Factory), and pumpkin pie. I usually aim for moderation (80 percent healthy food; 20 percent comfort food).

* * *

The lesson from all of this is simple. Eat well, exercise, don't smoke (smoking may be associated with mental decline in those who smoke more than twenty cigarettes per day between the ages of forty-three and fifty-three), and have regular physicals to monitor your blood pressure and blood sugars. This is the same advice that my grandmother gave me as I was growing up.

CHAPTER THIRTEEN

Managing Your Emotions

*"… if one's mood is positive, then one's associations, interpretations,
and impressions will also tend to be positive.
Conversely, more negative moods will negatively bias
the same cognitive processes." (David Barlow, 1988)*

So far, you have learned about the mental changes that unfold with normal aging as well as those involving disorders of memory. This chapter addresses emotions. The brain thinks, remembers, plans, evaluates, judges, reasons, directs movement, and emotes. If, for instance, I think back to my first and only traffic accident, I can recall a mental image of the accident and its location, as well as the emotions at the time and the subsequent anxiety I experienced when I drove near the intersection where the accident occurred. Alternatively, when I think back to the first time I saw my wife, Pamela, I can recall the details of where she was in the room and how she was dressed as well as the emotions of attraction that enveloped me as I first laid eyes on her. I also have countless emotions with no particular referent, such as waking up in a good mood, having a blue day, or worrying when there is no logical basis for worry. Emotion adds color and valence to life and recollection.

You have knowledge and memories of facts, places, times, and people, but you also have *memories of emotions*, some of which are positive while others are negative; they can be fleeting as well as enduring. You hold memories that bring joy and some that bring back sorrow or fear (think back to the death of someone about whom you cared). You also have emotional reactions as you anticipate your future (excitement in anticipation of your upcoming wedding, or worry about the progress of an illness in someone you love).

Emotions are also connected to changes in the brain. For example, individuals who have sustained a head injury or a stroke, or who develop Parkinson's disease, are at risk of experiencing depression as a symptom of neurological changes. Alternatively, depression may result as a reaction to having a serious illness such as cancer or Alzheimer's disease. Emotions are complicated, and they interact in complex ways with your memory and your brain structures (such as the amygdala).

You may describe yourself as being "stressed" by events around you, such as death, having too much to do, having too little to do, failing at something that matters, facing life transitions (graduations, weddings, having children, moving), vacations, or even being successful (promotion, awards, publishing a book). The word "stress" refers to either an internal physical response (feeling nervous, or feeling pounding or discomfort in the chest) or a psychological response (anticipation, dread, worry, avoidance, escape). Stresses may be nonspecific (anxiety, panic), or they may induce specific emotions (fear of snakes, of public speaking, of elevators). Many who have memory loss, as well as those who care for them, experience symptoms of anxiety and/or depression. This chapter centers on describing depression, anxiety, and stress, and on ways to manage these emotions.

DEPRESSION

Depression is often thought to be the most common emotional challenge of elderly people who *do not have* memory loss. Self-rating scales suggest that 15 to 20 percent of those over the age of sixty-five and living independently experience depressive symptoms. At any given time, about six million people in the United States suffer from depression. But these statistics may be the tip of the iceberg. As many as 50 percent of patients in primary medical care experience depressive symptoms.

Depression is associated with increased self-reporting of life stresses and daily hassles. For example, depression may develop as a result of a loved one dying, the loss of a job, divorce, being injured in an accident, or being diagnosed with a neurological disease such as Alzheimer's. Depression may occur if you become depressed at the loss or anticipated loss of ability and self-determination. Caregivers may experience depression as a result of lack of companionship, deprivation of affection, or having to take on tasks or challenges they never needed to do in the past, such as managing finances or a checkbook, doing laundry, maintaining a car, or preparing meals.

Depression is also associated with decreased frequency of social contacts, poor self-esteem, decreased comfort in interpersonal events, and diminished enjoyment of pleasant activities. Adding to the burden, pain or physical illness and depression are often intertwined; an increased severity of pain and illness contribute to greater severity of depression and vice versa. Medical conditions such as Alzheimer's disease, Parkinson's disease, hypothyroidism, Cushing's disease, stroke, and cardiovascular disease also add to depression. As was discussed in Chapter 12, depression appears to be a risk factor for developing Alzheimer's disease. Despite amazing resilience that most show during bereavement, 25 percent of bereaved elders may experience clinical depression during the first year. Depression is clearly a pervasive and often unrecognized complication of living and dealing with life and death.

Symptoms of Depression

It is no wonder that depression has been referred to as the "common cold" of mental health. Symptoms of depression vary across individuals but often include changes in emotion (sadness, guilt, anxiety), behavior (withdrawal from others, tearfulness), physiology (fatigue, changes in sleep and/or appetite), and thought patterns (loss of pleasure, feelings of worthlessness, hopelessness). Many gradations in the severity of depression occur, from mild demoralization to severe withdrawal from the world (spending large periods of time not getting dressed and not going out of the house). You may have a constant desire for escape, withdrawal, or death. Interestingly, some people with depression do not feel depressed or sad and may even be surprised if they were told they were depressed. *Depression is a state of sadness that does not pass in a matter of hours or a couple of days.* It is more than being "blue." Depression is a change in mood that endures for at least a matter of weeks and can last for months or even years.

Table 13.1 lists a number of symptoms associated with depression. You can use this as a self-test to determine whether you have symptoms consistent with depression. If you circle "marked loss of pleasure in life," "self-destructive thoughts," or "sadness," or you circle at least five items, you may be depressed. If you feel that you may be depressed, it may help to seek counsel from a professional (counselor, therapist, physician, pastor, psychologist, or social worker) whom you trust.

To determine if you might be depressed and, if so, how severely, complete this screening scale. Choose the best answer for how you have felt over the past week. Circle either "yes" or "no."

Score 1 point if you say "yes" to an item except items followed by an asterisk, in which case, score 1 point for a "no." If you score more than 5 points, you may be depressed, and I suggest professional evaluation. The higher your score, the more severe your distress.

Treatment for Depression

The two main strategies for treating depression are medications and counseling. Both can be effective in managing depression. Common medications (by their trade names) include Prozac, Zoloft, Celexa, Lexapro, Effexor XR, Remeron, Wellbutrin, Cymbalta, Pristiq, Fetzima, and Desyrel. Choosing the correct medication must be determined by your physician, psychiatrist, physician's assistant, or nurse practitioner. Successful treatment of depression often demands more than the use of medications. Indeed, many respond very well to non-medical treatments such as counseling or support groups. Furthermore, medications are most effective when accompanied by counseling/therapy. Although medications can help, they are not a miracle or instant cure (they often take a few weeks to work).

TABLE 13.1

MOOD ASSESSMENT SCALE — SHORT FORM

1.	Are you basically satisfied with your life?	Yes	No
2.	Have you dropped many of your activities?	Yes	No
3.	Do you feel that your life is empty?	Yes	No
4.	Do you often get bored?	Yes	No
5.	Are you in good spirits most of the time?	Yes	No
6.	Are you afraid something bad is going to happen to you?	Yes	No
7.	Do you feel happy most of the time?	Yes	No
8.	Do you often feel helpless?	Yes	No
9.	Do you prefer to stay in your room/apartment rather than going out?	Yes	No
10.	Do you feel you have more problems with memory than most?	Yes	No
11.	Do you think it is wonderful to be alive?	Yes	No
12.	Do you feel worthless the way you are now?	Yes	No
13.	Do you feel full of energy?	Yes	No
14.	Do you feel that your situation is hopeless?	Yes	No
15.	Do you think that most people are better off than you?	Yes	No

---

The fundamental psychological treatment for depression consists of reestablishing participation in life and becoming actively re-engaged in past activities that used to give you enjoyment. Therapies often focus on reducing self-defeating thoughts, such as "I am worthless," or "I can't," and helping you engage in active behaviors, such as accepting rather than refusing invitations from friends, going to a movie, or exercising. I often call the treatment for depression "Listerine Therapy" in that it may taste bad, but it is good for you. I never tell my clients to enjoy the activity that is their goal of the week. They don't need the pressure. Enjoyment is a bonus and will come in time by active involvement in life. The most effective treatments focus on overcoming the hallmarks of depression — the inertia of the withdrawal and inactivity. Depression makes you lose track of joy and interests. *Treating depression requires that you return to your past interests and pleasures even if you don't want to.*

One of the skills that I hope you will develop from reading this book is maintaining a good calendar habit. It will help you to set and accomplish goals and serve as a contract with yourself. Put things on it that you love to do as well as those you *have* to do. Your life will fill in around what is on your calendar. If you are blue or depressed, schedule events that interested you when you were not depressed (e.g., lunch with friends, shopping, reading a good book, exercising). Over time, increase the number of pleasing activities. The essence of this plan is to protect you from withdrawing into a protective cocoon and instead doing what you plan to do that you used to enjoy. You do not need a good memory to follow this plan; *you only need a good calendar habit.*

ANXIETY

If depression is the most common emotional challenge, anxiety runs a close second. Anxiety also affects your whole being and has physiological, behavioral, and psychological components. If you have ever been afraid, recall how you felt, and how your body reacted, and you will recognize the "symptoms" of anxiety.

Anxiety induces a mental and physiological state that is similar to fear. However, anxiety often does not have a specific, concrete, external object as a focus, which fear does. (You are afraid of the snake in the living room, but you are anxious about a snake that you might encounter in your backyard.) There are no life-or-death implications of a snake you never encounter or of having to give a speech, but you can become anxious if you *anticipate* something bad or dangerous, or if you have to talk in front of others. Anxiety is produced by a symbolic, vague, distant, anticipated, or unrecognized danger. You feel anxious about "losing control" or have the feeling that "something bad will happen."

Symptoms of Anxiety

Anxiety is often associated with depression, and the two may coexist and be difficult to differentiate. Anxiety also appears to increase with stress and daily hassles. The symptoms of anxiety are complex. Physical changes occur, such as rapid heartbeat, muscle tension, dry mouth, queasy stomach, and/or sweating. Behavioral symptoms also manifest, such as avoidance, reduction in the efficiency of thought, and inhibition of expression, all of which are maladaptive. Psychologically, anxiety is *perceived* as a feeling of apprehension and uneasiness. In its most extreme presentation, it can produce a feeling of extreme detachment or fear of dying or going crazy.

Anxiety may range in severity from a twinge of uneasiness to a panic attack. Panic attacks may be experienced as heart palpitations, disorientation, and terror. They are often "out of the blue" and may make you feel like you are having a heart attack; the symptoms can be very similar. Anxiety may be spontaneous or anticipatory, chronic or acute. Symptoms may last from a few minutes to hours. Anxiety may display itself as worry or dread. It is likely to arise from small hassles (not being able to find the TV remote) as well as from major stressors (losing your job, death of a loved one). Anxiety often is a signal of anticipated, imagined, or real danger. It is your internal-danger signal system that historically helped you to escape or avoid dangerous objects or situations and keep you out of harm's way. Unfortunately, this signal can work too well and induce you to avoid or escape situations that are not dangerous. For example, anxiety might keep you from asking out a person you're interested in or interviewing for a job you really want.

Although some anxiety is appropriate and reasonable, it can become extreme and may interfere with significant aspects of your life. Extreme or clinically significant anxiety is marked by its intensity and duration. It often leads to avoidance and/or escape. For example, if you are anxious about a medical test (such as having blood drawn to determine if you have cancer), you may wait too long to have the test and thereby undermine treatments that might have helped earlier. Or you may fear changes in your memory and then wait too long to seek a proper assessment, thereby reducing the control you have over current and future memory loss.

Anxiety Disorders

Various anxiety disorders are recognized by mental health professionals. Table 13.2 gives you a summary and brief description of these disorders. Most of us experience anxiety at one time or another, but the duration and intensity of the emotion can make anxiety maladaptive.

Treatments for Anxiety

Treating anxiety is easy, *in principle*. Reduce your anxiety by reducing your physiological reactivity (that is, by managing and/or reducing your symptoms). You can accomplish this through induced relaxation by using techniques such as massage, hypnosis, or deep breathing, or by means of medications such as antidepressants (Paxil, Effexor) or anxiety-reducing medications (BuSpar, Xanax, Ativan, Valium). You may also manage anxiety by *gradually* avoiding or escaping while you are in an anxiety-arousing situation. This is the way I managed my extreme speech anxiety. That is, I put myself in threatening situations by teaching, making presentations at professional meetings, taking a course on public speaking, etc. It took years (into my fifties), but I persisted and became a keynote speaker at several national meetings. I no longer had panic attacks to deal with before my talks. This is referred to as *"desensitization."* For example, if you are afraid of dogs, engage in a gradual and progressive exposure to them (preferably ones that are safe) until you are comfortable with a variety of them.

TABLE 13.2

FORMS OF ANXIETY

- **Panic disorder:** Intense, overwhelming fear without obvious cause

- **Agoraphobia:** Fear of open spaces that often leads you to become home-bound

- **Social phobia:** Possibly a form of shyness

- **Specific phobia:** Snakes, closed spaces, dentists, heights

- **Generalized anxiety disorder:** Persistent and maladaptive worry

- **Obsessive-compulsive disorder:** Spending many hours each day ruminating, cleaning, checking locks

- **Posttraumatic stress disorder (PTSD):** Reaction to a severe trauma such as surviving a major hurricane, assault, rape

- **Acute stress disorder:** Posttraumatic stress disorder but it resolves within four weeks

- **Anxiety disorder due to a medical condition**: Such as hyerthyroidism, pulmonary disease

- **Substance-induced anxiety disorder:** Such as overdose of caffeine or other substance

-

One of my clients cleaned houses for a living. One day she was cleaning the outside windows, which she had done dozens of times previously. The windows were inside a fence where pet dogs were free to roam. For some unexplained reason, the dogs savagely attacked her, leaving her scared and fearful of dogs. She sought treatment because her son wanted a pet dog, but first she had to resolve her dog phobia. We set up a hierarchy of cues, like pictures of dogs, going to a pet store, petting the pups in the store, and volunteering to walk dogs at the humane society. It took several months, but she succeeded and was able to get a dog for her son.

You also can manage your anxiety by altering what you say to yourself or how you think about events and situations that make you anxious. For example, when confronted by a difficult situation (such as going on a job interview or giving a speech), encourage yourself or "psyche yourself up." If you spill your coffee first thing in the morning, remind yourself that the entire day is not ruined. You do not have to be liked by everyone, and you don't have to be perfect in every task you undertake.

In short, anxiety can be managed through relaxation, physical exercise, imagery, desensitization, challenging any mistaken beliefs, assertion training, and/or taking medications. Fortunately, you can usually manage anxiety and depression by participating in enjoyable activities or by getting involved in more intensive activities that will distract you from anxiety-provoking thoughts. Table 13.3 (next few pages) presents useful activities for reengaging in the world if you are depressed. These also can be distractions if you are anxious or stressed, or if you are confronting the apathy resulting from neurological disorders. This list is not exhaustive.

(Note: Text continues on page 221)

TABLE 13.3

ENJOYABLE ACTIVITIES

	Have Done	Want To Do
PERSONAL		
Watching DVDs	________	________
Have a pet	________	________
Play computer games	________	________
Listen to music	________	________
Eat a nice meal	________	________
Keep a journal	________	________
Have a drink	________	________
Play board games	________	________
Take a day trip	________	________
Take a vacation	________	________
Get a massage	________	________
Get hair done	________	________
Get a manicure	________	________
Get a pedicure	________	________
Have time alone	________	________
Daydream	________	________
Relaxing	________	________
Take a bath	________	________
Gamble	________	________

(continues on next page)

TABLE 13.3 (continued)

ENJOYABLE ACTIVITIES

	Have Done	Want To Do
GET OUT		
Go to a movie	________	________
Go to a play	________	________
Go to a lecture	________	________
Go to a concert	________	________
Go to a bookstore	________	________
Go to a park	________	________
Visit neighbors	________	________
Go to a sporting event	________	________
Go to a museum	________	________
Go to a botanical garden	________	________
Go to an aquarium	________	________
Go to a zoo	________	________
Handle animals at a humane society	________	________
Work for Habitat for Humanity	________	________
Eat at a favorite restaurant	________	________
Eat at a new restaurant	________	________
Go shopping in town	________	________
Go shopping out of town	________	________
Go to a garage sale or auction	________	________

(continues on next page)

TABLE 13.3 (continued)

ENJOYABLE ACTIVITIES

	Have Done	Want To Do
GET OUT		
Go to an antique store	_________	_________
Take a walk	_________	_________
Go sightseeing	_________	_________
Go to a coffee shop	_________	_________
CREATIVITY		
Garden	_________	_________
Dance	_________	_________
Play cards	_________	_________
Paint	_________	_________
Draw	_________	_________
Take music, dance, art, acting lessons	_________	_________
Do needlework	_________	_________
Do woodwork	_________	_________
Write	_________	_________
Do puzzles	_________	_________
Collect (e.g., stamps, coins, pottery)	_________	_________
Astronomy	_________	_________

(continues on next page)

TABLE 13.3 (continued)

ENJOYABLE ACTIVITIES

	Have Done	Want To Do
SPORTS		
Play pool or ping pong	_______	_______
Go to a sporting event	_______	_______
Canoe or kayak	_______	_______
Go boating	_______	_______
Go skating or rollerblading	_______	_______
Hike	_______	_______
Play golf	_______	_______
Fish	_______	_______
Hunt	_______	_______
Play soccer	_______	_______
Water ski	_______	_______
Snow ski	_______	_______
Play racquetball or tennis	_______	_______
Bowl	_______	_______
Play basketball	_______	_______
Play football	_______	_______
Play shuffleboard	_______	_______
Play badminton	_______	_______
Play croquet	_______	_______

(continues on next page)

TABLE 13.3 (continued)

ENJOYABLE ACTIVITIES

	Have Done	Want To Do
SPORTS		
Play horseshoes	_________	_________
Play softball or baseball	_________	_________
LEARN		
Surf the Web	_________	_________
Go the library	_________	_________
Go to a bookstore	_________	_________
Go to a professional meeting	_________	_________
Take a class	_________	_________
Run computer programs	_________	_________
Read a newspaper	_________	_________
Read a magazine	_________	_________
Read a journal	_________	_________
Read fiction	_________	_________
Read nonfiction	_________	_________
Look at picture books	_________	_________
Learn a new language	_________	_________
Read comic books	_________	_________
Do photography	_________	_________

(continues on next page)

TABLE 13.3 (continued)

ENJOYABLE ACTIVITIES

	Have Done	Want To Do
SOCIALIZE		
Visit a friend	__________	__________
Go on a date	__________	__________
Visit relatives	__________	__________
Have people over	__________	__________
Go on an outing with a friend or family	__________	__________
Go to a party	__________	__________
Play with children	__________	__________
Go to an amusement park	__________	__________
Go dancing	__________	__________
Watch people	__________	__________
Volunteer	__________	__________
Go camping	__________	__________
Join a self-help group	__________	__________
Join a social club		
FITNESS		
Exercise	__________	__________
Work out at a health club	__________	__________
Go to an aerobics class	__________	__________

(continues on next page)

TABLE 13.3 (continued)

ENJOYABLE ACTIVITIES

	Have Done	Want To Do
FITNESS		
Walk	_________	_________
Jog	_________	_________
Run	_________	_________
Swim	_________	_________
Lift weights		
SPIRITUAL		
Go to church, temple, etc.	_________	_________
Pray	_________	_________
Meditate		
ENJOYMENT		
Cook	_________	_________
Bake	_________	_________
Fix something	_________	_________
Clean	_________	_________
Do some home improvement	_________	_________
Decorating		

(continues on next page)

TABLE 13.3 (continued)

ENJOYABLE ACTIVITIES

	Have Done	Want To Do
ROMANTIC		
Go on a date	_________	_________
Give or receive a massage	_________	_________
Have a romantic dinner at home	_________	_________
Shower or bathe together	_________	_________
Make love	_________	_________
Cuddle, kiss, hug.	_________	_________
Read together	_________	_________
Talk	_________	_________
Compliment each other	_________	_________
Have lunch together	_________	_________
Take a walk together	_________	_________
Enjoy music together	_________	_________
Dance	_________	_________
Relax together	_________	_________
Watch the sunrise or sunset	_________	_________
Go on a picnic	_________	_________
Go to a movie together	_________	_________
Tell each other jokes	_________	_________
Dress up and go somewhere fancy	_________	_________
Remind each other how much you love one another	_________	_________

STRESS

Although some stress may be good for you, constant stress can be debilitating and precipitate the development of depression and/or anxiety disorders. Three factors must be considered to understand stress. First, stress is a response to threatening or fearful events that may be either real (having symptoms that may be signs of serious illness) or imagined/anticipated (the lion in the bedroom). Second, stress is adaptive and serves your innate need for survival. By anticipating danger, you can either escape or avoid a dangerous object or situation. Stress is the activation of your "danger signal" system. And third, stress fuels your "fight-or-flight" response. That is, stress activates your body to either stand and fight or flee danger.

Coping With Stress

Your goal in coping with stress is to manage it rather than eliminate it. You cannot eliminate stress from your life. It is a normal reaction to both positive and negative life experiences, such as graduating from school, raising children, dealing with the death of a spouse, or retiring. *Stress is not a global response but rather a set of behaviors, thoughts, and reactions.* If you break down stress into components, you can develop strategies for managing difficult situations.

Start by focusing your awareness on the first, low-intensity cues that let you know you are feeling stressed. Then you can implement plans and strategies to manage your stress early in the process. If you wait for the heat of battle before you try to cope, you will be much less successful. For example, if you have to give a talk on Friday afternoon, don't wait until Friday morning to prepare for it. Indeed, the main message of this book has been to *start planning and managing early before you **need** to.*

If you have memory loss, it is not only a major stressor for you but also for those who live with or care about you. That's why you should seek assessment early. Don't wait for memory loss to become debilitating before you learn how to cope with it. Plan ahead. Consider your needs as well as those of your potential caregivers.

Problem-Focused Stress Management

The two general styles of coping with stress are problem-focused and emotion-focused, and both are important. *Problem-focused management*, discussed here, involves gathering and using information. You must plan and use logic and reasoning to manage your stressful situations. The specific steps for problem-focused coping include:

1. Gathering information
2. Problem-solving
3. Communicating
4. Managing time
5. Taking direct action

Reading this book and applying what works for you is an example of problem-focused coping. If you have memory loss, studying memory and learning all you can about memory loss will help you cope with the stress. If you have cancer, learning all you can about cancer will help you manage the stress. *Decide on goals you want to reach, and break them into small, manageable steps.* Then start moving forward one step at a time.

Emotion-Focused Stress Management

Emotion-focused stress management requires using *strategies* to manage your emotions rather than gathering information. Emotion-focused strategies include asking yourself questions ("Why is this happening to me?"). Support groups can help you manage your emotions because they allow social comparisons ("I am not alone").

I have long been involved with a support group for couples in which the husband, wife, or parent has mild memory loss (either Mild Cognitive Impairment or early Alzheimer's disease). These groups are excellent for gaining information about diseases of memory, but more importantly, they provide support and reduce the isolation for both the person with memory loss and the caregiver. These groups help participants to accept their lot (another emotion-focused strategy) without giving up and also show couples how to compromise (another emotion-focused strategy) rather than fight about issues. Group members may engage in activities, such as going to lunch or to a movie (diverting attention away from the problem for a time).

You may find yourself in denial (deny that your memory changes are indications of Alzheimer's disease. What's in a label anyway, as it doesn't really explain anything?). If you are actively doing what you need to do (being in a group, managing your lifestyle, taking appropriate medications), your stress will be reduced and the denial may be helpful. You also can go somewhere alone to scream and let out your frustration. Or, you can manage your stress by engaging in structured relaxation exercises (massage, deep breathing exercises, using relaxation tapes, apps, and videos) to induce periods of calm. This activity helps you break loose of the constant stress. All of these strategies can reduce stress by helping you to focus on reducing the intensity of your emotions.

Table 13.4 (next page) is a guide for managing stress and includes both problem- and emotion-focused coping strategies. Donald Meichenbaum (1985) has labeled this process as being "stress inoculation training."

ENGAGEMENT AND COGNITIVE STIMULATION FOR WHEN YOU FEAR ALZHEIMER'S DISEASE

The treatment for Alzheimer's disease needs to be proactive rather than reactive. You need to plan for a good life (everyone's long-term goal, regardless of memory) as you age.

A good treatment plan has two requirements. First, *build memory supports before you need them* — use the **One-Minute Rule**. Second, *build a life of engagement.* The popular advice is to learn something new or buy a brain-fitness program. I recently read a neurologist's suggested treatment plan for a client who had the amnestic (struggles to learn anything new) form of Mild Cognitive Impairment. The recommendation was for the client to learn a new language to stimulate his brain.

TABLE 13.4

COPING WITH STRESS*

- **Prepare for the stressor**
  - What do you have to do?
  - Develop a plan
  - Avoid negative statements about yourself and self-criticism
  - Minimize worry

- **Confront and handle the stressor**
  - Psych yourself up
  - Take one step at a time: "baby steps"
  - Stay relevant
  - Focus on the task at hand
  - Feeling tense is the cue for your coping skills
  - Reduce tenseness by relaxing: mindfulness, deep breathing

- **Cope with being overwhelmed**
  - When fear comes, pause
  - Focus on the present
  - Focus on what you have to do
  - Expect tension and fear
  - Manage your fear and tension

- **Reinforce yourself**
  - "I did it!"
  - "It wasn't as bad as I expected"
  - Be pleased with yourself. Tell others about your success
  - Do something good for yourself

* After Donald Meichenbaum (1985)

The problem here is that the client was being set up for failure. Learning a new language is difficult enough for most of us and is almost impossible for someone with diminished short-term memory. However, relearning or expanding on the skills or knowledge that you already have, as well as learning something new, can stimulate your brain. Participation in *any* engaging activity stimulates your brain. You do *not* have to put a load on your short-term memory.

I had a forgetful (Mild Cognitive Impairment) client who tried to learn a new language — Spanish. The class left her feeling frustrated and "stupid." After a discussion of her memory and talents (she was fluent in several languages, including English, Hungarian, and Russian), she decided to drop Spanish lessons in favor of French lessons — a language that was rusty but already in her brain. She thrived in French and felt good about herself again.

I recently had a client who asked if he should buy a computer program to stimulate his brain. As it turned out, he has mild short-term memory loss and is not good with computers — a new skill he would need to acquire before using a brain-stimulation program. We discussed the trade-offs based on how his memory was working in the context of his life skills and interests at this point in his life. As it turned out, he had learned to play the guitar as a youth but had not found the time to play it until recently. A long-term memory was already in his brain but was rusty. He thrived on returning to the guitar.

It's too easy to make simple things so hard sometimes. Enjoying your experiences and spending time well are important. No evidence exists that learning a new language or relearning to play a musical instrument is more helpful for the aging brain than immersing yourself into a passion you already have. Build on your long-term memory and interests. No matter how good or bad your memory, life is best spent in activities that you enjoy.

Review Table 13.3 on activities you might find engaging. See how many interest you. You may also think of others that are not on the list. Simply create a plan and use your calendar to make a contract with yourself.

CHAPTER FOURTEEN

Managing Your Future Today

*"Your memory is the best it will ever be.
Now is the time to learn memory management skills —
before you need them." (Bill Beckwith, 2010)*

In its earliest stages, Alzheimer's disease is relatively benign and mostly causes inconvenience and annoyance. As the disease progresses, it causes increasing adaptive and mental impairment until near its middle stage, when it causes substantial disability. Alzheimer's disease becomes more prevalent with age. For people who live into their sixties, the prevalence is less than 5 percent. However, for those who live to be eighty-five to ninety, the prevalence increases to nearly 50 percent, and by age ninety-five, the prevalence increases to about 60 percent.

Forgetfulness is usually the earliest sign of the disease (although different presentations, such as greater language impairment than memory impairment, are not uncommon). In the beginning, you usually become less able to manage higher-level finances, such as preparing taxes, balancing a checkbook, or paying bills. Further into the disease, managing home life becomes increasingly difficult. Keeping things organized, shopping, preparing meals, traveling independently, and driving become increasingly difficult and finally may fail. As the disease progresses, receiving care, monitoring, and supervision become more necessary. In the middle stages of the disease, self-care becomes an even greater challenge, and you may need more external assistance. In short, the disease unfolds over a trajectory of years to decades. Fortunately, the progression is typically slow, even without the use of medications. If you act early, time is your ally, *because you can plan your own future*. If you wait too long, others must do the planning for you.

You may have a long-range financial plan to cover your financial needs after retirement. You may buy insurance in case fire, floods, hurricanes, or death confronts you. You may plan ahead for your funeral. It only makes sense to also develop a plan that will act as a "safety net" in case you become cognitively or adaptively impaired with neurological or medical diseases that rob you of skills or mobility. It is far better to plan ahead than to have to react to an unanticipated outcome or crisis. *Planning allows control and self-determination.*

You can create a plan for possible changes in your mental and physical abilities at any time during your life and revise it as necessary for changing circumstances. Although you may have long-term care insurance, this does not help with the difficult and emotional decisions that you may have to make, such as when to stop driving or whether you should move to an assisted-living facility. It is never too early to begin to outline such a strategy. It is also important for you to make a living will, especially if you have strong feelings that you do not want to be on artificial life support in a vegetative state.

It is imperative for you to work out a safety net if you develop Mild Cognitive Impairment or you have a strong family history of memory loss. Figure out these plans while your memory loss is mild and your judgment and reasoning are strong. Decide how you would like to spend your time and where and by whom your care will be provided if you cannot care for yourself. Be specific about your desires regarding how any serious or terminal illness should be handled. Do you want mechanical life supports? Do you want to be resuscitated if your heart stops beating or your breathing stops? Under which circumstances should you stop driving, stop balancing the checkbook, begin to use companions, or move into an assisted-living facility or skilled-nursing home?

It is vital that your plans for your future care options be in writing. A written document serves as a permanent external memory aid so you can remind yourself of your decisions and the ways you want them to be carried out in case your memory fails. Periodically review this document, because the details will probably change as you age or face illnesses such as Mild Cognitive Impairment, Alzheimer's disease, Parkinson's disease, or cancer. Those who are closest to you must have access to this document as well so that they can know and carry out your wishes if your memory begins to fail.

VOLUNTARY TRANSFER OF DECISION-MAKING

Durable Powers of Attorney

Who will make decisions for you if you are unable to? Don't take it for granted that the person you want to manage your life will be able to do so. A durable power of attorney is a legal document specifying the circumstances for voluntary transfer of decision-making and to whom the assignment is to be made. Durable powers of attorney allow the voluntary transfer of decision-making in the event that you become incapacitated by events such as strokes, heart attacks, or dementia and cannot make decisions for yourself.

Make sure that these documents provide for a selected representative and at least one backup, often a spouse or children, to manage financial matters as well as healthcare decisions. A durable power of attorney appoints someone to act as your "attorney in fact" to make medical and/or financial decisions in your place. This document is different from a power of attorney, which allows for a time-limited representation for specific decisions, such as if I would give my wife my power of attorney to sell our house.

Trusts

Trusts or living trusts are more complex legal documents and are often set up during estate planning. Trusts may be either *revocable or irrevocable*. The latter is ordinarily a device for the very wealthy to minimize tax liability. A revocable trust appoints someone as a trustee to manage your assets and property. However, a clause in this document allows the trustor (the one who initiates the document) the right to revoke the trust at any time. An irrevocable trust does not contain this clause. Trusts and durable powers of attorney are complex legal documents and should be worked out in collaboration with an attorney.

The advantage of a durable power of attorney or trust is that it allows a person you choose to act on your behalf if you become incapacitated. These documents generally avoid the need for court interventions, such as guardianships (discussed next). A durable power of attorney or a trust requires advanced planning because it must be enacted while you have the memory and mental and legal capacity to make your own decisions. They are best completed before you develop diagnosable Alzheimer's disease or another dementing condition. They may require you to consult with an attorney, and if they are to cover changes that may occur in aging, *it is preferable to use an attorney who is familiar with elder law and related issues in the state in which you reside.* Clearly, having a predetermined transfer of powers is advantageous psychologically, economically, and practically. As is the case with buying insurance, durable powers of attorneys are documents for peace of mind that you hope you will never have to use.

Involuntary Transfers of Decision-Making Through Guardianships

Guardianships are actions involving the court and are required when you are already incapacitated (with dementia, coma, or delirium). Court proceedings to establish a guardianship are enacted as "protective." A guardian is a person who is appointed by a court to manage all or part of your affairs after a court-ordered evaluation and formal hearing before a judge. A guardian is appointed when you do not have sufficient mental capacity (due to conditions such as mental illness, mental retardation, or dementias such as Alzheimer's disease) to understand and make informed decisions, such as forming contracts, deciding where to live, or deciding on appropriate treatment for an illness or disease.

Guardianships are necessary when you lose your capacity to make decisions and have not planned ahead by prior establishment of durable powers of attorney or a trust while legally competent. A guardianship is formed when a court appoints a surrogate decision-maker who is given the legal right and responsibility to make decisions about where you can live, how to dispense your money and manage your property, what medical decisions need to be made, and so forth. These legal proceedings are usually conducted before a probate court of the county in which you live. This process is expensive and may cost several thousand dollars. Furthermore, being involved in court proceedings can be very stressful and, if you have an illness such as Alzheimer's disease, these proceedings occur when you cannot understand why this is happening to you. You may even think that you are being taken advantage of, or that you're in legal trouble. Therefore, it is much better to establish durable powers of attorney as "insurance" in order to try to avoid this emotionally and financially difficult outcome should you become incapacitated.

The Living Will

Most states have enacted laws to allow the "right-to-die." These laws were motivated by the famous case of Karen Ann Quinlan in 1976. Right-to-die laws allow you or your empowered representative to shut off life-support machines should your condition become hopeless, if that is your wish. A living will is the mechanism to convey your wish to *not* continue to live if you have a terminal illness and can only be kept alive with life-support machines or are in a vegetative medical state.

You will be kept comfortable and pain free as much as possible until your death. A living will makes your wishes known to your family and physician and is a legal document that is drawn up in consultation with an attorney. A physician who complies with this directive cannot be sued for honoring those wishes. This document should be a part of your medical file and discussed with your primary-care physician as well as with your attorney before there is a need for it. This is part of the safety net you are building for your own future.

Do-Not-Resuscitate Orders

You may also wish to consider a do-not-resuscitate (DNR) order. This is often confused with a living will but does not cover the same issues. A DNR provides medical workers with a clear directive about whether or not you wish to be revived if you stop breathing. In effect, it directs emergency-service personnel not to administer cardiopulmonary resuscitation (CPR) or electrical stimulation to restart your breathing or your heart if it were to stop on its own. Obviously, this is a document that you need to consider carefully. It is typically formed if you have a serious and often terminal illness or a progressive neurological disorder. The decision to enact a DNR may change with your age or the state of the disease you have. I've had clients in their late eighties and nineties who are fearful of death and do not have a DNR order. On the other hand, another client in her early nineties had her DNR laminated and wore it on a chain under her blouse.

Decision-Making About Daily Activities

It is interesting that we commonly make detailed funeral plans but fail to make plans to cover everyday life situations, such as how to decide when it is time to stop driving or under what circumstances we (and our family) might be better served if we had a companion, or we moved into an assisted-living or skilled-nursing facility.

No formal or legal processes are available to protect your rights and allow you to plan your own course in terms of your everyday activities. However, if you experience mental or physical decline, you still have avenues by which you can plan prudently for yourself in these areas.

In order to create the right safety net if you are vulnerable to progressive mental decline, you need to consider a number of issues. You also need to discuss these with your spouse and family or close friends. These discussions can be difficult, but they will allow you to gain advance control of how any difficult situations may be handled. Put your wishes in writing for future reference. When you talk about these issues with your significant others before you develop Mild Cognitive Impairment, you will have control over your wishes and will save your family from having to make agonizing decisions at a time of great stress.

LEGAL AND FINANCIAL RISK MANAGEMENT

"Alzheimer's epidemic puts advisers — and their practices — at risk."
(InvestmentNews.com, February 26, 2013).

"Clients with Alzheimer's pose 'scary' legal risks."
(InvestmentNews.com, February 13, 2012).

"Money woes can be early clue to Alzheimer's."
(New York Times, October 2010).

The worry has been there for some time. The problem of risk management is as clear as is the solution. Alzheimer's disease unfolds over the course of decades, progresses slowly, and does not produce disability until it is well advanced. Progressive dementias unfold like reverse development. First in, last out. We learn walking and talking very early in life. Managing the checkbook and finances comes much later. It's no wonder that an inability to make complex decisions, like investing money and making legal decisions, are early signs of decline and catch family and advisors off-guard. Decline appears to sneak up on us — *but it does not.*

Alzheimer's disease gives adequate warning to allow you to develop a proactive plan that gets ahead of any changes and unfolds based on feedback from objective data and self-determination — just like long-term investment strategies and advanced directives that you don't put off until you are eighty. The solution is obvious. You must quit waiting for a medical diagnosis that puts you in a reactive rather than a proactive stance.

The earliest symptoms are progressive and measurable short-term memory decline accompanied by declining self-awareness. *You would not plan your investment strategies without looking at long-term data.* It's also best to have advanced directives *before* you sustain a serious head injury or stroke. A brain scan or a memory screening (e.g., MMSE score) does *not* detect mild changes in judgment or awareness. *Managing finances is not a medical problem.*

If you are a professional (financial or legal), you have an obligation to your clients to help them monitor their own memory and reasoning with objective and quantifiable assessments. As you gather data to set up financial and/or legal estate planning, you must have your clients begin a thorough cognitive and memory assessment as part of their program from the start. You must help your clients make their decisions fully informed of how well their cognitive abilities are working. You need them to be proactive and act in their own best interests before their decline becomes more than just minor forgetfulness.

It is clear that physicians, neuropsychologists, and neurologists are reluctant to discuss money matters, and financial advisors are reluctant to discuss cognitive skills. It is my opinion that psychologists, financial advisors, and attorneys need to change their practices, because their clients are the ones who are getting short-changed.

DRIVING

For most of us, driving equals independence. We can just "hop in the car" to do errands, go golfing, run to the store, or travel. Therefore, the decision to hand over the car keys is difficult. *Aging changes driving behavior for all of us.* Older drivers make subtle alterations to compensate. For example, older drivers drive less, restrict driving to familiar locations, drive more conservatively, and limit driving at night.

Consider purchasing a later-model car that has safety technology. These vehicles are equipped with 360-degree or rear-view cameras, warning signals when a car is in your blind spots, and radar so you can keep a safe distance when using cruise control. Many of the newer features help make you a safer driver for longer than if you drive an older-model car without these features.

Aging brings with it physical and mental changes that impact your driving skills. You may experience a decline in your vision (e.g., slower adaptation to changes in lightness/darkness, cataracts, glaucoma, macular degeneration, and stroke), slower reaction times, and slower thinking times. Decreased strength, medical conditions, and/or medications may compromise safety. Changes in memory, attention, and the ability to multitask also present challenges as you age. Throw in the effects of even mild dementia, and the decision about whether to drive can become very difficult.

Research directed toward driving by patients/clients diagnosed with Mild Cognitive Impairment suggests an increased risk for driving. Mild Cognitive Impairment shortens the time between realization of a hazard and time to collision and lowers safety ratings on road tests. Clients with Mild Cognitive Impairment and depression make more errors in a driving simulator. As might be expected, more severe cognitive impairment presents greater risk. On the positive side, *training on a driving simulator improved performance.*

But to say that no one with a mild dementia should drive is as unfair as saying that everyone over the age of eighty should no longer drive. As many as 76 percent of those with mild dementias can still pass road-driving tests. (Passing a road test does not guarantee that you are a safe driver, but if you can't pass a road test, you should no longer drive.) However, if you have dementia, you cannot reliably assess your own driving skills. Caregivers who rated demented spouses as marginal or unsafe drivers were often correct. On the other hand, although 94 percent of those with Alzheimer's disease reported they were safe drivers, only 41 percent could pass a driving test.

We all want to drive as long as we are safe drivers. And we would all probably agree that we should stop driving if we no longer have the skills behind the wheel of a car (or golf cart or motorized scooter) that allow us to be safe.

However, progressive or sudden changes in mental and motor functions increase the risk of driving. How can you decide when to stop driving? I often hear clients say, "I'll know when it's time." Nevertheless, the essential dilemma presented by dementing conditions is that, despite good intentions, you probably will *not* know when it is time to stop driving. Poor insight into your own deficiencies and poor judgment are cardinal features of most dementias. Furthermore, *short-term memory loss means you may not remember your close calls or your accidents* (such as the client who had five accidents in the previous month but could not recall any of them and thought she was a safe driver). Nor may you recall the many people who honked at you because of poor decision-making in your car. Therefore, you need to decide early about *how to determine* when you should stop driving (well before the actual decision of stopping driving), and *put it in writing*.

I suggest that you make a pact with yourself. This especially holds true if you are experiencing even very mild changes in memory. You need to make this decision *before it is needed*. Appoint some agreed-upon person (the "bad guy") to tell you that you need stop driving because you are no longer safe by your own prior agreement. This hopefully helps to ensure that you will stop driving in case you don't voluntarily keep your agreement. A relative or professional who knows about your agreement with yourself can help you enact it.

You can schedule a formal driving evaluation with an on-road test or consider including the following contract as part of your advanced directives:

"I realize that I may not be the best judge of my own driving skills. Therefore, I agree to have (name of person whom you trust to be honest with you) ride with me at least once every six months. If that person is concerned about my skills in driving, or if I am making poor decisions, I agree to stop driving. If I do not voluntarily stop driving, (name of person who will tell you) will send a letter to the Department of Transportation indicating that I am no longer safe to drive. The following errors suggest that I may no longer be a safe driver.

- Incorrect signaling or failure to signal at all

- Poor navigation
- Moving into the wrong lane
- Confusion at exits
- Failure to notice traffic signs or roadside activity
- Parking inappropriately
- Hitting curbs frequently
- Driving at inappropriate speeds
- Having delayed responses in unexpected situations
- Using poor judgment on left turns
- Not anticipating dangerous situations
- Making frequent scrapes or dents in your car, garage, or mailbox
- Having unexplained collisions
- Getting lost in familiar locations
- Experiencing near-misses
- Confusing the brake with the gas pedal
- Stopping in traffic for no apparent reason
- Having a car accident as a result of the above errors"

Finally, decide on how you will manage if you can no longer drive. *Make plans for alternative forms of transportation so you do not become home-bound.*

I hope that you will never have to execute your plan. However, you must remain proactive about your driving. *You can make hard decisions.* Don't drive a day longer if you think you are unsafe, and don't trust your own judgment about whether or not you are safe.

Besides memory loss, other medical factors may impair your driving; it is important to be aware of these, because they may affect your ability to drive safely.

- Sleep apnea
- Narcolepsy
- Uncontrolled epilepsy

- Foot abnormalities
- History of falling
- Limited field of vision
- Limited neck rotation
- Sedating medications
- Neurological diseases

GUNS

Older adults have a high rate of owning guns, which means that if you have significant cognitive decline, you need to address this issue in your care plan. Evaluations for cognitive decline do not, as a standard practice, inquire about gun ownership. Indeed, health-care professionals are obligated to report clients who are no longer safe drivers, but they do not need to report if the patients own guns.

Access to guns for the cognitively impaired increases the risk of suicide and accidental shootings. Family and caregivers are especially at risk. There are no legal proscriptions about what to do about firearms, because gun ownership rights are restricted for individuals with mental illness but not for those with dementia.

This issue needs to be debated, and a policy needs to be established that will include assessment of gun ownership as a standard part of evaluations for those experiencing cognitive decline. This is a matter of public and individual safety. We need to have new "red-flag laws" permitting authorized professionals to remove access to guns from those who are too impaired to use them safely.

Throughout this book, I have suggested a proactive approach to managing cognitive decline by putting safety nets in place *before you need them.* One suggestion you might consider is creating a "firearms retirement date" as part of your safety plan if you own guns. This needs to be part of your advanced directives and in put into writing.

OTHER AREAS OF POTENTIAL DIFFICULTY

When should you stop using the stove and /or the microwave? You may forget that something is on the stove and start a fire. You may put materials in a microwave or an oven that will start a fire. When should you no longer have credit cards? I know people who have given thirty-dollar tips for a ten-dollar meal. I know others who were previously extremely responsible with their money run up thousands of dollars in credit-card debts. When should you give up preparing the taxes? When should you stop doing a checkbook? When should you no longer be able to access your main financial accounts? When should someone else manage your medications? When should you stop traveling?

You may need to make all of these difficult decisions if you develop a dementia. The decisions are not always clear-cut. They may involve *sequential steps* based on your retained abilities. However, making these decisions goes much smoother if you have thought through them and have developed a general plan to which you commit in writing.

Monitor yourself in these areas, but also find someone trustworthy to monitor you in case you cannot perceive or remember your own limitations. Be aware how competent you are in managing your checkbook, preparing food safely, and taking your medications reliably. If you make mistakes, develop a plan to eliminate the mistakes (use a timer, hire a companion, move to assisted living).

Also, if you are struggling, consider having a trustworthy person take over your high finances and checkbook. Reduce the credit limits on your credit cards to the amount of money you can afford to lose, or destroy your credit cards and cancel the accounts. Carry only as much cash with you in your purse or wallet as you can afford to lose. Keep important papers safely secure and where someone you trust can always have access to them (such as in a safety deposit box). Be sure this person has a key or knows its location.

DAYCARE

Stimulation enhances your brain's efficiency. For example, if you are feeling a little sluggish, go on a short walk, see a movie, or attend a concert. Your brain is built to respond to change and thrives on stimulation (*but not overstimulation*). This is true if you have normal memory or if you experience memory loss. Indeed, if you have progressive memory loss such as Alzheimer's disease, keeping yourself engaged is an essential ingredient of any treatment plan. Competence doesn't matter. *It is in the doing that counts.*

Adult daycare programs were created for those who need stimulation and for caregivers to have a respite. If you attend a well-run daycare program for the memory impaired, you will receive "palliative" memory rehabilitation through engagement therapy. In essence, this allows you to engage in joyful and stimulating activities such as walking, socializing, thinking (e.g., word games, watching movies, art therapy, music therapy) that fit your interests and retained abilities. It is not a warehouse or adult babysitting service. It is essential that you start these programs early when your memory and other cognitive skills are working relatively well.

Daycare programs are usually at a specific location where participants gather in a room(s) and enjoy activities run by a staff member. Naples, Florida, where I practiced the last ten years of my career, has a number of excellent programs (Millennium House, Ardent Manor, and The Care Club). However, they are limited by your *need* to be in a place like a "senior center." Not everyone needs this kind of setting, and not everyone does well engaging in group activities.

Why not develop daycare without walls? The concept is simple. If you love to fish, keep fishing. If you love ballet, keep going to the ballet. The range of activities is limitless: movies, lunch, concerts, museums, art, or exercise. You can do these by yourself or with a small group of two to four participants.

Fortunately, Jim Moran and I created CompanionPlus to meet this need in Naples in 2009. We carefully selected participants who could go somewhere individually or in small groups to enjoy activities of common interest. Their first outing was a group of three who went to a Twins spring practice game in Fort Myers. Others enjoyed golfing or going to lunch. Still others preferred supervised exercise. At this point, most participants use the program for one-on-one outings in a safe, relaxed, friendly environment.

What types of activities work best? Jim reported, "Activities with movement, such as golf, biking, tennis, and walks on the beach are ideal, because they enhance body, mind, and spirit. Also, lunch, movies, and ball games are popular. Just being out is the most important aspect of the program. Not only do the participants benefit — so do family members and caregivers, because they have time to relax and recharge."

Jim was enthusiastic about his experiences. He said, "It's been very gratifying." Caregivers have said, "We both really needed that." "This program was sent by divine intervention." According to Jim, one wife called and told him her husband needed to "get out with the Roosters." Jim knew exactly what she meant. It's important for men (and women) to spend time with male (female) friends in activities they enjoy.

We need more programs like this to add joy to those who won't remember what they did despite the happiness the outing created, and the respite that was given to their caregivers. We need to create more safe programs for those with memory loss who cannot be alone outside their home. Such programs also need to include activities that are not limited to just one physical location.

ASSISTED LIVING

Assisted living can help you manage daily living if you have a mental or physical impairment that prevents you from independently caring for yourself. For example, not being able to manage a checkbook means that you need assistance with that. Not being able to drive means needing someone else to get you from one place to another that is too far to walk. Sometimes, a family member provides this assistance. If you have the financial assets, or if you have good long-term care insurance, you can hire the help you need. If the assistance is greater than a family member can or will manage, then you need assistance from another source.

Assistance can take many forms. Friends may help. Neighbors may help. Compassionate groups and organizations, such as church groups, may help. Or, you may prefer more formal assistance that would require paying someone to help. For example, you might hire a companion or a home health service. You may prefer to use day programs that provide the necessary supervision along with activities that stimulate and reward you. You may choose to move to a formal assisted-living facility or a skilled-nursing facility, where the available care is more extensive. How you decide to obtain the care you need is up to you and those who care about you.

If you need this level of care, it's helpful to personally visit a few local options before you decide which one may best fit your needs. It can be stressful but is worth the time, stress, and effort during advanced planning. Put the tentative plan in writing and review it periodically. Hope that you never have to use it, but enjoy the confidence that comes from knowing that you have a clear plan.

You need to be creative when developing a plan for possible assistance. This is best accomplished by pre-planning. As much as you feel that you would never want to use any resources outside of family for your care, if you never consider the use of a skilled nursing facility, you are only making things worse for your caregiver. Yes, you are always happiest in a familiar environment with your loved ones as caregivers, but this is not always possible. Discuss possible ways to manage your care ahead of time. Also, consider the *triggers* that will lead to your need to incorporate various levels of assistance. This can save you a great deal of anxiety, anger, and guilt. An example may help clarify this point.

I assessed a seventy-year-old single man who had mild Alzheimer's disease. After the assessment, we went over his strengths and weaknesses. He had few local supports, and his prognosis was for continued and progressive decline over the course of months to years. He decided to move from his house to a large retirement community as part of his plan to remain as independent as possible for as long as possible. He chose the particular retirement community because it had care ranging from independent living to assisted living to skilled-nursing care as continuous services. He moved into an independent apartment and used a home-health aid and a companion to help him with meal preparation and shopping. His son, who lived in another state, managed his finances.

We also discussed his interests and needs. He was physically very active and wanted to continue playing tennis and billiards and riding his bicycle. He had the financial resources to hire a companion who played tennis and billiards with him most days of the week (so he would not forget to play often). In short, we kept his activities intact so that, as his memory loss progressed, he continued to do what brought him joy.

As his illness progressed over the next couple of years, he was no longer able to drive, shop, or prepare meals. He expanded his companion time so that he could stay in his apartment, continue with his activities, and go on rides and out to lunch. He developed close relationships with his companions.

Although he was unable to tell someone what he did each day or each week, he kept his life full of the joyful activities that were meaningful to him because of the companions. He also kept himself out of the assisted-living facility for several years, because he had set up such good routines and supports earlier in the course of his illness. He did not have to remember what to do to enjoy life.

I have worked with several other individuals and couples in making creative use of companions and routines to keep their life intact and to delay their need to move into more structured care. These plans must be flexible and created in light of your background, needs, joys, activities, and desires, along with those of your primary caregivers. The plans must be fluid and flexible and be revised periodically. If you wait until you need the elements of the plan, you may be too impaired to institute and develop a plan to secure your own future.

A Practical Approach to Caregiving

One of the most difficult lessons for caregivers of persons with Alzheimer's disease or other dementias is to *not fight futile battles. The "mind over matter" strategy does not work.* You may be used to negotiating, teaching, or even coercing your partner into doing things you wish. You may think that if you say something often enough, loud enough, and emphatically enough, it will stick. Have you ever seen someone use this strategy on a person who speaks a foreign language? The problem with loss of short-term memory is that *new things, promises, and schedules do not carry over.* This is *not* intentional, motivated resistance or orneriness.

No matter how often individuals with memory loss meet people, they never remember the names of those people. Furthermore, if "forgetting that they forget" sets in, they tend to believe that their memory is fine and that the world is wrong. Going toe-to-toe does not work. Caregiving — whether in a facility or at home — needs to be built around *what still works.* You must set up the environment to elicit a behavior (i.e., if gardening stills brings engagement, then take the person to the garden with tools already set up). You also should *set up more external prompts* to initiate the retained skills of the patient.

One of the clever caregivers with whom I worked had enjoyed golfing with his wife. She declined to the point where she no longer had the skill to set up a shot. He would place the ball in a tee, give her a club, point her in the right direction, and tell her to swing. He then praised any attempt to hit the ball and she squealed with delight. She even beamed when he told me they had golfed that day.

Areas of Care That May Induce Conflict and Situations to Consider

1. **Informing and explaining the diagnosis of dementia** can be tricky. Individuals being evaluated have a right to know their diagnosis. Undertake this discussion with sensitivity, compassion, and support. If

these clients engage in "denial," don't push it. Negotiate a way to have them accept the needed interventions despite their belief that they are fine. Remind yourself that *they forget that they forget,* no matter how many times or how loudly you say something. Denial in this sense is blindness to symptoms driven by neurological deficits. It is not intentional or "psychological."

2. **Those in early to middle dementia have lost the capacity for making financial, legal, or medical decisions.** They can neither provide a reliable self-report nor report back what they are told to do. They need an advocate but are resistant to the intervention. The best solution is to *go together to medical, legal, or financial appointments as a team.* It's also a good idea to engage confused individuals with the interactions taking place. It's better to talk *with* them rather than *about* them in the third person. Rather than confront them on the spot, set up an independent communication, such as an e-mail, a teleconference, or a note to provide accurate details. For example, one client of mine had done all of the investing during the couple's marriage and still talked to his broker regularly to suggest changes. The broker listened as in the past. However, the broker made no changes without verification by his wife. My client enjoyed doing the finances "independently" without risk.

3. **Decisions about driving.** It's best to have already discussed this as part of life planning before cognitive changes occur. If your spouse is not the principle driver, consider having *him or her take over driving to improve his or her skills.* For example, I do most of the driving while Pamela looks around, surfs the internet, or navigates in complex situations so I can focus on traffic safely. My suggestion is for me to have a conversation with her, asking her to let her do the driving to enhance her skills should I no longer be safe to drive.

4. **When to enact the Durable Power of Attorney (DPOA).** Doing such tasks as finances should be shared with those who will be legal

surrogates on a regular basis. It's best to implement this plan before confusion sets in, if possible. For example, most couples divide duties like paying bills, finances, planning trips, and so on. I am suggesting that the tasks be done together. This helps the potentially impaired spouse to get used to having someone else "look over his or her shoulder." Furthermore, it helps *the unimpaired* spouse to learn things like passwords, account numbers, and how to access safety deposit boxes. And, as mentioned, it helps each spouse to be comfortable with being monitored.

5. **Sexual activity.** This can be a thorny issue. What about sexual activity (masturbation, holding hands, sexual encounters) among those placed in assisted living? When can't a person give consent legally? For example, a husband was charged with statutory rape for having what was consensual sex with his wife under the guise of her inability to legally give informed consent. He was acquitted in court, but the stress and expense were considerable. How do you handle inappropriate sexual behavior toward caregivers and adult children (like the father who tried to climb in bed with his daughter because he was confusing her with his deceased wife)?

6. **Those in early to middle dementia often have progressive decline in standards of dress and grooming.** They need at least supervision (sometimes prompts) to maintain activities of daily living (ADLs). Forgetful persons may need daily assistance with caring for their teeth and gums, shaving, bathing, choosing their clothing, and changing into clean clothes. These are areas where conflict can be intense. Standards such as how many showers per week or whether it is really important to shave each day need to be considered in the light of which battles are worth the energy to fight. How many showers a week are really necessary? Do clothes have to match well? One couple solved the conflict over showering by showering together. Another made dressing a pleasing activity rather than a chore by using soothing music in the background.

7. **Those in early to middle dementia have significant decline in judgment as well as in the ability to play well with others.** They also are at risk of getting lost on outings. Consider a client who was a lifelong avid tennis player. Unfortunately, he had alienated all friends with whom he had played because he threw tantrums and challenged all shots that did not go his way. The solution was to hire a caregiver who played tennis with him three times a week. The caregiver went with the flow and always allowed the client to be "right."

8. **Those in early to middle dementia need stimulation via routine and regularity.** Forgetful persons need to be engaged in the familiar, not the new. They need activities that focus on productivity rather than on competence and short-term memory. If forgetful individuals can still play the piano, give them the opportunity to play the piano each day, and guide them to the piano with an invitation. If they enjoy movies, going to lunch, playing bridge, doing art, or playing golf, invite them, don't ask them. It's better to say, "Let's go to a movie" rather than asking, "Do you want to go to a movie?"

9. **What if the client refuses necessary medications?** Do you put the medications in food (known as covert administration)? Again, informed consent is the issue. Does a legally determined incompetent person have the right to refuse medications? What about "therapeutic lies?" How many times do you inform someone that his or her parents are long deceased? Is it okay to set extra places at the table or say that they are on vacation and will return soon? How many times do you need to make someone re-grieve?

10. **When do you administer antipsychotic medications?** These medications are controversial for use with the elderly and have back-box warnings (e.g., increase risk of stroke, diabetes, death). If used, how long do they stay in place? When do you stop administering "anti-dementia" medications?

11. **Have you discussed desires regarding end-of-life issues (hopefully before decline)?** When do you use palliative care or hospice? What about resuscitation?

12. **No one can provide 24/7 care alone without paying a substantial price.** Caregivers for those in early to middle dementia need support, respite, and guidance. They need to accept assistance from family, friends, and services such as daycare (without walls, if available). *Don't go it alone.*

I hope this discussion gives you, as a caregiver, some ideas on how to reduce power struggles you cannot win. Managing those with dementias can often go much more peacefully if you choose your battles carefully and don't make unrealistic demands on either the person with memory loss or yourself. Sometimes it's best to just go with the flow.

ADVANCED DIRECTIVES THAT WE ALL NEED

Listed below are questions that you need to consider doing *now*, before your cognitive skills decline due to stroke, a head injury, or a progressive neurological disorder. Leaving so much to chance, just because these topics are often uncomfortable to discuss and plan for, is *not* a good idea. Put your plans in writing and keep them safely (safe against fire, flooding, winds) so you will know where they are when you need them. Circle the number next to each of these tasks that you have completed and have in writing. Start working on the ones you have not done.

1. What is your financial plan (social security, savings, IRAs, Roth accounts, working) for your future income to meet needs and desires? What are the essential elements of your lifestyle that you want to protect as you get older? Take into account that you may have different needs at age seventy than you will at age eighty or ninety.

2. What is retirement to you? How will you make the transition? How will you spend your time? What hobbies and activities for continued engagement and stimulation have you developed or do you need to develop?

3. Do you have a DPOA? Does it cover both heathcare and financial decision-making? Who is your primary proxy? If your spouse becomes impaired first, do you have a plan for transfer of decision-making?

4. Do you have a Living Will? What issues do you want it to cover? Is it on file with your healthcare provider? Have you discussed your desires in detail with your family? Do they know where all of the paperwork is located? Do they have account numbers, passwords, and access?

5. Would you be better served by a trust? Consult your attorney to find out. Whether you have a trust or DPOA, how will you decide when to have a proxy take over? It's better to decide your possible contingencies in advance rather than making decisions under stress and emergencies.

6. Are you ready for a Do Not Resuscitate (DNR)? If you feel this is important to you, contact your physician and discuss it with him or her. This is not covered in a Living Will.

7. When should you no longer carry a credit card? Carry cash? What mistakes would you consider critical for you to turn over your financial planning to your proxy? What mistakes would you need to make to feel that you should no longer do a checkbook? Who will take over these tasks? How will you monitor yourself for errors?

8. When should someone else manage your medications?

9. When should you stop traveling alone? When should you stop traveling with family or friends?

10. Have you planned for your funeral and discussed your desires with your family? How do you want your remains handled? What do you want for a service?

11. Do you own any firearms? If you do, consider a plan to give up access to guns and establishing a firearms retirement date.

Important Documents

We often forget about important documents when we put them "where we will remember them" rather than in a *defined location*. Circle the documents that you have below. Make a check mark next to the ones that you can find without looking. Do you know where they are? Does your proxy (e.g., spouse, children) know where they are? Does your proxy know and understand your system for managing finances and documents? Does your proxy periodically check to be sure you are not making mistakes that you don't realize? Are your documents "backed up" and in a safe place in case of disasters (floods, hurricanes, tornadoes, fire)?

It is better to not do these tasks alone. You will head off your paranoia if you allow someone you trust to do things for you, like balancing your checkbook.

The following is a list of potentially important documents that you and your "backup" should be able to easily locate and understand:

- **Identity:** Birth certificate, marriage license, driver's license, divorce decrees, naturalization/immigration papers, passport, social security card, insurance cards, military records, funeral desires and pre-arrangements.

- **Financial:** Bank and credit card accounts, savings accounts, certificates of deposit, deeds, life insurance, bonds, stocks, trusts, loans, tax records, IRAs, pensions.

- **Legal:** Durable Power of Attorney (DPOA), living will, Powers of Attorney, wills, and Do Not Resuscitate documents.

***

As you have learned in this chapter, it is important to *manage your future today*, before you show signs of mental decline. Organize your papers and written desires for your future now, and store them in a safe place. And always share your plan with a friend, loved ones, a spouse, or someone else you trust, and let this person(s) know where everything is located.

CHAPTER FIFTEEN

Putting It All Together

"Age is an issue of mind over matter.
If you don't mind, it doesn't matter."
(Mark Twain)

We have covered a lot of territory. As I reflect on what I've written, I'm left with an essential question: Can we age "successfully" as our memory becomes less efficient as a consequence of aging or under the more trying circumstances of developing a memory disorder? I hope I have convinced you that you can manage memory changes successfully by *planning well ahead*. When you practice good memory techniques, you will create a safety net for yourself that addresses your personal joys, skills, and needs. If you have any concerns, seek the counsel of a memory expert as early as possible.

I also hope I've convinced you to do all of this *before* you need it. Let's review the main concepts involved in developing a plan that is suitable for you in managing your own future.

Memory Is Complex

Memory consists of many modules. This is fortunate, because even if you have significant memory loss, you will often retain many *kinds* of memory. When treating memory loss, your decline in short-term memory is what presents the most difficult challenge in that it underlies your ability to adapt. You must make use of other memory systems and mental skills to cleverly compensate for the challenges you will face in *new learning* as you age or develop a memory disorder.

Although Aging Does Not Destine You to Lose Your Memory, Your Memory *Efficiency* Declines as a Natural Consequence of Aging

You will not have the same efficiency of memory now as you did ten years ago. This means you will have to spend more time and energy *planning on how to remember* by implementing *memory supports* as you grow older. There are no shortcuts. Still, this *doesn't* mean you will lose your memory or develop Alzheimer's disease. Indeed, if you live to be ninety, you will have about a 50 percent chance of having a normal memory — for a ninety-year-old.

Many Things Can Increase Your Likelihood of Forgetting

Forgetting is a natural component of human memory. However, you can control many facets of your life that will help reduce forgetting. For example, you can keep your living and work spaces organized. You can reduce clutter. You can increase your attention by minimizing distractions. You can give your attention a boost by doing more demanding mental tasks when you are more efficient, which is in the mornings for many but later in the day for others. You can manage your use of drugs and alcohol, because they often reduce the efficiency of memory and attention. And you can keep your vision and hearing as sharp as possible with corrective eyewear and hearing aids.

Anticipate and Plan for Likely Areas Where Your Memory May Become Unreliable

Short-term memory becomes less efficient in a number of areas as you age. You may sometimes forget what people tell you. You may forget appointments if you don't write them down and refer to your calendar regularly. You may have increasing difficulty following complex sets of characters and plots in novels and movies. You may sometimes forget where you parked your car. You may forget phone messages and names more often than you used to. You may repeat yourself to your spouse or friends because you forget that you already told them the same thing. And you may sometimes even forget that you forget. It's okay to forget where you parked your car; it is not okay to forget that you *have* a car.

Use external memory aids to support your memory. Whether you're simply anticipating the memory changes of aging or are experiencing the early stages of a memory disorder, it is best to implement your plan while your memory is normal for your age. As I mentioned early in the book, your memory is the best it will ever be right now. You will not be able to develop the skills you'll need to manage your memory if you wait until you *need* those skills. If you ever grow concerned about your memory, seek a professional consultation with an expert in memory assessment and treatment. I hope I have convinced you that you needn't fear Mild Cognitive Impairment. This is a stage of memory decline in which you have a great deal of control and can develop the skills you need to create a safety net for the future.

Use Cleverness and Long-Term Memory

Short-term memory and attention are usually the culprits that make new learning increasingly difficult. Therefore, seek stimulation by doing what you like and know well. Develop routines and set goals that are based on what you want and need to do with your time. Create and re-create your life history in a concrete form. Organize your life's memorabilia, such as the pictures you may have stuck in boxes in your closet or garage or make slide shows and/or albums if you store pictures digitally.

Implement the General Rules for Managing Memory

Memory loss cannot be cured. Therefore, you need to use your remaining skills and external memory aids liberally. *Now* is the time to develop the skills and habits of implementing memory aids so that you will have them if you need them. Start by beginning a calendar habit in which you write down what is important and also what is pleasurable in your life. You also can develop the habit of using audio recordings. Cope with fatigue and stress. Keep learning sessions short and frequent. Develop a plan to become and remain more organized. Spend more time and more effort with those things that are important for you to remember.

Use External Memory Aids

External memory aids are not crutches. They are adaptive tools to enhance success. As mentioned above, develop a good calendar habit, because it is a plan for spending time you enjoy and can be used as a personal contract with yourself (like starting or refining an exercise plan or spending time reading). It's useful to keep both a *master calenda*r that stays at home and a *daily calendar* or appointment book that you carry with you at all times. Use a digital watch and clock (smart phones are a perfect and convenient tool for keeping track of time and activity). Begin a diary or journal to recall trips, family visits, or other things in your life that are important to you. Use timers and to-do lists.

Create a *takeaway spot* where you put everything that needs to leave the house with you, and develop the habit of using that spot without fail. And while you're at it, decide on a place for everything and develop the habit of putting everything in its place — every time. Unfortunately, *good intentions do not make for good memory*. You cannot always count on your short-term memory, but external memory aids can keep you efficient. This is because they use other skills and parts of your memory. *If you lose your short-term memory, the habits and supports you develop now keep your life together well into progressive decline.*

Manage Your Biology

Modify your diet to eat fruits, vegetables, and fish as the foundation rather than meat. Implement a "Mediterranean" diet. Exercise most days of the week — and keep your exercise plans in your daily calendar. It's important to include stretching, aerobic, and strength training in your exercise routine.

Plan Ahead

You hopefully have insurance and investments/savings for future needs. You wouldn't wait for a car accident, a serious or chronic health problem, a lightning strike, a plumbing leak, or a hurricane to buy insurance. Of course, you never want to collect on your car, health, or home insurance, but you're ready just in case. Hopefully, you have also planned ahead to have money for your future. If you wait until you retire, it may be too late to set aside enough money for you to enjoy a more comfortable retirement. You plan ahead for your health by exercising, attempting to eat right most of the time, and diligently managing cardiovascular issues (e.g., hypertension, diabetes) and as part of your wellness plan. You also need to create the skills you need for retirement. Unfortunately, most people learned well *how to work* but *not how to not work*. This is something you plan for by scheduling (in your calendar) time now for developing interests and hobbies.

Also, plan for your memory to be less efficient than it is now. Use more external memory aids and integrate them into your lifestyle. If you never really need them, great. If you have not already done so, set up a will, a Durable Power of Attorney, and a living will (you might consider completing the Five Wishes document that can be found online). In short, don't be reactive to aging, be proactive — on as many fronts as you can.

*****

I have worked with many individuals who have aged successfully. I have worked with many who have planned ahead and managed their own memory loss or memory loss in someone for whom they care. Having memory loss does not have to lead to a loss of joy in life. Aging is not a disease that you must defeat. However, successful aging requires you to *manage* disease. You must spend time *now* considering what is really important to you. And you may need to revise your plans several more times as your life changes.

THREE THINGS

I was invited to participate in a panel discussion at Avow Hospice in Naples, Florida. The theme was, "What are the three things that you want all of your clients to know?" This is an interesting challenge for two reasons. First, panel members had only ten minutes to make their point. And second, I had recently turned seventy and decided to retire. What do I need to know for myself, because I am not immune to the complex cognitive and physical changes that accompany both normal senior moments and abnormal aging? The following discussion covers the issues that I think are essential in dealing with progressive neurological diseases like Alzheimer's disease.

1. **We do not yet know what causes Alzheimer's disease.** A recent issue of the AARP newsletter states that the problem is a lack of research funding. But the issue is more complex. Where do we put the money? Amyloid treatments are a bust, despite the fact that we have dedicated millions of dollars for clinical trials of amyloid-altering drugs that have failed over the last three decades. When it comes to amyloid theories (first formulated in 1906), we appear to have mass tunnel vision within the scientific and medical communities. (*New Frontiers in Alzheimer's* (2020), published by *Scientific American,* presents an excellent, understandable description of the many factors that are being evaluated currently to understand mechanisms contributing to and potential treatment approaches for Alzheimer's disease. It is well worth reading.) A strong disconnect occurs between putative amyloid pathology and Alzheimer's disease, and this disconnect presents a conundrum. Consider the following facts:

   - A significant number of people have the pathologic features of Alzheimer's disease (amyloid and tau protein density) than they do the clinical symptoms.
   - For every three persons with the pathology, only one has clinical symptoms.

- About 80 percent of those who are eighty and older have the *biological signs* of Alzheimer's disease *without clinical symptoms*.
- Between 25 to 50 percent of elders complain of memory loss.
- Some of those with clinical symptoms perform competently in everyday life.
- Some who are diagnosed with Alzheimer's disease stay stable for years without treatment.
- Amyloid may be a contributor to Alzheimer's disease, but it is neither specific to nor the root cause of Alzheimer's disease.

2. **We need a paradigm shift.** Variability is the norm for the course of Alzheimer's disease. The term "Alzheimer's disease" is too broad. We have focused on the amyloid hypothesis for decades and tested hundreds of compounds to no avail. The most recent failures were with solanezumab (Lilly) and gantenerumab (Roche). This was a particularly dramatic failure in that participants were volunteers from individuals with the inherited form of Alzheimer's disease.

3. **A number of disorders have been subsumed under the term Alzheimer's disease, and other neuropathologies share plaques and tangles.** Advances have been made in measuring tau that are currently being studied. However, it doesn't appear that Alzheimer's disease has a simple, single cause. It is not clear to me where or how to direct the search. Multiple threads seem worth exploring.

For example, inflammation appears to be a key but neglected player marking cascading events, with amyloid as the match and tau as a brush fire. Once neuroinflammation starts, cell death speeds up (Rudolph Tanzi, 2020, p. 78; quoted by Karen Weintraub, *New Frontiers in Alzheimer's*).

Alzheimer's disease is not an infection like a common cold, but pathogens like viruses, bacteria, or fungi may trigger the disease.

Blood (and brain) glucose and insulin share a complex relationship with cognitive functions, including memory. This finding has led to the theory that a third form of diabetes exists, in which insulin is insufficiently utilized (or deficient) in the brain, thus contributing to Alzheimer's disease. Intranasal administration of insulin has been helpful to some.

A smattering of other findings that may be helpful in the future understanding and treatment of neurocognitive disorders include the following:

- Elders who use trazodone as a sleep aid show slower decline.
- The highest levels of cortisol (a stress hormone) are correlated with worse scores on cognitive testing. However, so far no evidence has been found that reducing levels of cortisol reduces the risk of Alzheimer's disease.
- Deep brain stimulation has been associated with a slower decline and improved brain glucose metabolism. Although results have been mixed, can a "memory prosthesis" be devised?
- Magnetic resonance imagery (MRI)–guided, focused ultrasound can be used to open the blood-brain barrier in a safe, reversible, and non-invasive way, allowing better drug delivery to the brain.

The good news is that Alzheimer's disease gives advanced warning; therefore, you can make plans to have a good life in the face of future memory loss. Furthermore, not everyone with the pathology of Alzheimer's disease becomes demented, and not everyone with dementia has Alzheimer's disease. Given the right structure and advanced planning, you can still have a good life, even if you can't remember it. Anterograde amnesia forces you to live in the moment, and the key to improving your life if you develop short-term memory loss is to create good moments.

Treatment of Alzheimer's disease requires treatment of short-term memory. Changes in the ability to learn new information or skills —

changes that unfold over at least a decade before dementia (read as disability) sets in — are becoming more available. You will have adequate time to strategically plan how to compensate for memory changes and how to create a higher quality of life if you become forgetful. This applies to those who live with you as well. Make your life plan before you forget that you forget.

In the following list, based on findings from the ongoing "Rush Memory and Aging Project: A Religious Orders Study" (David Bennett, 2020, "Banking Against Alzheimer's Disease," in *New Frontiers in Alzheimer's*, pp. 820-976), Bennett suggests ways to reduce your risk of Alzheimer's disease:

- Choose your parents well for good genes, add a good education, and learn a second language or musical instrument.
- Engage in regular cognitive and physical activities.
- Strengthen and maintain your social ties.
- Get out and explore new things.
- Chill and be happy.
- Avoid people who are downers — especially family members.
- Be conscientious and diligent.
- Spend more time in activities that are meaningful and goal-directed. (See Victor Frankl, 1946, *Man's Search for Meaning*).
- What's good for the heart is good for the brain.
- Eat a Mediterranean-style diet.

Treating short-term memory loss requires planning how to remember — the One-Minute Rule. Anything given less than one minute of thought will fade from your memory. Moreover, the more minutes you spend with something, the better you will remember it. Quit *trying* to remember. *Plan on how you will remember*. A well-placed Post-It note trumps a good intention. Write things down in an organized way. Live by your calendar, which contains both what you love to do and what you have to do. *Organize your memory tools. The time and effort pay off.*

Time and recollection are your most valued gifts. If you plan well the things that are important to you, you can use your time in the future to meet the goal set by Carl Rogers, a famous psychologist: "Rather than growing older, I plan on being older and growing."

Antonovsky, A. (1979). *Health, Stress, and Coping.* San Francisco: Jossy-Bass. We all face periods of stress and illness at some time in our lives. How you make sense of the world determines how you handle stress and disease. In this and the next book listed, Antonovsky develops the concept of *sense of coherence* to explain how your perception of being in control versus being controlled by forces outside of yourself (internal versus external control) affects your coping with health and disease.

Antonovsky, A. (1988). *Unraveling the Mystery of Health: How Many People Manage Stress and Stay Well.* San Francisco: Jossy-Bass.

Barlow, D.H. (1988). *Anxiety and Its Disorders: The Nature and Treatment of Anxiety and Panic.* New York: Guilford. A comprehensive coverage of origins, dynamics, and treatment of anxiety and its disorders. It's the best textbook about anxiety and its disorders that I have seen. A second edition was published in 2018.

Beckwith, B.E. (2010). *Managing Your Memory: Practical Solutions for Forgetting.* Naples, Florida: Memory Management.

Bright, J.G., and Lang, J.M. (2007). "Robert McNamara: Then and Now." *Daedalus,* Volume 136 (1). A fascinating essay that reflects on McNamara's reflections on his life and the difficult decisions he made as Secretary of Defense. This is a discussion of his use of hindsight to evaluate the outcomes of his past decisions.

Brul, A.B., and Sahaian, B.J. (2016). *Drugs, Games, and Devices for Enhancing Cognition: Implications for Work and Society.* New York: Annals of The New York Academy of Sciences.

Carr, N. (2010). *The Shallows; What the Internet Is. Doing To Our Brain.* New York: W.W. Norton & Company.If you ever wondered how technology and the Internet affect human memory, this is a must-read. It is clear and entertaining while explaining how computers have compromised the need for reflection and understanding. He discusses the impact of the Internet on learning and memory.

Deardoff and Grossberg. (2016). "Drug Design, Development and Therapy," 10: 3267-3279, PMID: 27757016.

Dittrich, L. (2017). *Patient HM: A Story of Memory, Madness, and Family Secrets.* New York: Random House. A splendid biography of the most studied and famous case study in history, HM (Henry Molaison). HM suffered a brain injury as a child and as a young adult underwent neurosurgery to treat a serious seizure disorder by removal of his hippocampi (he was the only person ever to receive this neurosurgery, because it resulted serious memory loss after the surgery). And the surgery did rob him of his memory. The study of HM provided the foundation for our understanding of anterograde amnesia, which underlies many disorders of memory.

Draaisma, D. (2012). *Why Life Speeds Up As You Get Older.* Cambridge: Cambridge University Press. A scholarly, entertaining, and informative book — another of my favorite books on memory.

Draper, B., and Withill, A. (2016). "Young Onset Dementia." *Internal Medicine Journal* 176: 779-786.

Gould, S.J. (1981). *The Mismeasure of Man.* Norton: New York. A rigorous and readable history of intelligence testing and psychometrics. The book goes well beyond just explaining nature versus nurture. It presents a critical review of how our theories and cultural biases have shaped the use and misuse of data.

Harari, Y.N. (2015). *Sapiens: A Brief History of Humankind.* Harper: New York. The best history book I have ever read. It describes the impact of the cognitive revolution as it facilitated the evolution of culture. It is thought provoking and encyclopedic.

Herrmann, D. J. (1990). *Super Memory*. London: Blandford.

Hua, Hildreth, and Pelak. (2016). "Effects of Testosterone Therapy on Cognitive Function in Aging: A Review." *Cognitive and Behavioral Neurology* 29: 1221-1238.

Huff, D. (1954). *How to Lie With Statistics*. New York: W.W. Norton & Company. A humorous and entertaining guide to the misuse of statistics.

Infurna, F. J., Gerstorf, D., and Lachman, M.E. (2020). "Midlife in the 2020s: Opportunities and Challenges." *American Psychologist* 75: 470-483.

Jackson, M. (2009). *Distracted: The Erosion of Attention and the Coming Dark Age*. New York: Prometheus Books. How information overload and social media (e.g., Twitter, Facebook) have transformed us into a society with "attention deficit disorder." What is the impact of being constantly on? How did we get to the point of going to dinner and looking at our phone rather than engage in conversation with our companion?

Kandel, E. (2006). *In Search of Memory: The Emergence of a New Science of Mind*. New York: W.W. Norton. An exceptional autobiography that not only presents the life and intellectual history of a renowned memory researcher but also describes his creative process and the neurobiology of memory.

McNamara, R. (2007)."Robert McNamara: Then and Now." *Daedalus* (Winter): 120–123.A fascinating essay that reflects on McNamara's reflections on his life and the difficult decisions he made as Secretary of Defense. This is a discussion of his use of hindsight to evaluate the outcomes of his past decisions.

Meichenbaum, D. (1985). *Stress Inoculation Training*. New York: Pergamon Press. By far the best book on stress management that I have ever read.

New Frontiers in Alzheimer's 2020. (2020). *Scientific American*: New York. A clear, brief, nontechnical, and readable update on Alzheimer's disease.

Reisberg, B., Ferris, S.H., de Leon, M.J., and Crook, T. (1982). "The Global Deterioration Scale for Assessment of Primary Progressive Degenerative Dementia." *The American Journal of Psychiatry* 139: 1136-1139. A foundational work to scale cognitive decline.

Sapolsky, R.M. (2017). *Behave: The Biology of Humans at Our Best and Worst*. New York: Penguin Books. A tour de force. The best book on brain function as it relates to aggression and social interactions that I have ever read. Explains how brain function brings out the best and worst in us. Includes a description of how tribalism is related to biology.

Schacter, D.L. (1997). *Searching For Memory: The Brain, The Mind, and The Past*. New York: Basic Books. A comprehensive, readable, and understandable description of human memory as it relates to art, literature, and everyday living.

Schacter, D.L. (2001). *The Seven Sins of Memory: How the Mind Forgets and Remembers*. New York: Houghton Mifflin. Schacter presents a framework for understanding how memory is more than just the facts. He presents the context of how everyday memory is an active process subject to biases such as blocking (can't get at the word you want), transience (memories become less clear over time), bias (justification of beliefs rather than objective recounting), and persistence (memory for trauma that doesn't fade over time).

Shenk, D. (2003). *The Forgetting: Alzheimer's: Portrait of an Epidemic*. New York: Doubleday. An approachable review of the state of understanding of Alzheimer's disease at the turn of the century. A good summary of the thinking and findings about Alzheimer's disease.

Wheelan, C. (2012). *Naked Statistics: Stripping the Dread From the Data.* New York: W.W. Norton & Company.An intuitive approach to understanding the uses of statistics. Our daily life is inundated with statistics. This is the best non-mathematical treatment of statistics that I have seen. Wheelan gives us a way to learn about statistics that is understandable, humorous, and loaded with everyday examples of how to interpret statistical findings.

Wingfield, A., & Byrnes, D.L. (1981). *The Psychology of Human Memory.* New York: Academic Press. A comprehensive and readable textbook on human memory. Describes how much of human memory is a reconstructive process rather than a playback of past experience. Explains in detail how memory is a multifaceted process with many components.

Wurman, R.S. (2001). Indianapolis: QUE. A gem. Although written for businesses, this is a comprehensive treatment of how to manage ourselves in an age of information.

About the Author

Dr. Bill Beckwith has been studying, researching, and teaching about memory for more than forty years. He earned advanced degrees in Experimental Psychology and Clinical Psychology from The Ohio State University.

His extensive career as an educator spans decades of teaching students in preschool, junior high school, and graduate school. As a Professor at the University of North Dakota, Dr. Beckwith was honored with several teaching awards. As a researcher, he broadened our knowledge of neuroscience, learning, and memory. He has published extensively in these fields.

During the twenty-five years before his retirement, Dr. Beckwith focused on the needs of people with memory loss and their caregivers by developing important new approaches and programs. He was clinical director and cofounder of the Memory Disorders Clinic in Fort Myers, Florida. He also established the Department of Behavioral Health and created the innovative Center for Excellence in Memory Care for a large, continuing-care retirement community.

Aware of the increasing need for practical knowledge about memory, this renowned educator brings his expertise to broader audiences. Dr. Beckwith and his wife, Pamela, are founders of the Life and Memory Center, an educational resource company dedicated to aiding people in planning and managing their memory assets through seminars, workshops, publications, and consultations.

Dr. Beckwith lives in Omaha, Nebraska, with his artist wife, Pamela, and their two cats, Gracie and Vanna.

INDEX